COLLEGE STUDENTS' SENSE OF BELONGING

Belonging—with peers, in the classroom, or on campus—is a critical dimension of success at college. It can affect a student's degree of academic adjustment, achievement, aspirations, or even whether a student stays in school. This book explores how belonging differs based on students' social identities, such as race, gender, sexual orientation, or the conditions they encounter on campus. The second edition of *College Students' Sense of Belonging* explores student sub-populations and campus environments, offering readers updated information about sense of belonging, how it develops for students, and a conceptual model for helping students belong and thrive. Underpinned by theory and research and offering practical guidelines for improving educational environments and policies, this book is an important resource for higher education and student affairs professionals, scholars, and graduate students interested in students' success.

New to this second edition:

- A refined theory of college students' sense of belonging and review of current literature in light of new and emerging findings;
- Expanded best practices related to fostering sense of belonging in classrooms, clubs, residence halls, and other contexts;
- Updated research and insights for new student populations such as youth formerly in foster care, formerly incarcerated adults, and homeless students;
- Coverage on a broad range of topics since the first edition of this book, including cultural navigation, academic spotting, and the "shared faith" element of belonging.

Terrell L. Strayhorn is Professor of Urban Education and Vice President for Academic and Student Affairs at LeMoyne-Owen College, USA. An internationally recognized student success expert on equity and diversity issues, he also owns a private educational consulting firm, Do Good Work LLC.

COLLEGE STUDENTS' SENSE OF BELONGING

A KEY TO EDUCATIONAL SUCCESS FOR ALL STUDENTS

Second edition

Terrell L. Strayhorn

Routledge
Taylor & Francis Group

NEW YORK AND LONDON

Second edition published 2019
by Routledge
711 Third Avenue, New York, NY 10017

and by Routledge
2 Park Square, Milton Park, Abingdon, Oxon, OX14 4RN

Routledge is an imprint of the Taylor & Francis Group, an informa business

© 2019 Taylor & Francis

First edition published by Routledge 2012

Library of Congress Cataloging-in-Publication Data
A catalog record has been requested for this book

ISBN: 978-1-138-23854-1 (hbk)
ISBN: 978-1-138-23855-8 (pbk)
ISBN: 978-1-315-29729-3 (ebk)

Typeset in Sabon
by Deanta Global Publishing Services, Chennai, India

This book is dedicated to my parents, Wilber and Linda Strayhorn; my two children, Aliyah Brielle and Tionne Lamont Strayhorn; my maternal grandmother, Creola Evelyn Warner, who devoted over 50 years of unwavering professional service as a public school teacher. She taught me to "love many, trust few"—one of her life mottos—and to dare to believe in the impossible. I dedicate this second edition of the book to my beloved godsister, Kimberly Yvette "Fat" Williams, who won a three-year battle with cancer in July 2017, just as I was finishing up edits for the publisher. She was a major supporter, "a biggest fan" as she would say, and always took pride in me and my work. "Kim, though I can't hold you anymore, I will always hold you in my heart. *You belong* there." All of these people—those mentioned and those implied—have helped me to believe that I matter, that I am important, and that I am cared about, all of which are key components of *sense of belonging*. Because of them, I am and this book is complete.

Contents

Foreword by Quartez Harris

I am a paper thin book
without pages of camaraderie.
While on this brittle shelf
of worldwide publishers
I am encumbered by thick dust of loneliness,
missing the touch of another.
The swarm of students bypassing me,
with enough storage in their backpacks
never browse the tarnished pages of my emptiness
They assume I am not alone
but they are blinded by the shadows of their assumptions
These sills are nothing more than hardcover books
that never dared to breathe me into their stories.
I am just waiting for somebody
to read each chapter of my loneliness,
while I linger in this crowded room of a library.

Quartez Harris is a graduate of The Ohio State University and award-winning spoken-word artist. A native of Cleveland, Ohio, Mr. Harris continues his creative expressions through multiple forms of media.

Foreword by Walter R. Allen

"I am somebody! I am somebody! I must be respected! I must be protected! I am God's Child! I am somebody!" This is how Reverend Jesse Jackson opened Saturday morning meetings of Operation PUSH. These words gave meaning and power to disenfranchised Black people in Chicago and across the United States. These words also held profound meaning for me, a Black graduate student swimming upstream in the sea of whiteness at the University of Chicago. Family, tribe, community—the Black nation—had affirmed, embraced and sustained me on my journey through unwelcoming, oftentimes hostile, white spaces. Without these places and spaces where I truly belonged; where I felt safe, valued and "normal," I surely would have been lost.

This important book by one of the world's leading experts on the subject, Professor Terrell Strayhorn, speaks to that predicament and the lived experiences of college students from a multitude of different backgrounds who share the common challenge of finding ways to "fit in," to matter, and to belong. Their quest predicts whether they will achieve social, emotional, personal, and academic success. Whether they will persist, dropout, or transfer institutions. And college student educators—faculty, practitioners, and administrators—play a critical role in creating environments where all students can thrive and belong. They have the power to help students who feel lost find their way.

In this book, Terrell Strayhorn masterfully spans and connects wide literature and empirical data sources to help us understand the basic desire of humans to belong, especially in learning contexts. He skillfully weaves Maslow's concept of basic human needs with a version of Beverly Daniel Tatum's thoughtful question, "Why do all the [diverse or vulnerable] children sit together in the cafeteria" and provides clear answers, innovative ideas, and effective practices that link research to practice, policy, and theory. The result is a compelling, creative, rigorous examination of how belonging relates to healthy development and academic success for all college students.

The power and relevance of this book is revealed as Dr. Strayhorn probes the existential linkages between student experiences of belonging and successful student outcomes. He helps expand our understanding of how best to achieve the elusive goals of diversity and inclusion; how best to join increased access AND success in higher education. Strikingly this book offers a promising formula for achieving broader student success. Whether the student is from the majority or minority, s/he will maximize their "best self" with the scaffolding and support belonging provides. We all share the essential, human need to belong, especially in places and times when we are prone to feel like an outsider or invisible, and Strayhorn makes these theoretical linkages crystal clear in this 2nd edition.

"I see you," is one way young folks affirm and embrace each other in popular vernacular. This statement embodies age old yearnings. It joins "Me" with "We" and "Us" with "Them" to build, maintain, and promote community. Only from community can we expect to grow the fruits of success. When we truly "see" and value diversity—each other, magic happens, moving higher education closer to her ideals of inclusive excellence, student-centeredness, and democracy. Achieving this is difficult, but this book not only calls us to a higher place, it offers the promises and practices we need to help save future generations from feeling lost to finding hope and belonging in college.

Walter R. Allen
Allan Murray Cartter Professor of Higher Education
Distinguished Professor of Education, Sociology
and African American Studies
University of California–Los Angeles

Preface

The idea for this book evolved out of my own personal experiences as a student turned professor. Thinking back to my undergraduate years, there were certainly times when I felt like I did not belong in college. Several years later these feelings would return while I was pursuing my doctoral degree as a graduate student at Virginia Tech. And just when I thought that I had experienced everything, they arose again (and in different contexts) as a professor at two major research universities. Indeed, sense of belonging matters.

It is my hope that this book will contribute to the body of knowledge in at least one of several ways. First, it might represent a worthy contribution to the national discourse about degree completion, career and college readiness, student success, and the impact of college on students. Sense of belonging affects all of these and, in my opinion, has been missing from the proverbial conversation nationally. Second, it might be viewed as a powerfully useful tool or guide for undergraduate and graduate students, educational researchers, and faculty members who have an interest in these issues. Finally, if nothing else, I hope it begins to address some of the unanswered questions that lurk and linger regarding college students' sense of belonging.

Keep in mind, gentle reader, that many of the explanations presented are provided to render the complex, simple; realizing that a degree of accuracy is lost in the process. While more detailed than the first edition, this version of the book is not entirely exhaustive but provides a starting place for those who want to know (and read) more about college students' sense of belonging.

Future reviewers of this text may wonder why I decided to use my own work as useful illustrations of how this topic could be investigated in college student research. To be sure, countless other examples abound in the extant literature (most are cited in the book) and my work is by no means the grand exemplar by which all other studies should be judged. However, the decision to feature my own work was both important and necessary to the goals of this text, as it allowed me to "unpack and unveil" my thinking as I moved through the research process, to share with readers on paper what might otherwise go unsaid and unwritten, implied yet rarely admitted, and to make the inexplicit, explicit. With these goals in mind, I release this volume to you. Let's talk about how it is organized and then turn attention to the intended audiences.

ORGANIZATION OF THE BOOK

In keeping with the overarching objectives, this volume was organized around four major questions that serve as the primary foci. First, what is sense of belonging? Second, what are the central tenets and key concepts of sense of belonging? Third, how has sense of belonging been examined in prior work, some of which is my own? And fourth, how does sense of belonging apply to various student populations? All of these are addressed over the course of the volume.

The book consists of 11 chapters, divided into two parts. Part I includes three chapters. Chapter 1 serves as the introduction to the book and provides a detailed discussion of sense of belonging and a general description of its content. Chapter 2 focuses on reviewing the relevant literature on or about sense of belonging, framing it in ways that are consistent with the overall objectives and the tenor of my main arguments. Chapter 3 briefly describes and outlines the broad contours of a sense of belonging model that will prove useful to several chapters in the second part of the book.

Part II includes seven chapters. Chapter 4 highlights the role that sense of belonging plays in the success of Latino collegians. Gay students are the focus of Chapter 5 in a national study of gay male collegians of color. Chapter 6 draws upon data from first-year students participating in a summer bridge program to demonstrate the influence of educational interventions on college students' sense of belonging, while Chapter 7 examines the belonging experiences of students in science, technology, engineering, and math (STEM) fields. Chapter 8 devotes attention to the belonging experiences of Black male collegians, while Chapter 9 focuses on graduate students. In Chapter 10, I review much of what is known about involvement and engagement, and argue for a theoretical link between these two constructs and sense of belonging. Using students' participation in campus clubs and organizations as a lens, I offer insights that distinguish these concepts theoretically, while also demonstrating how they might be related in service to educational success. Chapter 11 is the epilogue, which recalls the purpose of the book and key points raised in the volume. A robust set of references is placed at the end of the book—perhaps rightfully so—pointing readers to the sources of information upon which several of my arguments stand. Organizing the book in this manner was a deliberate decision on my part; I thought it necessary to cover a wide range of contexts and populations for the book to be applicable to broader audiences.

WHAT'S NEW IN THIS EDITION?

The basic message communicated in the first edition has proven as useful and powerful today as when I first shared it in 2012. It is undeniably clear that sense of belonging is a basic human need, vital for optimal human functioning and critical for students' learning and development. Everybody wants to belong and one's need to belong is heightened in contexts and settings where individuals are prone to feel alienated, invisible, (pre)judged, stereotyped, or lonely. In fact, I am *more* convinced today about the importance of belonging and its ability to predict college students' success than I was years ago when I wrote the first edition. This second edition provides far more detailed information about sense of belonging, how it develops for students, and insights about the extent to which it matters in college.

The research base of belonging has evolved as the world of theory, policy, and practice has changed too. For instance, education as a field has witnessed the advent of sense of belonging interventions such as attributional retraining and expansive campus-wide civility campaigns that celebrate the dignity, humanity, and worth of all beings. Nowadays, sense of belonging is incorporated in campus strategic plans, enrolment management strategies, and faculty development workshops. This second edition includes much of what we have learned through research and best practices since the publication of the last edition.

I have also found that many people in higher education and private sector organizations have used the previous edition of this book in classroom settings, faculty development workshops, staff trainings, and independent research. Though this book is intended mostly for educators, leaders, managers, planners, and stakeholders of education policy organizations, I have also discovered that a surprising number of college students themselves use the book to assess the importance of finding a sense of belonging, as well as to identify effective strategies for achieving belonging and success. The second edition of this book includes a number of significant enhancements including:

- A significantly expanded and refined theory of college students' sense of belonging (Chapter 3) that can serve as a framework for guiding future research discoveries;

- Countless best practices related to fostering sense of belonging in students in college classrooms, clubs, residence halls, and other contexts;
- New results from more recent studies on the college student samples addressed in this volume, as well as insights for new student populations such as youth formerly in foster care, formerly incarcerated adults, and homeless students;
- New "call out" boxes or vignettes that address a broad range of new topics that have evolved from my research since the first edition of this book, including cultural navigation, academic spotting, and the "shared faith" element of belonging, to name a few.

FOR WHOM WAS THE BOOK WRITTEN?

College Students' Sense of Belonging was written with several audiences in mind. First, college student educators and student personnel administrators, who work with students directly, will likely benefit from the research-based recommendations presented throughout the book. For instance, student activities directors and staff members may consider my recommendations about advising students to "see" involvement as a way of establishing a sense of belonging on campus, not just a résumé filler (see Chapter 10). Similarly, summer bridge program staff may find the information in Chapter 6 particularly helpful as they work to revise existing or formulate new curricula and activities for students.

Campus administrators and college student educators will likely find the practical recommendations for nurturing students' sense of belonging provocative, useful, and possible to enact on their own campus. For example, STEM outreach coordinators, STEM advisors, and faculty may consult information in Chapter 7 to adopt or refine practices such as student orientation programs, living-learning communities, or summer research opportunities as a way of promoting belonging among students. Even graduate advisors and deans may find themselves revisiting Chapter 9 for ways to build belonging among graduate students.

That the book focuses on students' experiences inside and outside the classroom should appeal to higher-education professionals in both academic affairs (e.g., provosts, deans, faculty) and student affairs (e.g., student activities, housing). Consider that several chapters turn attention to what happens in the classroom or related spaces (e.g., Chapters 7–9), while other chapters place an accent on the out-of-classroom, extracurricular, or social spheres of college life (e.g., Chapters 4 and 10). Again, this was an intentional design, reflecting my belief that sense of belonging, too, has academic (cognitive) and social (behavioral) dimensions.

The main substantive chapters present new findings from research studies that employ quantitative, qualitative, and mixed-methods approaches; thus, educational researchers and scholars from related fields (e.g., psychology, sociology) may be attracted to the book's empirical base, the various ways in which data were used to achieve the book's purposes while "telling the story" of students from various backgrounds whose voices are virtually silent or "silenced" (hushed by power) in the extant literature. It may also be useful to researchers to find so much information about sense of belonging under a single cover. This can potentially reduce the amount of time spent in the library (or online) hunting for references to the relevant literature.

Lastly, students may stand much to gain from this book. Graduate students in Student Affairs and Higher Education programs may find the book useful for enhancing their understanding of sense of belonging, its relation to student success, and the role they can play in nurturing sense of belonging in various educational settings. It is not a far stretch to think that college students themselves may benefit from the book's content as well. I have tried to articulate my thesis about sense of belonging via words (and numerical data) provided by students themselves. Having their belonging experiences reflected back at them through the words, vignettes, and responses of students who share their interests and backgrounds may lead student readers to nod their head in passionate agreement, to gasp in amazement that others share experiences closely mirroring their own, or to read the book cover-to-cover in a single sitting. If nothing else, I hope this book calls attention to sense of belonging as a critical ingredient in the recipe for student success. I hope it demonstrates to students that college student educators care about them and want to work to create campus conditions that promote their belonging in college. Conversely, I hope the book demonstrates to college student educators that not only are all students capable of learning or able to achieve, but also yearning to belong. Information in this book may even inspire some students to connect with the campus in ways that they might not have imagined otherwise.

Note. This second edition of *College Students' Sense of Belonging: A Key to Educational Success for All Students* includes new images, photos, and diagrams to illustrate the function and structure of sense of belonging in postsecondary contexts; these new photos and images are also instructive in showing belonging's applicability to various scenarios. Unless otherwise noted, all illustrations, photos, and graphics were created by the Author or made available for use in the public domain at: www.publicdomainpictures. net or www.public-domain-photos.com. Both sites authorize "use of images for any purpose, including commercial."

Acknowledgments

Any undertaking of this magnitude leaves the author indebted to a number of individuals. First, I want to thank my wonderful advisees and research assistants over the years for their help with the various projects that form the basis for this book. Special thanks to Amanda Blakewood (PhD, Tennessee), James DeVita (PhD, Tennessee), Derrick Tillman Kelly (PhD, The Ohio State University [OSU]), Joey Kitchen (PhD, OSU), Fei Bie (MS, OSU), Todd Suddeth (PhD, OSU), Michael Steven Williams (PhD, OSU), Royel Johnson (PhD, OSU), Leroy Long (PhD, OSU), and Marjorie Dorime-Williams (PhD, Illinois), all of whom have served as members of my research team through one of the three academic research centers that I have directed. Other members of my research teams over the years have contributed in meaningful ways to these works too: D.J. Baker, Chrissy Hannon, Karl Jennings, Fred Calvin McCall, Shanna Pendergrast, Demetrius Richmond, Chutney Walton, William Roberts-Foster, Eric Stokes, Porche Wynn, Aaron Hatchett, and Feven Girmay (UCLA). Without the competent support of my graduate students, this book—first or second edition—would not have been possible.

I benefited greatly from the generous financial support of the American College Personnel Association's (ACPA) Commission for Academic Affairs Administrators, the Tennessee Higher Education Commission in partnership with the US Department of Education, and from professional development grants available through the Provost's Office at The University of Tennessee, Knoxville and The Ohio State University. External grants from the National Science Foundation Division of Research on Learning has supported my research on science, technology, engineering, and math (STEM), some of which is featured in this book.

I've said it before and I must say it again, my family gave me the encouragement and motivation to start this project, especially my son and daughter. While my family provided the fuel to start this project, it took the constant support and encouragement of my close friends to sustain me over time, long after I thought I had written the "last line." Special recognition to Jamaal Brown, Elias Fishburne, Leon Howell, the late Darren Harris, Joshua Johnson, Evelyn Leathers, Joseph Terrell Lockett, Belinda Bennett McFeeters, Jeremy Morris, Tonya Saddler, and Herbert Smith. This second edition was particularly helped along by candid conversations with and indirect support from TJ Andrews, Xavier Killebrew, and Royel Johnson.

I wish to thank several "higher ed colleagues" who have encouraged me over the years that I've worked on this book project too. Without their contributions to our collective knowledge, my understanding of higher education, student development, and college students' sense of belonging, while still incomplete, would be far too limited to write an entire book about it. Thus, I recognize the encouragement and support of Don Creamer (my doctoral advisor), Marybeth Gasman, Joan Hirt, Sylvia Hurtado, Steve Janosik, Susan Komives, George Kuh, Norma Mertz, Amaury Nora, Laura Perna, Kris Renn, Vincent Tinto, Frank Worrell, Dante Dixson, and DeLeon Gray. Special recognition to my former faculty colleagues at The Ohio State University for their support, direct and indirect, during the first edition. So much of this second edition was done with support from new OSU faculty colleagues (Matt Mayhew, Marc Johnston, Anne Marie-Nunez) and leaders across the country including Jamie Washington, DL Stewart, Menah Pratt-Clarke, Vern Granger, to name a few.

Finally, I thank Dr. DeLeon Gray and the many other graduate students, scholars, and practitioners with whom I spoke and those with whom I worked as I carried out this second edition. Our conversations, questions, and confusion served as a basis for my additional thoughts about college students' sense of belonging. Special thanks to Heather Jarrow, Kate Lalor, and the editorial staff at Routledge; your enormous patience was appreciated as I worked to produce the edition that I *wanted* to write, not the one that I had time to write in light of so many life transitions. Working with you on this second edition has been literally amazing and I hope we'll do this again soon. To all of you and those who are implied, but not listed, I offer a multitude of "thanks."

Here's to belonging.

Chapter 1

Introduction

If both the physiological and the safety needs are fairly well gratified, then there will emerge love and affection and belongingness needs, and the whole cycle already described will repeat itself with this new centre. Now the person will feel keenly.

(Abraham Maslow)

This is a book about sense of belonging. Say this: "I belong here." Now, turn to someone near you and say it again: "I belong here." If you're alone, grab your cell phone and text someone: "I belong here." What's their reaction? What's yours? If you receive affirming nods in agreement or feel a sense of warmth, then pause and connect with the moment. That's your mind (cognitive), body (behavioral), and soul (affective) converging on the sentiment that you are important, that you matter to others around you, and you belong. If your declaration is met with blank stares, disagreement, dismissive laughter, or the all-too-familiar text reply (??! ☺) then take a moment to sense your feelings. Channel them toward your mind. What are you thinking? What do you want to do now? What meaning do you make of the entire exchange? Connect with those emotions before moving on. All of this is the essence of sense of belonging, a phenomenon that we will talk about over the course of this entire volume.

BACKGROUND

On September 8, 2009, former President Barack Obama delivered a widely televised, though hotly contested, "Back-to-School Address" at Wakefield

High School in Arlington, Virginia. Thousands of students across the country, from kindergarten to 12th grade and beyond, tuned in as the then President offered encouragement and inspiration to America's future about their potential. During his 15-minute address, the country's first Black President recalled his experience as a child raised by a single mother who struggled at times to make ends meet. "There were times when I was lonely and felt like I didn't fit in." He went on to explain how important it is for students to feel safe and have a sense of belonging in educational settings. His comments implied that safety and belonging were correlated with success in school. And his comments certainly align with the evidence base presented in this book, namely the link between social isolation, loneliness, perceived fit, and belonging.

If we know anything at all, we know that belongingness is a basic human motivation and all people share a strong need to belong (Maslow, 1962). As Maslow explained in the quote that opens this chapter, "If both the physiological and the safety needs are fairly well gratified, then there will emerge ... belongingness needs." Many definitions of belongingness abound. **Sense of belonging generally refers to a feeling of connectedness, that one is important or matters to others** (Rosenberg & McCullough, 1981).[1] The absence of a sense of belonging typically is described as a "sense of alienation," rejection, social isolation, loneliness, or "marginality," which has been linked to negative proximal and long-term outcomes such as dissatisfaction, low self-esteem, depression, substance abuse, and suicide (Hagerty, Williams, & Oe, 2002). Lack of a sense of belonging can undermine academic performance (Walton & Cohen, 2007) and even one's plans to stay in college (Berger, 1997). Students who do not feel like they belong rarely stay in college. In fact, students "who do not have a sense of belonging complain that their college experience is like 'stopping by the mall' to get what they need on the way to somewhere else" (Jacoby & Garland, 2004–2005, p. 65).

We've also learned from dozens of studies that posit sense of belonging as a function of perceived support from one's peers, teachers, and family members (Hoffman, Richmond, Morrow, & Salomone, 2002–2003; Johnson et al., 2007; Strayhorn, 2008a). For instance, scholars have documented that students' sense of belonging is greater if and when they socialize with peers whose backgrounds may differ from their own[2] (Maestas, Vaquera, & Zehr, 2007; Strayhorn, 2008c). For college students, peers play an important and powerful role in facilitating sense of belonging, as it is the peer group that provides the feedback and support necessary for the achievement of this need (White & Cones, 1999). And since we know that peer interactions can produce or inhibit sense of belonging, it is critical for college student educators to encourage positive interactions among students through conditions that *really* matter in college, ranging from advising networks to cocurricular involvement, from learning communities to peer mentoring, to name a few (Kuh, Kinzie, Schuh, Whitt, & Associates, 2005). I will say this many times in different ways: positive interpersonal, peer interactions increase students' sense of belonging and sense of belonging leads to student success so those charged with increasing college student success should think just as much about campus climate and policies governing social interactions as they do about predictive analytics, intrusive advising, curricular alignment, and early alert systems. It all *really* matters.

Although a good deal is known about sense of belonging as a basic human motivation, factors that influence students' sense of belonging, and the influence of sense of belonging on important outcomes such as achievement, adjustment, and plans to stay in college, comparatively little is known about differences that exist in terms of college students' sense of belonging, as well as social identities and campus environments that create a sense of belonging for such students. And, more recently, researchers and policymakers have called for a change in the focus of educational research from "research for research's sake" to purposeful examinations that lead to empirically based recommendations for institutional transformation by improving educational practices, policies, and programs, given that in the past "the results of scholarly research on teaching and learning [were] rarely translated into practice" (US Department of Education, 2006). With this in mind, the second edition of *College Students' Sense of Belonging* was designed to achieve these larger objectives as well.

PURPOSE OF THE BOOK

The book has several main purposes. First, the Introduction and leading chapters will offer a substantive review of the extant literature on sense of belonging and critique that literature in light of new and emerging scientific discoveries. Second, the book's review of literature will lead to a synthesis of several theoretical threads and conceptual components that represents the book's overarching organizing framework. The resultant model will be outlined generally, defined explicitly, and illustrated graphically, mostly in Chapter 3.

Third, the book presents new and recent research findings from quantitative, qualitative, and mixed-methods studies conducted by the author and many other scholars across various fields/disciplines throughout the country. As was mentioned in the Preface, the second edition includes studies published since the previous edition too. And, finally, *College Students' Sense of Belonging* offers college student educators what's really needed by translating research into practice—practical recommendations for improving educational environments, practices, policies, and programs in ways that facilitate students' sense of belonging on campus. Before proceeding with a critical review of existing literature and theory, let's establish a "working definition" for sense of belonging that will level our understanding of this concept.

A WORKING DEFINITION

Quite often, before scholars can mine an idea for its empirical worth, it is necessary to attend to basic definitions and concerns. For the purposes of this book, sense of belonging is framed as a basic human need and motivation, sufficient to influence behavior.

> In terms of college, sense of belonging refers to students' perceived social support on campus, a feeling or sensation of connectedness, and the experience of mattering or feeling cared about, accepted, respected, valued by, and important to the campus community or others on campus such as faculty, staff, and peers.

It is a cognitive evaluation that typically leads to an affective and/or behavioral response.

Sense of belonging is relational, and thus there's a reciprocal quality to relationships that provide a sense of belonging. Each member benefits from the group and the group, in a sense (no pun intended), benefits from the contributions of each member. It is the proverbial "I am we and we are each" phenomenon. Under optimal conditions, members feel that the group is important to them and that they are important to the group. Consider the student who is a member of a collegiate sorority—she likely feels important as a member and the group serves an important role in her life, partly because it satisfies one of her fundamental needs and that is to belong. By the same token, the sorority means nothing without members who constitute its very existence. The group satisfies the belongingness needs of the individual—in exchange for membership, members will be cared for and supported. The group needs its members, however, to exist and the members yearn to be part of the group as it also gives meaning and purpose to their existence. So, in essence, **sense of belonging is a "feeling that members matter to one another and to the group, and a shared faith that members' needs will be met through their commitment to be together"** (McMillan & Chavis, 1986, p. 9). (Question: Do you think college students today feel like their institutions need them to exist and vice versa?)

Let's consider another example that illustrates these points in a college environment. Meet James. James is a first-year student from a rural neighborhood in southwest Virginia. New to college, and first in his family to attend beyond high school, James spends a lot of time contemplating questions about his future. *Will I make friends? Will other students like me? Will I "fit in" in my residence hall? And, can I do it?* During summer orientation, he learns that the university offers a freshman living-learning community called "Explorations" for students who are interested in science careers. Despite his relatively modest upbringing in poorly resourced public schools, James has always done well in science and had given considerable thought to becoming a scientist or engineer someday. Notwithstanding initial uncertainties, he moved quickly to sign up for the living-learning community without consulting his parents, academic advisor, or friends.

Why would a first-year, first-generation college student from a rural community make such a hasty decision without seeking further advice? Simply put, the "Explorations" learning community seemed to meet one of James' most basic needs: a sense of belonging, of being around and accepted by others who may share common interests. Recall that definitions of **sense of belonging generally refer to "an individual's sense of identification or positioning in relation to a group or to the college community, which may yield an affective response"** (Tovar & Simon, 2010, p. 200). By participating in the "Explorations" learning community, by engaging peers who likely share common interests, and by living in a university space sanctioned for those interested in science or engineering careers, James reduced his worries about making suitable friends, satisfied his need to connect with others on campus, and increased the likelihood that he would feel a sense of belonging in a space that was otherwise foreign, unfamiliar, lonely, and unwelcoming. This example not only reflects key elements of sense of belonging such as involvement or mattering, but in part, reveals my approach to examining this important dimension of students' experiences in college. There are many decisions that students make that trace back to their basic belonging needs.

Conceptually, my approach reflects a social cognitive perspective on achievement motivation. That is, sense of belonging, as I explain it here, is part of a larger motivational framework. Such a framework maintains that individuals have psychological needs; satisfaction of such needs affects behaviors and perceptions, and characteristics of the social context influence how well these needs are met. In this book, I frame sense of belonging as a basic human need that takes on heightened importance in *certain* social contexts where *some* individuals are prone to feeling unsupported, unwelcomed, or lonely, or in *some* social contexts where *certain* individuals are more likely to feel that way. Recall that James worried about making friends and feeling accepted—his need to belong was heightened as a first-generation, first-year student in an unfamiliar college environment where he expected to stand out, stick out, or even feel lonely and left out. Given the importance of belonging, he moved quickly, even without advice, to join a learning community where his need to belong and matter could be satisfied. Illustration of my approach to this topic leads to an important question, which is addressed below.

WHY WRITE THIS BOOK?

I decided to write this book for at least three reasons. First, over the years, I have conducted a number of large-scale research projects examining the experiences of college students in various contexts. Viewed as a social scientist whose primary interests center on the academic study of students in postsecondary and higher education, I have several lines of work that focus on student access and achievement, issues of equity and diversity, as well as student learning and development. Whether studying the role that summer bridge programs play on low-income racial/ethnic minorities' preparation for college, the academic supports that enable the success of minority men in science, technology, engineering, and math (STEM) fields, or the meaning-making processes of gay men of color, I have uncovered a preponderance of evidence suggesting the importance of community, support, membership, and acceptance, all core elements of the book's central topic, *sense of belonging*. So, I wrote this book because data from my research, over the years, suggested the need for it.

It's not only the number of times that sense of belonging has been identified in my research as an important factor in the success of college students that demonstrates the compelling need for this book, although I think that certainly deserves mention. Rather, it's the nature in which students talk about sense of belonging that underscores its significance to the college student experience. As you'll see in the next chapters, college students stress the importance of social acceptance, support, community, connections, and respect to their own identity, development, mental health, wellbeing, and academic success. When I started thinking seriously about writing a book on college students' sense of belonging, I was working with members of my research team to complete a wave of interviews for a mixed-methods project. Following one of the interviews, a participant asked, "What will you do with this information?" As usual, I shared that aggregated information would be published in journal articles and presentations (you know, the usual "IRB 101" stuff), but I also added that I was contemplating a book on sense of belonging. The participant's eyes lit up and she proclaimed, "YES [emphasis added], you've got to ... Sense of belonging is so important. It can literally be a matter of life or death for some students, like me." So, I wrote this book because my informants over the years encouraged it. The book's topic is important, weighty, and has gravity for students' success in college—I wrote it to help all students succeed.

There is a third reason why I wrote this book. In graduate school, my doctoral advisor, Don Creamer, would say to students, "It's hard to write a paper when you have nothing to say." Simple, yet profound wisdom. And if it's hard to write a paper without something to say, imagine trying to fill enough pages to constitute a book! I firmly believe that reading should usually precede writing, jump-starting one's impulse to write. And, for me, I began (this book) by reading (other people's work), which led to writing (and thinking) my own ideas, and more reading, which, in turn, led to more writing (and thinking) on a topic about which I feel strongly. I didn't start writing this book because I *wanted to*; rather, I had to. The more I read about campus environments, the more I wrote about community and vice versa. I wrote this book because, simply put, I felt like I had something to say about the topic. Sense of belonging is a topic about which I feel strongly; those feelings compelled me to begin writing and sustained me as I completed the previous edition of this book. Surprisingly, similar convictions and feelings fueled my work on the present (second) edition of the book too.

Before concluding this chapter, I should mention one other aspect of the book's design that relates to *why* and *how* I wrote it. You will notice that each substantive chapter begins with at least one quotation, some preserved from the first edition and some new to this second edition. Quotes were drawn from participants in my previous studies or were spoken by politicians, philosophers, educators, and entertainers. I found this a useful way to jump-start my thinking about sense of belonging in particular arenas. In other cases, I thought the quote was appropriate as it captures the essence of sense of belonging as I am framing it in this book. Where possible, I attempt to use the quotation to launch a discussion of sense of belonging in terms of the chapter's specific focus, but I also strive to return to the quote at the chapter's end as a way of "circling back" to the thoughts that initiated our conversation in the first place. For instance, in this chapter, we will return to the words of former President Barack Obama before moving on to the next chapter.

CONCLUSION

Echoing the words of Barack Obama that began this chapter, I, too, recall times growing up when I did not belong. I was in grade school—a rising fourth grader—when one of the assistant principals decided that I would make a good addition to the "football gang," as it was called, which of course is fundamentally problematic is so many ways. The "football gang" consisted of mostly young Black men who attended the predominantly White elementary school where I was enrolled. They were known amongst teachers, staff, and some students as "brutes," "thugs," "jocks," and even "monsters" mostly because they were taller, bigger, stronger than most of our peers. Standing at nearly under 4 feet and so small that I was often mistaken as a third grader, I'm not sure why the assistant principal thought that I would *find community* in this group (except for obvious and *racist* reasons). Looking back, it's clear that *race mattered* even in fourth grade at my award-winning, highly ranked elementary school that boasted very large numbers of veteran teachers with master's degrees and hundreds of graduates who scored highest on standardized assessments. Regardless of what we shared in phenotype—mostly boys of color, ranging from chocolate brown to caramel yellow in skin tone—I knew that I would stick out like a sore thumb. They wanted to skip class and I wanted to get there early so I could sit up front near the teacher. They wanted to throw food in the cafeteria as a way of inciting a riot and I wanted to eat my food quickly (including my dessert) so I could be dismissed early and spend time working alone in the computer lab. They wanted to play football, tackle each other, and make touchdowns—I wanted none of this. Just because we looked alike to some people, we actually shared very little in common. I did not belong. I felt like I didn't matter. And I was rejected many times over once they all learned that I knew very little about football (and didn't care to), had no intention of ever being tackled, and would drop the ball before I would ever let one of them drop me. I was always one of the very last to be "chosen" by team leaders and usually that moment was met with pregnant pause, rolling eyes, and something like: "Shucks, we got Terrell." Not exactly the most welcoming refrain. My time with the "football gang" was lonely; though surrounded by dozens, I felt alone.

Although it is clear that I shared very little in common with members of the "football gang," there was hardly a time when I felt unsafe (with the exception of a few times that someone came close to tackling me). Generally speaking, I felt safe and secure at school, which according to Maslow's (1954) hierarchy of needs brought my love and belonging needs to the fore. I can recall times in high school when I did not belong and my safety was threatened. For instance, I ran for office in the Student Government Association (SGA). I ran on a strong platform arguing to give more visibility to students, their needs, and wishes. My campaign slogan was upbeat and optimistic, but I also championed issues of diversity in my campaign speech. I remember it like it was yesterday—my speech closed with a cadence as I rhythmically recited the words etched on my paper about creating community, unifying bands of students, and strengthening the bonds of *personhood* in the school. Just as I reached the last paragraph, I crossed over into my best imitation of "Kermit The Frog" and declared: "It's not easy being green." I sang the entire song in that disguised voice. It was a metaphor, hinting lightly at what it was like for students of color (like me) in the predominantly White, highly selective high school that I attended.

Everyone rose in ovation at the end and my music teacher was so impressed that she was crying in the corner of the stage. The next day, I arrived at school and found that dozens of my campaign flyers had been defaced with the word "Nigger" written across my photo. I was devastated. I was hurt. I felt lonely. I was afraid. I felt unsafe. Quickly, I worked with my team and school personnel to remove the flyers and produce new ones. News spread fast and pretty soon I was getting help from people who I had never even met. That support, outpouring of love and care brought light to a dark situation and restored my faith in our school spirit. I won the election and people cheered. I felt a strong sense of connection to that school, the people ... like I was there on purpose and I belonged.

I've said it before and I'll say it many times again: sense of belonging is a basic human need, a fundamental motivation, sufficient to drive behaviors and perceptions. Its satisfaction leads to positive gains such as happiness, elation, wellbeing, achievement, and optimal functioning. Given its significance in various social contexts, as well as its consistent association with positive health, and social and psychological outcomes, I think its importance cannot be stressed enough. Much of what we do, we do to establish and maintain a sense of belonging in the contexts and fields that constitute our ecology, our lives, our world. In many public talks and lectures across the globe, I point out for audiences that humans go to almost any length to *feel* as if they belong or to "find their people," "their village," or "mi gente," as one Latino undergraduate told me years ago. People will change their style of dress, buy a new car, build a brand-new home, change academic majors, join a fraternity or sorority—even despite expensive membership dues—cut their hair or dye their hair blue to gain acceptance, to experience community, or to feel a sense of belonging. It's crucial, important, and related to student success in college. Until the next chapter ...

NOTES

1 The first edition of this book included a reference to "fitting in" as a feature of belonging. However, since that time, I have come to disagree with my previous point. True belonging is not about fitting in; it's about being authentically oneself, flaws and all. I'll say more about this later in the book.
2 Even though conventional wisdom may lead one to believe that homophily—being amongst one's own kind—is a precondition for belonging.

Chapter 2

Insights from Literature and Research

We are driven by five genetic needs: survival, love and belonging, power, freedom, and fun.

(William Glasser)

I've always been shy or had a shyness about me. I think I learned how to use sports and athletics as a way of breaking out of that shell and as a way of belonging to a particular group of others, a way of feeling special.

(Ricardo Lama, second-year undergraduate, Latino male)

PRELIMINARY THOUGHTS

Before rolling in the deep about what has been written about sense of belonging, a few preliminary comments seem warranted. Throughout the text, I refer to students who have participated in my research studies over the years. Here you meet Ricardo. Keep reading, and you'll meet Vincent. And much later in the book, you'll come to know a bit about Tiffanye and Malika, to name a few. All of these are pseudonyms selected by the students. In most cases, students picked pseudonyms that reflect aspects of their ethnicity, gender, and cultural naming practices. In other cases, the pseudonym may have little to do with the student.

Armed with this information, let's roll up our sleeves and grapple with the existing literature. First, I review the cast of published definitions about sense of belonging. Next, I use some of that information to articulate why sense of belonging is important. Then, given its importance, I review the extant literature, largely from education, that addresses sense of belonging among students in learning contexts.

DEFINITIONS OF SENSE OF BELONGING

Sense of belonging is one term with many meanings. Reflecting the difference of opinions is the vast diversity of terms or labels attached to this experience: belongingness, relatedness, membership, community, acceptance, support, and affiliation, to name a few. No matter the term, they all deal with an individual's psychological experiences and, importantly, their subjective evaluation of the level of integration in a particular context such as family, school, or college. Others examine people's experiences of social support and involvement when studying sense of belonging. To be sure, there's a fair amount of disagreement in the literature about the specific definition of sense of belonging. Consider the following:

1. Sense of belonging refers to "a feeling that members matter to one another and to the group, and a shared faith that members' needs will be met through their commitment to be together" (Osterman, 2000, p. 324). See "Episode 2.1: A Moving Email" for further discussion of this point.
2. Sense of belonging characterizes a person's perceived belief of indispensability within a system (Anant, 1966).
3. Sense of belonging is defined as "an individual's sense of identification or positioning in relation to a group or to the college community, which may yield an affective response" (Tovar & Simon, 2010, p. 200).
4. Sense of belonging refers to "students' sense of being accepted, valued, included, and encouraged by others (teachers and peers) in the academic classroom setting and of feeling oneself to be an important part of the life and activity of the class" (Goodenow, 1993a, p. 25).

EPISODE 2.1: "A Moving Email"

In the first edition of this book, I quoted that sense of belonging refers to a "feeling that members matter to one another and to the group, and a shared faith that members' needs will be met through their commitment to be together" (Osterman, 2000, p. 324). In public talks and lectures across the nation, I have shared that I *wrote* that statement in 2012 (in the first edition) but I *truly understood* the statement in 2016, nearly four years after the book had been published. That's not to say that I wrote the statement initially without any understanding of what it meant in terms of our work with students—as the book makes clear, my research suggests that belonging is a feeling, a sensation, a belief that one matters to others around them and that someone else cares about them and their outcomes (aka "success or failure") almost as much as they do. But I spent time thinking deeply about *when* and *how* students came to develop "faith" in us *as educators* and even more so "us" *as institutions*. One of my most pivotal insights came on August 11, 2016, while visiting the State University of New York-Binghamton (SUNY) to give a campus-wide lecture on belonging and several workshops with faculty, staff, and students.

At one point in the day, I was scheduled to speak to over 300 resident assistants (RAs) about the important role they play on campus as RAs. I was excited to share them, stressing their *unique* opportunity to serve as a "peer educator" by working together to create a curriculum for their residents—not just a menu of disconnected activities and programs (like I did when I was an RA at UVA)—but a set of well-aligned experiences designed to *teach* their residents the knowledge and skills that they believe they need to possess. So, my presentation really started with a question: That is, what will I teach my residents this year and why? Then, I coached them through working as an educational team (not just a group of RAs), alongside educational consultants (e.g., staff, faculty), to assemble a set of learning experiences (i.e., what we typically call "programming"), ranging from guest speakers to book clubs, from field trips to hall celebrations, that provide opportunities for residents to learn and master the skills intended. Just before taking the stage to address the RA group, I had time to check email in a private "green room" tucked away in the auditorium. When I launched the mail client on my cellphone, the following note loaded immediately:

From: CHUCK

Date: Thursday, August 11, 2016 at 11:35 AM

To: T Strayhorn

Subject: moving in

would it be possible for me to move in a day early? because my mom got the dates confused and booked a hotel for me on the 15th so that way I can be ready to move in by the 16th but we have just come to the realization that the program doesn't actually start until the 17th and the hotel and everything is already booked. So we want to know would it be at all possible for me to move in a day early. We can't afford to pay for all this right now. :-(

Have you ever received an email that was clearly <u>not</u> intended for you? One that was so misplaced and misguided that the words didn't even seem to make sense? That's how I interpreted this email initially. I thought: "Wait, what?! Move in ... who's moving in, where? My mom did what with the hotel ... how does he know my mom?!" I was deeply confused, and my initial reaction was to hit DELETE and move on, as the email didn't seem to be intended for me. But, as I've shared many times, it's ever-more difficult to research, teach, and write about student success and *supporting all students* on one hand, and ignoring a student who may need help on the other. So I sat with the email awhile and tried to decipher its cryptic message. Upon closer inspection, I realized that there was a small chance that the author intended to contact me, so I replied: "Help me understand what you're referring to ... move in where?" Pretty soon he responded and explained that he was a new first-year student moving to campus in a few days. We exchanged a few emails and I connected him with a few *trusted colleagues*—cultural navigators (Strayhorn, 2015)—who I knew would reach out to help him while I redirected my attention to those at SUNY-Binghamton. After a soft punt or "touch pass" to one of my colleagues in housing/residence life, I went on stage, gave my talk, answered questions, and then returned to email to check on "the moving email" thread.

There had been several exchanges between housing staff and the incoming student, so I started with the most recent email first. It read:

Dear Dr. Strayhorn,

YOU ROCK ... and my mom loves you! Thanks so much for your help with everything today. I can't think Nancy, Tom, and Leroy enough for telling me what to do to make this work out. I haven't even gotten [*sic*] to campus yet and I can already tell that I'm going to love it there. Thanks again, chuck

Like Chuck, I was happy to know that things worked out but still curious why he reached out to me as I don't work in housing, residence life, or student affairs. I thanked my colleagues (Nancy, Tom, Leroy) via email for following-through and helping Chuck and his mom resolve the matter so quickly. I wrote a separate note asking Chuck how he found me, worried that my name was etched on some bathroom wall that read: "Hey, need to move-in early? Contact

Strayhorn at 1-800-FUN-SIZE!"[1] He replied with another short note that read:

> That's an easy one! No, you're one of the first
> people that me and my mom met during one of
> the campus visit days. You were the keynote
> speaker. And at the end of your talk, you said:
> "If there's ever anything I can do for you,
> please don't hesitate to contact me. **I'm here
> to help!**" so when all this started happening,
> my mom said: contact that little fun-size pro-
> fessor ... he said he's here to help us!

And like finally discovering the "missing piece" of a complicated puzzle, it clicked for me. *That's when students start to develop faith in us*, as individuals and institutions. When we say things like: "We're here to help" or "Let me know if I can do anything for you" or "Tell me what I can do to make things better for you." Students, their families, siblings, guardians, and friends are all listening to us, vetting the words that we share, and hoping that they can trust us to do what we say. What have you said to students that shapes their "faith" in us and their belief that we're here to help them get what they need out of college? And what can you do today to increase their faith? Sense of belonging is a feeling, it's about groups or community, and it's a shared faith.

Since the first edition of this book, I have witnessed many experiences that illustrate the essence of these definitions. For instance, during a visit to Carthage College in Kenosha, Wisconsin to speak at a campus event, I met a student who had been running frantically at near lightning-fast speed to make it inside the elevator, just before the closing doors caught his trailing foot. He made it just in the nick of time but was clearly out of breath, as he gasped for air and rolled around on the wall until his heart slowed. "Where are you rushing off to," I asked, worried that he was en route to an emergency or running late to a time-restricted exam. "I'm off to class ... Biology and we can't be late for THIS [emphasis implied] class," he replied. Surprised and confused since the young man was already late, I proceeded: "What do you mean you *can't* be late for *this* class? You can be late for other classes?!" Laughing, he clarified:

> No, no ... it's not like I can't be late for this class and others don't count. It's
> just that *this* professor told us at the beginning of the term that we can't be

late ... he really needs us there every day. He said he can't teach without us. And if you're not there, he contacts you by phone or email to find out what happened. He called me once when I was out and told me he missed me, that class really wasn't the same without my perspective. He always says that he has a lot to teach us, but it won't matter much if we're not there in class. He does a lot of discussion, debate, and stuff ... and you can't really do that without students (laughing). If I'm late or not there, I'll feel like I'm letting him down, you know.

Just then the elevator doors opened and my new "student informant" darted away to his Biology class. I, on the other hand, took out my iPhone and jotted down notes for this second edition about how much of his story mapped on to feeling cared about, mattering, and sense of belonging in college. This professor seemed an expert in making students feel like they matter—we feel like we matter when we play *important* roles, when we feel like others *depend on us*, and when we command others' *attention* such that our absence does not go unnoticed.

On a separate occasion, I was in northwest Ohio speaking at Marietta College. After a full day of workshops with faculty members and small group meetings with staff, they hosted a small dinner for me to meet a few members of the planning committee and three student leaders. I sat across from one student leader named Mario, a full-framed African male who stood at nearly six feet. He asked about my undergraduate majors, fondest memories of the University of Virginia (my alma mater), and what motivated me to become a professor. In response, I asked about his major, memories, and motivations, but also asked him if he felt like he played an important role on campus. His eyes brightened, just as his posture straightened and he said:

I didn't at first. When I first enrolled here, I thought I had made a big mistake. In fact, I had because I thought "Marietta College" was in Georgia, not Ohio. So when I got here, I thought that I wouldn't stay. I didn't like it at all ... but I hadn't given it much of a chance either. Then, I joined a club for Black students, mostly African Americans. Still, I met other Africans and that's when I realized that I had something to offer the campus ... that it needed me. Ever since then I have been working to connect African students to each other and to form a student organization. That's given me a sense of purpose ... like an important role to play. And it's nice because I feel like other people—faculty and staff—also feel like what I'm doing is important. Like I really matter now.

Fascinated by the clarity and depth of his response, I affirmed that his feelings align with notions of belonging. And I etched a summary of his story on the back of a paper napkin so I could share it with readers in this second edition of the book.

Other definitions imply that belonging may be synonymous with or closely related to community. For instance, McMillan and Chavis (1986, p. 9) define belonging as community, which refers to "a feeling that members have of belonging, a feeling that members matter to one another and to the group, and a shared faith that members' needs will be met through their commitment to be together." Community, by definition, can't exist until members experience feelings of belonging, trust in others (and self), as well as safety (Furman, 1998). Most readers will be familiar with Ernest Boyer's (1990) *Principles of Community* that enumerate the characteristics of academic and social dimensions of campus community life: (1) educationally purposeful; (2) open (i.e., rights are protected); (3) just; (4) disciplined; (5) caring (i.e., wellbeing of members is valued); and (6) celebrative (i.e., heritage is remembered, rituals affirm traditions). I argue that sense of belonging, then, is a precursor to community, and while closely related to community, it is not its exact equal; rather it is the feelings, perceptions, and mindsets that accompany gaining true membership in a community. You may notice, too, that the "working definition" presented in Chapter 1 (as well as the one coming up in Chapter 3) represents a smooth blend of elements drawn from many of the definitions cited throughout the volume. Rather than split hairs about *which* of these best reflects sense of belonging, I have offered a critical definition of belonging in both chapters that's almost all of them at once.

CONSEQUENCES OF SENSE OF BELONGING

As I argue in other parts of the book, sense of belonging is a basic human need and fundamental motive, sufficient to drive human behavior. By that I mean, everyone feels a need to belong, to matter, to be accepted by others (even at the expense of self sometimes). Consequently, individuals are motivated to satisfy their need for love and belongingness, just as they are compelled to satisfy more basic physiological needs like the need for air, water, food, sleep, and shelter. Belonging is a fundamental need *for all people,* people are motivated to satisfy their belonging needs, and, thus, people are driven to do things in the hope of gaining a sense of belonging. In pursuit of belonging, some people have joined clubs and places of worship, while others have run marathons, cycled in support of a cure, married their partner, gone to college, changed academic majors, studied abroad, handled snakes, and even connected with cults.

A fairly conclusive body of evidence has amassed to suggest that sense of belonging is important for human functioning and a critical factor in the psychological wellbeing of individuals (Hagerty, Lynch-Bauer, Patusky, Bouwsema, & Collier, 1992). Without it, people suffer from a number of pathologies. For instance, Tom Joiner's (2005, 2010) research on suicide suggests that suicide or suicidal ideation—that is, thoughts of suicide—are directly, positively related to perceived burdensomeness and thwarted belonging or social alienation. When these two psychological states are present at the same time and they persist in the person long enough, then the desire to die by suicide develops. Said differently, when one feels like they're a burden to others—that others would be better off without them—and they also feel socially alienated (i.e., belonging needs unsatisfied), then thoughts of suicide increase in frequency and intensity.[2] Satisfaction of one's need to belong not only prevents suicidal thoughts, but also leads to a variety of positive emotions such as joy, elation, calmness, and happiness in life (Baumeister & Leary, 1995).

A fair amount of research has shown that sense of belonging is also associated with numerous positive, prosocial, and productive outcomes in specific domains such as education. For instance, sense of belonging positively influences academic achievement, retention, and persistence (Hausmann, Schofield, & Woods, 2007; Rhee, 2008). Quite often, students' academic and social involvement influences their sense of belonging on campus and vice versa (Strayhorn, 2008d). By interacting frequently and in positive ways with others on campus, students establish meaningful relationships (e.g., friendships) with peers and personnel, which, in turn, affirm that they are seen, cared about, and needed by others. Supportive relationships of this kind become critical resources that can be brought to bear on the college experience. Strong support networks tend to enhance students' commitments, campus connections, and, consequently, retention. Indeed, sense of belonging is "a critical aspect in retaining all students and particularly students of color" (Maestas, Vaquera, & Zehr, 2007, p. 238).

Just as an absence of sense of belonging generally leads to decreased or diminished interest and engagement in ordinary life activities (Joiner, 2005; Weiss, 1973), the same holds true in education. When students' needs are not satisfied in educational settings, research also shows that their motivations are diminished, their development is impaired, they become disengaged, and they perform poorly on assignments and tests (Deci & Ryan, 2000). It is clear that students have difficulty sustaining academic engagement and commitment in an environment where they do not feel personally valued and welcomed (Goodenow, 1993b). So, the takeaway point seems clear: To excel, students must feel a sense of belonging in schools or colleges, and therefore educators must work to create conditions that foster belongingness among all students. And we do this through any number of ways, including engaged teaching, providing academic supports, campus activities, positive messaging (see Figure 2.1), and striving to build learning communities where everyone's voice matters. And when educators do not concern themselves with students' sense of belonging, they conspire in the academic failure of their students.

Research also has documented that needs are domain- and situation-specific (Maslow, 1962). Students may experience belongingness in school

Figure 2.1   Sign on building at Kent State University is a good example of positive messaging and its ability to impact students' sense of belonging.

but not sports, in history but not science, or in campus clubs and organizations but not classrooms, and consequently, they will function better in the context where their needs are satisfied (Osterman, 2000). The following is an instructive, personal example:

> I am a classically trained pianist, who studied piano and voice as a music major at the University of Virginia. My primary instruments are my voice and most keyboards, including those on which I was trained (e.g., acoustic piano,

electric piano, digital keyboards). However, I am not a pipe organist! So, you can imagine my surprise (and escalating anxiety) when I was invited to play the opening selection for "MLK Day" at St. Stephen's Episcopal Church in front of hundreds of congregants. I had always "felt at home" in front of the piano or keyboard, but this massive pipe organ was unfamiliar, uncomfortable, different, intimidating, and extremely loud. My completely ordinary (and less than amateur) performance that night had little to do with my musical skills, but everything to do with how "out of place" I felt in the cold shadow of this towering pipe organ. Worried that I had lost my touch, I played the Black National Anthem, "Lift Every Voice and Sing" again that night at home on my little Korg workstation in D-flat. Like magic, there it was again ... harmonic chords flowing effortlessly from memory.

So, what explains the difference between my broken, amateur "plunking" on the pipes and the virtuosic "chording" on the Korg? Sense of belonging; and the fact that we tend to function better in contexts, settings, environments—yes, even college classrooms or campuses—where feelings of isolation and intimidation give way to connections, caring, and community. Under the threatening shadow of the monstrous pipe organ, I was fighting to remember my notes and play without hiccup, although a portion of my "working memory" (see next section) was preoccupied with anxiety, worry, and fear of this unfamiliar instrument. Consequently, feelings of loneliness, intimidation, and doubt hijacked my musical abilities that night. Once back home—a place that I find comfortable, familiar, and warm—more of my working memory was available for use and my performance was optimized by feelings of confidence, safety, and security.

WHY SENSE OF BELONGING IS IMPORTANT

I covered a bit of this in Chapter 1, so I won't go into too much detail here. Suffice it to say that sense of belonging is important and it takes on heightened importance in contexts where individuals are inclined to feel isolated, alienated, lonely, or invisible. Early research on belonging suggested its importance as a basic human need and motivation for behavior. For instance, Maslow (1954, p. 20) explained, "If both the physiological and the safety needs are fairly well gratified, there will emerge the love and affection and belongingness needs." At this point, individuals will strive to belong, to connect with others, to make friends, motivated by the unsatisfied hunger for contact, intimacy (in a literal sense), and community. Until the need to belong is gratified, other (and higher-order) needs like self-actualization, creativity, and innovation cannot gain ascendency or "may become simply non-existent or be pushed to the background" (Maslow, 1954, p. 16).

Sense of belonging also takes on heightened significance in certain contexts, at certain times, among certain people. For instance, belonging needs take on increased significance in environments or situations that individuals experience as different, unfamiliar, or foreign, as well as in contexts where certain individuals are likely to feel marginalized, unsupported, or unwelcomed (Anderman & Freeman, 2004). Recall my story from the previous section about the gargantuan pipe organ. Other examples of feeling marginalized run the gamut from students of color at predominantly White institutions (PWIs); to women and/or minorities in science, technology, engineering, or math (STEM) fields; to gay students in largely heteronormative and homophobic environments; to low-income entering freshmen at highly selective and high-priced private universities. As Hurtado and Carter (1997, p. 324) rightly implied, sense of belonging is particularly meaningful to those who "perceive themselves as marginal to the mainstream life [of college]."

All of this has implications for college students. As mentioned earlier, without sense of belonging students' motivations are diminished, their development is impaired, and they perform poorly on assignments and tests (e.g., Deci & Ryan, 2000). Theoretically, this makes sense from the stance of motivation theory. Sense of belonging is part of a larger motivational framework. Motivation theory posits that individuals have needs. Satisfaction of such needs leads to optimal functioning; deprivation of or insufficiently meeting needs leads to pathology. So if an individual lacks a particular need such as food or housing, then s/he/z develops an appetite for that missing element. Virtually all of their time, energy, and concentration is devoted to the quest to fulfill that need.

Interestingly, contemporary social psychology research advances the idea that individuals have what's called a "working memory" that they use to complete tasks associated with daily life. Any activity—from ironing clothes to checking email or using FaceTime on one's iPhone—draws upon one's "working memory" and uses up a fraction of its capacity. Trying to manage too many activities simultaneously can overdraw "working memory" (also known as one's "bandwidth") and lead to poor output, loss of quality, or failure. Similar wisdom holds for college students craving a sense of belonging. After basic physiological needs (e.g., air, water, food) are met and safety/security needs are in place, virtually all of their strivings can be interpreted as attempts to satisfy their need to belong. And the more they have to do to feel a sense of belonging, the less resources available for them to devote to studying for class, acing a test, or engaging in undergraduate research, just to name common examples. It's also instructive to note that time and energy devoted to worrying about basic needs—like food, water, shelter, and safety—reduces the psychological resources available for hungry, homeless, and vulnerable students to direct toward finding a sense of belonging or excelling in college. In short, deprivation of belonging in college prevents achievement and wellbeing, while satisfaction of college students' sense of belonging is a key to educational success for all students.

WHAT WE KNOW

An extensive review of the literature on sense of belonging led me in a number of directions. Initially, I set out to read critically all that had been written on sense of belonging in higher education, with most references dating back to the mid-1990s (e.g., Hurtado & Carter, 1997). My search for belonging literature took a sharp, and unanticipated, turn when I stumbled across a reference to sense of belonging in schools rather than colleges, with references dating back to the early 1990s (e.g., Goodenow, 1993a). Information about related concepts like mattering and community took me back even further (e.g., Rosenberg & McCullough, 1981; Schlossberg, 1985) until I settled on the idea that belongingness is a basic human need, which took me back to the beginning of time (Maslow, 1954) ... or at least well before I was ever born. Be that as it may, the review that follows of existing literature on college students' sense of belonging is organized into three major categories: belongingness as a concept; circumstances that promote (or thwart) belonging; and the relation between belonging and other outcomes or behaviors. Where possible, I made decisions to constrict our conversation to literature drawn from educational contexts, as these sources were deemed most relevant to the whole issue of college students' sense of belonging. By no means is this review exhaustive or encyclopedic, but it serves to introduce readers to several primary sources to which they should turn for more information.

Early research on belonging stressed its importance as a basic human need and a fundamental motivation, sufficient to drive behavior and beliefs (Maslow, 1954). The importance of belonging(ness) as a conceptual construct has been well established (Goodenow, 1993a; Hagerty, Williams, & Oe, 2002; Ostrove, 2003). For instance, grounded in the work of Bollen and Hoyle (1990), sense of belonging relates to "an individual's sense of identification or positioning in relation to a group or to the college community, which may yield an affective response" (Tovar & Simon, 2010, p. 200). The psychological dimension of belonging refers to feeling valued, needed, and significant within a system or environment. And, indeed, all of us yearn to belong. Consider this point: "In their desperation to belong and to feel worthwhile some may join a gang and also worship Satan" (Clark, 1992, p. 289). Good news is that in their quest to belong, many others engage in a number of healthy, productive, prosocial behaviors too, such as joining the military in service to one's country, starting a family, going to college, choosing a major, picking a job, making friends, and even succeeding in college.

Considerable work has documented the circumstances that promote students' sense of belonging in schools and colleges (Baumeister & Leary, 1995; Hagerty, Williams, & Oe, 2002; Hoffman, Richmond, Morrow, & Salomone, 2002–2003; Strayhorn, 2008c). For instance, Velasquez demonstrated how interactions with White students affected Chicano students' sense of belonging. Hoffman and his colleagues identified the important role that peer interactions, faculty support, and campus climate play in sustaining students' feelings of belonging. As yet another example, Hagerty, Williams, and Oe found that participating in a sport fostered a sense of belonging among college students (see Chapter 9 of this volume). So encouraging positive peer interactions, connecting students with supportive faculty, and providing opportunities for student involvement help them to feel a sense of belonging. Write that down—that's three more ideas of promising practices for fostering students' sense of belonging in college.

A subgroup of studies exists within this larger category that tends to focus on determinants of sense of belonging—that is, factors, not just circumstances, that promote or prohibit belonging in education (e.g., Hurtado & Carter, 1997; Maestas, Vaquera, & Zehr, 2007; Museus & Maramba, 2011). For example, Hurtado and Carter (1997) analyzed survey data from 272 respondents at 127 colleges. They found a strong, positive association between sense of belonging and reports of frequent discussions with others about course content, tutoring other students, and frequency of talking with faculty members. Interestingly, their results suggest that academic performance does not necessarily promote or diminish sense of belonging and students who were members of religious clubs and sororities/fraternities had a significantly stronger sense of belonging than non-members. Membership in community outreach organizations, student government, and athletics or sports teams also tended to be associated with a greater sense of belonging. It may be the case that these are the kind of involvement opportunities that should be suggested to students who are struggling to feel like members of the campus community.

Drawing on data from The Diverse Democracy Project, Maestas, Vaquera, and Zehr (2007) analyzed longitudinal survey data from 421 students at the University of New Mexico to study how various factors affect sense of belonging. Findings indicate that academic and social integration, along with experiences and perceptions of diversity, positively impact students' sense of belonging at a Hispanic serving institution, accounting for 30 percent of the variance in belonging. For example, they found that participating in academic support programs, faculty interest in a student's development, living on campus, and socializing with students whose race/ethnicity differs from one's own increased sense of belonging. Results add to the weight of evidence showing that faculty members play a critical role in students' success and academic support experiences like tutoring, peer mentoring, and TRIO programs matter too.

Museus and Maramba (2011) analyzed survey data from 143 Filipino Americans at a large, highly selective public research university located on the West coast, using structural equation modeling, to examine the influence of cultural factors on Filipino American college students' sense of belonging.

Results suggest that cultural factors are related to Filipino American college students' sense of belonging. Specifically, ease of adjustment to campus culture was positively and directly associated with sense of belonging; ease of adjustment to campus culture was directly and negatively influenced by perceived pressure to sever ties with those who share one's cultural background—what many authors call "cultural suicide" (i.e., greater perceived pressure was related to more difficulty in adjustment)—while maintaining connections with one's culture of origin led to greater ease in adjustment. They also uncovered differences by generational status, with second-generation students reporting the greatest pressure to commit cultural suicide, and the weakest connection to their cultural heritage; first-generation students, on the other hand, reported the lowest sense of belonging.

A third and final stream of inquiry focuses on the relationship between sense of belonging and other variables (Hausmann, Schofield, & Woods, 2007; Johnson et al., 2007; Ostrove & Long, 2007; Strayhorn, 2008a, 2008d). For instance, Ostrove and Long conducted a study with 322 students attending a small, liberal arts college. They found that only background variables were related to sense of belonging. Specifically, measures of social class such as access to basic needs and ease of life were significant predictors of sense of belonging, which affirms the hierarchy posited by Maslow (1954) and the theoretical underpinnings of my model. As another example, Johnson and her colleagues examined sense of belonging among a national sample of first-year students. They found that social dimensions of college life, residence hall arrangements, and perceptions of campus climate were significant predictors of belonging.

In a previous study (Strayhorn, 2008d), I analyzed data from 289 Latino and 300 White students who responded to a wave of the College Student Experiences Questionnaire (CSEQ), employing hierarchical regression techniques with a nested design to estimate the influence of academic and social collegiate experiences on Latino students' sense of belonging, controlling for other effects. Results suggest that grades, time spent studying (a proxy for academic effort), and interactions with diverse peers positively influenced sense of belonging, with greater effect ($R^2 = 11\%$) on Latino students than Whites. This may indicate that sense of belonging matters more for Latino students at PWIs than White students at similar institutions, which seems to support the notion that sense of belonging takes on heightened importance for *some students* in *certain contexts*.

WHAT WE NEED TO KNOW

Despite the growing body of literature that speaks to college students' sense of belonging, there is still relatively limited understanding of its malleable character and the complex interaction of forces that give rise to it. Much of what we know (or at least *think* we know) about sense of belonging is impartial or incomplete at best and misleading or wrong at worst. For example, there is a good deal of confusion in the literature about the differences between involvement, engagement, and other increasingly circulated terms such as sense of belonging. As a result, we have been given the mistaken view that students' investment of time and energy into the college experience is involvement, engagement, and belonging, all at once. Essentially, we've equated what *students* do with what *institutions* do and we have confused what students *do* with what students *need* and *feel*. Clearly, these are not equals, although it is not always clear how they are distinguished either. Information is needed to clarify the distinctiveness of sense of belonging, and guidance about how it is marked off from involvement, engagement, and related concepts. This topic is taken up in Chapter 10.

What has amassed, to date, is best described as research on *individual* students' sense of belonging in college. Virtually everything that has been written, particularly in postsecondary contexts, comes from the perspective of the individual student. And while certainly useful, the current literature base does not help us to understand how organizational or institutional attributes, conditions, ethos, and practices influence college students' sense of belonging, directly or indirectly. Nor does the existing literature enable us to understand why it is that similar students may experience similar situations in college but arrive at very places in terms of sense of belonging. That this is the case is no reason for surprise; remember, much of what's known, up to now, focuses on individuals, where they are located, what they do, and how they engage others on campus. Absent are sufficient references to the fact that belonging is also a function of the ethos that pervades the daily life of college. Even when scholars make respectable attempts to note the role of institutional environments, they rarely, if ever, explain the mechanisms by which those environments affect sense of belonging. For instance, how does attending a private elite university shape a Muslim students' sense of belonging on campus? Or, how might an HBCU context influence the extent to which an affluent, Black male finds a sense of belonging there? We will return to this point in the next chapter.

There are other gaps that need to be filled. Despite having acquired information from a variety of sources about the myriad ways in which college students connect or "plug in" to campus life (e.g., Astin, 1984; Guiffrida, 2003; Tinto, 1993), we have yet to discern specific attributes or experiences that are most likely to yield the outcomes that we desire for students. With the advent of new student success data systems and early alert protocols by high-tech providers like Starfish, Education Advisory Board, and Civitas, advising personnel are in a much better position to advise intrusively, where advisors anticipate the challenges and needs of struggling students before it's too late for them to recover. Consider a student who's doing poorly in college math, missing home, and not making many friends. What might an advisor prescribe for them to do to achieve belonging? And which intervention or prescribed activity yields the biggest bang for their effort—joining a club, getting to know a professor, seeking counseling, getting supplemental instruction, all or none of these? This is the kind of nuanced information that we still need about college students' sense of belonging. Without such information, it is difficult for us to inform administrators, practitioners, and those charged with student success about practices that hold considerable promise for nurturing a college student's sense of belonging. Up to now, our advice has been quite generic and very institution- or sample-specific. Over and above more research, what is needed is a synthesis of what we know about sense of belonging, which, in turn, gives order to the growing body of research on this topic by suggesting a theoretical model of college students' belonging that can be employed in a variety of settings and communities in which students reside. It is to the description of that model that we now turn.

NOTES

1 The term "fun size" is often used to refer to my physical build, size, stature; a light-hearted way to characterize the fact that I am 5 feet, 6 inches tall (but appear even shorter), about 130 pounds, and can easily fit a boy's size large (smile). It's also a term that college students have used to describe how they receive me as a speaker and teacher: "Smart but fun sized, energetic, and down to earth." I preserve use of the term in this book, not to downplay its scholarly texture but to stay as true as possible in recounts and recollections of stories and experiences with students on campuses across the globe.

2 I learned about Joiner's (2005, 2010) research on suicide after the first edition of this book. It is an interesting body of work and I found it tempting to think about his interpersonal-psychological theory of suicidal behavior in the context of higher education, similar to the way in which Vincent Tinto (1993) drew upon sociological notions of suicide to propose a college student attrition theory. For instance, it's likely true that a college student will not feel a sense of belonging on campuses or in classrooms where they perceive themselves as a burden to the instructor, peers, or larger community; neither are they likely to feel a strong sense of belonging where they experience social alienation, strained relationships, or where no one and nothing seems familiar. This awaits empirical testing in college contexts—a ripe avenue for future research.

Chapter 3

From Plausible Explanation to Evidence-based Theory

We don't recognize the little things in life, or appreciate the little things in life like belonging. A sense of belonging is a big thing today.

(James Caan)

I think, therefore I am. I do, therefore I belong.

(Terrell L. Strayhorn[1])

INTRODUCTION

I had written this chapter six or seven times, over and over again, in the margins of my mind while walking around campus, in my dreams while sleeping, in my mental rolodex while running early morning in the park (which had become my custom), on the creased corners of paper napkins while eating lunch at P. F. Chang's (lemon chicken being my favorite), while flying in the air enjoying the complimentary beverage service ("cranapple juice with no ice, please"), or while sitting in the barbershop tuning out the "noisy chatter" about "last night's [ball]game," awaiting my turn in the chair. No matter how many times I wrote and re-wrote mental drafts of this chapter, several points would appear time and time again.

Initially, I interpreted this as a psychological by-product of my own insanity—doing the same thing repeatedly, yet expecting different results or revelations. As time passed, I started to see this a bit differently— perhaps a mutant form of writer's block that I had not encountered previously (and I rarely experience writer's block because I refuse to take up a pen to write before I've read everything that's needed, at least within reason, to inform my thoughts about a topic). It wasn't until much later, almost eight months into the first edition of this book project, that I realized it was neither insanity nor writer's frustration, but rather something much more personally rewarding and intellectually productive—saturation. Yes, saturation—saturation of my thoughts and insights about the concept of sense of belonging. Saturation of single findings from my numerous studies on (or about) sense of belonging that provide the empirical basis for several chapters in this book. And saturation of my handwritten notes, mental memos, electronic notecards, email correspondences, and undocumented daydreams about sense of belonging. All of these converged on seven key elements of sense of belonging, which form the organizing structure of this chapter and the emerging model highlighted herein.

Once I realized that saturation was the proper diagnosis for my condition—not insanity or influency—I fetched my pen to start writing it down in some logical order. For I had done it. I had struggled sufficiently with the material and immaterial conditions surrounding my work on sense of belonging and arrived, admittedly mentally drained yet intellectually stimulated, to the point where I knew what needed to be done. I knew where I was going with my thoughts, how to get there, and what to do upon arrival. I felt compelled to transfer my thoughts and notes from paper to computer screen. This proved even more difficult in this second edition of the book, as I worked to synthesize notes and comments, images, tweets, texts, "napkin notes," and a typhoon of Post-Its® that accumulated over the last six years since the first volume. Here I offer you the result of this exquisite experience.

SENSE OF BELONGING DEFINED

Sense of belonging is one term with many meanings. A review of the extant literature revealed a litany of lists, a diversity of definitions, a menagerie of metaphors (I could keep going) related to sense of belonging. For instance, McMillan and Chavis (1986, p. 9) used the term "sense of community," which refers to "a feeling that members have of belonging, a feeling that members matter to one another and to the group, and a shared faith that members' needs will be met through their commitment to be together." Another example is Goodenow's (1993a) use of sense of belonging or "membership" in school settings, which refers to "students' sense of being accepted, valued, included, and encouraged by others (teachers and peers) in the academic classroom setting and of feeling oneself to be an important part of the life and activity of the class" (p. 25).

In my previous work, I have defined sense of belonging as students' perceived social support on campus, a feeling of connectedness, or that one is important to others, in consonance with understandings rendered by previous scholars (e.g., Jacoby & Garland, 2004–2005; Rosenberg &

McCullough, 1981; Taylor, Turner, Noymer, Beckett, & Elliott, 2001). Consider the following two instances. Analyzing survey data from 289 Latino and 300 White students, I conducted a comparative study predicting students' sense of belonging, which was operationally defined as their perceived sense of integration on campus (Strayhorn, 2008d). In that article, I went on to say that "sense of belonging reflects the social support that students perceive on campus; it is a feeling of connectedness, that one is important to others, that one matters" (p. 305). And as sense of belonging may be particularly important for students who perceive themselves as marginal to campus life, such as Latino students, I posited a theoretical connection between belonging and mattering. We will return to this point later.

In a separate study of 231 Black and 300 White male collegians, I conceptualized sense of belonging as a "subjective evaluation of the quality of [students'] relationships with others on campus" (Strayhorn, 2008a, p. 505). Similar to Hurtado and Carter (1997), I noted:

> Sense of belonging consists of both cognitive and affective elements. An individual assesses his/her position or role in relation to the group (cognitive), which, in turn, results in a response, behavior, or outcome (affective). Sense of belonging, then, reflects the extent to which students feel connected, a part of, or stuck to a campus ... for example, some scholars measure sense of belonging as how much others would miss you if you went away (Rosenberg & McCullough, 1981).
>
> *(Strayhorn, 2008a, p. 505)*

Since the first edition, I have clarified my understanding of the three dimensions and questions that swirl around each of these, which is reflected in the revised model published in this edition. And though less apparent, my use of the term "supportive relationships" in a quantitative multi-institutional study of Black male collegians was conceptually related to sense of belonging (Strayhorn, 2008c).

For the purposes of this book, sense of belonging is framed as a basic human need and motivation, sufficient to influence behavior. In this way, it is not only an important aspect of college student life but relevant to life for *all of us*, although it may take on heightened importance for college students given where they are generally in their personal development—traditionally at the crux of identity exploration and vulnerable to peer influence. Sense of belonging may also be particularly significant for students who are marginalized in college contexts such as women, racial and ethnic minorities, low-income students, first-generation students, Muslims, returning military veterans living with disabilities, and gay students, to name a few.

In terms of college, sense of belonging refers to students' perceived social support on campus, a feeling or sensation of connectedness, the experience of mattering or feeling cared about, accepted, respected, valued by, and important to the group (e.g., campus community) or others on campus (e.g., faculty, peers). Indeed, it is a cognitive evaluation that typically leads to an affective response or behavior in students. As was mentioned at the end of Chapter 2, this process is conditioned by environmental or institutional factors and ethos.

One other important point about my operational definition of sense of belonging deserves mention. Note that I refer to sense of belonging throughout the book, but also allude to its chilly cousin, *alienation*, in some places. In my mind, the absence of belonging is marginalization, isolation, or alienation from others. Alienation is defined as "a withdrawing or separation of a person or a person's affections from an object or position of former attachment," according to the *Merriam-Webster Dictionary*. I would protract that definition in a number of other directions; for instance, alienation may also refer to resistance to or rejection of a person or a person's affections from an object or society to which one belongs (or aspires to belong). Though related, I tend to focus on belonging versus alienation as the goal or outcome of effective educational practices in education. Belonging, not alienation, is what we, as educators, hope to foster for all students. By focusing on belonging rather than alienation, I intentionally employ an anti-deficit, strengths-based perspective that yields powerful and promising insights for clarifying our understanding of college students, improving our programs and services, as well as enhancing our practices and policies in education so as to increase student success. Before presenting the scope and details of the model, let us discuss the seven core elements of sense of belonging.

CORE ELEMENTS OF SENSE OF BELONGING

As mentioned earlier in this chapter, my constructive review of the existing literature and theory related to sense of belonging yielded a fairly consistent list of core elements that deserve explanation. In the section below, I identify seven core elements of sense of belonging (see Figure 3.1) and explain each in the context of existing literature and how it applies to the main thesis of this book. Let's begin.

1. *Sense of belonging is a basic human need.* It is important to note that there are two basic types of needs: latent and expressed. Latent needs (also known as hidden needs) are those of which the individual is unaware and, consequently, they are not actively requested by the user but very much needed. Latent needs are typically implied and located in one's subconscious feelings and thoughts. As such, they can be enormously difficult to capture, gauge, track, or trend with any degree of certainty. Traditional research methods (e.g., surveys, interviews) are

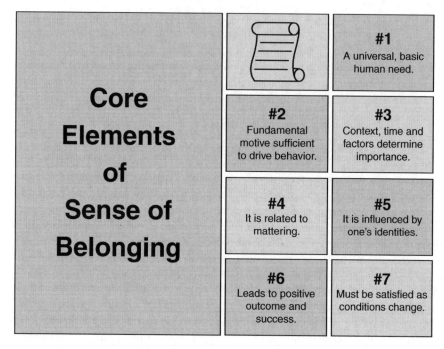

Figure 3.1 Core elements of sense of belonging.

Source: Strayhorn, T. L. (2012). *College students' sense of belonging: A key to educational success for all students*. New York: Routledge.

largely ineffective in identifying latent needs since consumers are *not aware* of their unmet needs in the relevant domain. When latent needs are met by a product, service, or experience, consumers are both surprised and delighted. For example, years ago, international business travelers were content flying multiple times per week, collecting frequent-flyer miles by the hundreds, while packing multiple adapters in their carry-on luggage that would fit power outlets across the globe. It wasn't until Fuji, the Japanese electronics conglomerate, released the first-ever all-in-one unit that combined all the connectors needed to fit any outlet in the world that *unknowing* overseas travelers recognized how much space was taken up by multiple adapters. The all-in-one unit met a latent need and sales hit high records in the very first period. Similar lessons were learned from Apple's invention of the iPad or when microcomputer software companies like Microsoft met consumers' *unexpressed need* for convenience and usability by developing copy-paste or pinch-zoom capabilities for gadgets. Expressed needs, on the other hand, are conscious and present. They show up in traditional research settings and can be tracked for understanding.

Indeed, the need for belongingness is universal and applies to all people but there are times when belonging needs are obvious and expressed; other times when they are latent. Satisfying the need for belonging is a necessary precondition for higher-order needs such as the desire for knowledge, understanding, and self-actualization (Maslow, 1962). Recall that Maslow located "love and belongingness needs" in the middle of his motivation hierarchy; these needs do not emerge until more basic needs (e.g., air, water, food, safety) are met. Deprivation of middle motivations, like belongingness, also prevents movement toward knowledge and understanding, both of which are related to the consummate goals of higher education. See Figure 3.2 for a review.

There are several applications of this to our conversation about sense of belonging in college. First, if sense of belonging is a basic human need, then it also is a basic need of college students. And if sense of belonging is a fundamental human need—second only to more basic needs such as food and safety—then it takes on equal importance in higher education. A college student's need for belonging must be satisfied before any other higher-order needs such as knowledge and self-actualization, which some would argue are the desired outcomes of a college education (Strayhorn, 2005). Go glance at a few institutional mission statements. Notice the goals stated: knowledge production, technology proficiency, active participation in democracy, and, yes, global citizenship. None of that is possible without belonging. As I have said elsewhere, we could surmise that the consummate goals of higher education cannot be

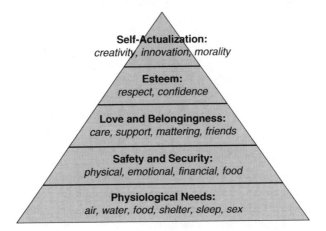

Figure 3.2 Basic human needs hierarchy, based on insights from Maslow (1954) and the first edition of this book.

achieved (or even pursued) until students feel a sense of connect-edness, membership, and belonging in college. That's deep! Sense of belonging is just that important. And as previous scholars have explained, "if psychology has erred with regard to the need to belong ... the error has not been to deny the existence of such a motive as much as to underappreciate it" (Baumeister & Leary, 1995, p. 522). Fulfillment of our educational mission rests, in part, on making sure that students (and the faculty/staff who teach them) feel a sense of belonging in college.

2. *Sense of belonging is a fundamental motive, sufficient to drive human behavior.* Sense of belonging is not only a basic human need, but it also is a motive that can affect human behavior(s). Motive is defined simply as "something (as a need or desire) that causes a person to act," according to the *Merriam-Webster Dictionary*. Needing to belong compels individuals to act. And there's no shortage of exam-ples for this in our daily lives. It's the underlying principle for why some people choose the neighborhoods in which they live. It's why some people join particular churches and faith groups. It's why some soldiers joined the military in the first place. And why some little girls join "The Brownies" or become a girl scout. But, let's be honest. The need to belong does not always compel individuals to act in ways that are prosocial or productive. In their desperation or longing to belong (no pun intended), to feel worthwhile some impressionable youth "may join a [street] gang or also worship Satan" (Clark, 1992, p. 289). It's also why some people establish new or stay in existing romantic relationships, even when they're detrimental to their own physical and psychological wellbeing. And it is why some National Merit scholars with sky-high IQs subject themselves to obvious risk and life-threatening dangerous hazing just to gain admittance to a social fraternity or sorority. It's because all people want to feel special, part of something larger, cared about by others, needed, valued, sup-ported, and somewhat indispensable as the object of someone else's affection (this latter point reminds me of Beyonce's "Irreplaceable" single). I digress, but it's a contemporary example of the point being made. Imagine the personal testimony of an alum who felt indispen-sable to their alma mater—what would they say and how would they talk about their "college days" to new and prospective students? To those who work in alumni relations, imagine how much of their dis-posable income would be donated to the institution or their favorite club, organization, or department for meeting their need to belong, no matter how expressed or latent.

In educational settings, the need to belong can drive students' behaviors to or against academic achievement norms. For example, those who feel unsupported or rejected by adults (e.g., teachers) or achieving students may appeal to the interests of peer groups with anti-academic norms for acceptance, resulting in disidentification with school or disinvestment from academic goals. Under these circumstances, some students build bonds of support, trust, and friendship with members of groups that are marginalized, devalued, and worse, punished in educational settings such as schools and colleges. For instance, several interview participants over the years have talked about their "decision" to break school rules by joining the proverbial "troublemakers" as a way of finding community and connectedness with others who accepted them in school. Other participants described how they learned to goof off in class by joining the "class clowns" group, known for their pranks and stunts rather than their intellectual aptitude. Still, there were other participants who spoke fluently about joining a group of "apathetic learners" by refusing to pay attention or complete assignments, while the most alienated learner may have joined a street gang, all in pursuit of the same thing: community, connectedness, acceptance, love, and belonging. Almost without exception, students described personal histories and academic journeys that placed them in moments where they developed an appetite for belonging, disidentified with adults and achieving peers in schools, and consequently, satisfied their need to belong by affiliating with those who promised them security, community, and support in exchange for their commitment to certain values that challenge school rules (e.g., imposing fear over friendliness) and a code of conduct comprised of anti-academic beliefs and behaviors. These outcasts, throwaways, or what Ferguson (2000) calls "Bad Boys" (although in my experience they're not always male), gratify their need to belong in much the same way as anyone else—by doing something with others who share their commitments, interests, values, and goals. Indeed, sense of belonging "stimulates goal-directed activity designed to satisfy it" (Baumeister & Leary, 1995, p. 500).

Consider the following questions based on information shared in the previous sections

1. What are some goal-directed activities that could be useful for engaging or re-engaging disengaged students?
2. What struck you in this section that might be helpful for working with "Bad Boys" or disengaged students on your campus?

3. *Sense of belonging takes on heightened importance* (a) *in certain contexts,* such as being a newcomer to an otherwise established group, (b) *at certain times,* such as (late) adolescence when individuals begin to consider who they are (or wish to be), with whom they belong, and where they intend to invest their time and energies (Chickering & Reisser, 1993; Sanford, 1962), and (c) *among certain populations,* especially those who are marginalized or inclined to feel that way in said context (for more, see Goodenow, 1993a).

Belonging is a universal characteristic and a basic human need (Maslow, 1962). Belonging may also offer a shared sense of socially constructed meaning that provides a sense of security or relatedness. Generally speaking, people strive to be accepted by others, valued, and respected as competent, qualified individuals worthy of membership in a defined group or particular social context. It is part of the currency that makes the "Ivy League" so prestigious—the fact that some institutions by nature and virtue of their history and fiscal endowment *belong* to the exclusive group, while other world-class universities do not. The existence of the Ivy League meets an obvious need of the institutions that comprise its membership—a need to feel different, exclusive, special, or uniquely prestigious. And in exchange for bona fide membership, "the League" expects the institutions to adhere to certain values, practices, and codes that animate the group's character. It is why there are neither "open access" Ivy League schools nor Ivies with a strong agricultural and technical thrust to the academic program. What it means to belong and what it takes to belong, in part, depends on when and where one wants to belong.

That is to say, the experience of belonging is context-dependent, such that sense of belonging in a particular context (e.g., campus, department, classroom) has the greatest influence on outcomes (e.g., adjustment, achievement) in that area. In fact, some research suggests that issues of inclusion and belonging can predominate to a point that "until members resolve where they stand in a *particular social setting* [emphasis added] they face difficulty in attending to the official tasks at hand" (Goodenow, 1993b, p. 88). Applied to higher education, I argue that college students face serious difficulty in attending to the tasks at hand like studying, learning, and retaining information until they resolve one of their most fundamental needs—a need to belong in learning spaces. A quick example: I once interviewed a campus student leader who struggled to find her footing in a college calculus course. She loved her school and never hesitated to share her school spirit with others through cheers, tweets, and stickers. She attended math class daily—usually arriving on-time—but struggled to comprehend the subject matter. Simple equations made sense, even to the point of geometric functions and graphs. Logarithmic functions, computing limits, and derivatives? Totally foreign. She felt out of place as if she (or her academic advisor) had made a terrible mistake by enrolling her in the course. Before you know it, she was preoccupied with worries about her place in the class that she couldn't focus on the lecture and that simply avalanched thoughts about her "fit" for *college-level* calculus (emphasis added), which, in turn, surfaced insecurities about whether she was "college material" (whatever that is) at all. Just a few weeks into the course, a spirited student leader was converted—feelings of assurance and confidence in her **sense of belonging in college** were eroded by the energy that fueled her anxiety, worry, and **sense of alienation in the classroom.**

It is important to note that sense of belonging is context-specific for other reasons too, one of which relates to the notion of normative congruence. Normative congruence suggests that individuals seek environments or settings that are congruent with their own expectations, values, attitudes, and positioning. It is quite clear, however, that campuses have a broad range of values and normative contexts in which students interact and construct affiliations (Hurtado & Carter, 1997). If campus environments are broad and diverse in their norms and values, then so too will be the factors that facilitate students' belonging in that environment. To this, conventional wisdom holds: what's good for the goose (in situation A) may not be good for the gander (in situation B). Just as these waterbirds that belong to the same family (Anatidae) may experience birdlife differently, college students might experience a sense of belonging in different ways. To help someone achieve a sense of belonging, one needs to know something about their expectations, values, attitudes, interests, goals, and so on. (I've always wondered why we don't share this kind of baseline information about students with all first-year instructors in college, as they work to help students find their purpose for belonging.)

There is substantial evidence to support the notion that sense of belonging takes on special prominence at certain times such as (late) adolescence and early adulthood when individuals begin to consider who they are (or wish to be), with whom they belong, and where they intend to invest their time and energies (Goodenow, 1993b; Sanford, 1962). Sense of belonging assumes heightened relevance in moments and circumstances that threaten the most basic of human needs (e.g., air, water, food, safety) or when belonging needs are left unsatisfied. For instance, cues that suggest possible harm (e.g., danger signs, nightfall) or uncertainty (e.g., life transitions, uncontrolled futures) seem to increase the need to be with others (Baumeister & Leary, 1995). It is why people want someone to hold their hand when they get their first tattoo. It is why most people go to haunted houses in groups or walk through together packed so tightly that they're constantly stepping on each other toes. And it is why college students started creating "Facebook groups" for members of their incoming class long before campuses knew anything about it—students wanted to make sure that they would know someone on campus upon arrival. Sense of belonging is just that crucial.

I think this point is also reflected in the words of one of my past interview participants, Armond, an African American male who identifies as Haitian, stands at 5 feet 10 inches, and wore smoky gray Gucci glasses to the one-on-one. When asked, "What were your initial thoughts about college?" he replied, "I was terrified. I was scared. I remember feeling unsure. I didn't know how [college] would be. And no one in my family had gone so they couldn't tell me much about it really. I didn't really want to think about it ... I just wanted my momma [laughing]." In the face of uncertainty that marks the transition from high school to college and the anxiety that all incoming freshman feel upon arrival, Armond shared that he wanted to retreat, to resist the unfamiliar in favor of the known, to cling to that in which he found comfort and support: his mother.[2] Sense of belonging is a basic human need, sufficient to motivate certain behaviors and it takes on heightened importance at times and in places where individual feel vulnerable.

4. *Sense of belonging is related to, and seemingly a consequence of, mattering.* Indeed, the weight of empirical evidence lends fairly persuasive information to support the idea that mattering matters. By definition, mattering refers to feeling, rightly or wrongly, that one matters, is valued or appreciated by others (Schlossberg, 1985). Rosenberg and McCullough (1981) identified five dimensions of mattering: (a) attention or being noticed in positive ways, commanding interest; (b) importance or feeling cared about, special, as the object of another's concern; (c) dependence or feeling needed by others; (d) appreciated or feeling respected; and (e) ego extension, which refers to experiencing self in others who share in our failures and successes. Generally speaking, mattering turns attention to the relational aspect of sense of belonging. Interactions with others that are affectively positive or pleasant are necessary but not sufficient for experiencing belongingness. To satisfy the need for belongingness, the person must believe one cares.

It is also true that mattering (to others) can act as a motive. For example, sociologists have argued for years that people tend to internalize and project the values of others around them—those to whom they feel related, connected, and important as a member of the group.

This very same logic explains the perceived cohesion of families, the cultural solidarity of streets gangs (Clark, 1992), and much of what is known about intergroup contact theory (Pettigrew, 1998). "Primarily one identifies with and emulates the practices of those to whom one is or might desire to be attached" (Ryan & Stiller, 1991, p. 121). People might feel like they matter when they command attention or feel needed. But people might also create circumstances where they feel needed, like others depend on them. Imagine a librarian who keeps all of the recent serials behind the counter so that others have to ask for access. Years ago, I met a man who worked for a *Fortune 500* company who refused to share all the codes and passwords for digitizing workflow in his unit. When I asked him why he wouldn't release the codes, his answer was simple: "Then they won't *need* me." He wanted to be wanted—for others to need him and rely upon him for access. Indeed, mattering motivates all sorts of behaviors.

Based on information shared in this section, respond fully to the following questions:

1. How does mattering relate to your experience with students on your own campus?
2. How, and in what ways, have you seen students behave in ways that reflect the four dimensions of mattering?
3. In your opinion, are there things educators should keep in mind when creating conditions where *all students* feel like they matter and are special to the campus?

5. *Social identities intersect and affect college students' sense of belonging.* Although the need for belongingness is universal and applies to all people, it does not necessarily unfold for all people equally. My research on college students' sense of belonging lends fairly persuasive argument to the point that individuals experience belonging in new and different ways. Quite often, social identities such as race/ethnicity, gender, class, sexual orientation, and religion converge and intersect in ways that simultaneously influence sense of belonging. For instance, as one Asian gay male shared in an interview conducted by my team: "Every part of me really shapes how I feel about belonging here [in college]. It's not my Asian side saying, 'Yes I fit here because I'm smart in science,' while the immigrant or working-class side of me says 'You're alone here, so go home' ... it's actually all of them at once saying a combination of both things, I guess."

Simultaneously negotiating multiple dimensions of complex identities is a bit challenging to describe in words on two-dimensional paper when we know, from research (Jones & McEwen, 2000), that the process is much more dynamic, synergistic, and three- or four-dimensional (i.e., 3D or 4D) than previously understood. To understand students' belonging experiences, one must pay close attention to issues of identity, identity salience or "core self," ascendancy of certain motives, and even social contexts that exert influence on these considerations. And while researchers find it necessary to disaggregate this always intersecting, dynamic experience into discernible steps, stages, and transitions, students experience it seamlessly and would find it difficult to isolate a single aspect of self that is responsible for a particular behavior, belief, feeling, or sense of their belonging in college. The point here is simple. Social identities intersect and often simultaneously affect college students' experiences of belonging. A few examples are useful.

Very early in my academic career, one of my graduate students encouraged me to think about extending my research on African American students to include members of the gay and bisexual or queer community. Pretty soon thereafter we were joined by another student in conducting qualitative research on Black gay and bisexual men in college. One afternoon, we gathered for a focus group interview and met five or six guys who were recommended for the study by campus administrative staff. During the interview, one Black guy (Justin) shared how he would "never be caught *alive* (emphasis added) in the Black cultural center" on campus that was often assumed to be a "home away from home" for Black students. He explained how his sexual orientation made him a target for harassment (i.e., verbal teasing to physical assault) especially among Black male peers who were presumed to be heterosexual. Despite shared racial/ethnic ancestry, his sexual orientation combined with his racial identity (and other dimensions of difference) to shape powerfully what he watched on television, how he spent his discretionary time, and, consequently, what he shared in common with his same-race male peers in the cultural center. Just like his "straight peers" who spent lots of time relaxing in the center bragging about their sexual conquests, Justin wanted to share about his love life and interests but struggled to do so in the cultural center where there were very few other "openly gay guys." The cultural center was "not a place where [Justin] felt like he belonged." In fact, Justin felt like "it's a place where [he] should not be, not if [he] wanted to be [his] true self." His sentiments affirm a deeper revelation about sense of belonging that occurred to me *after* publication of the first edition of this book in 2012—that is, that *true* sense of belonging is not about "fitting in" but rather about accept-ance, authenticity, and finding community as one's true self, just as you are.

6. *Sense of belonging engenders other positive outcomes.* Satisfying the need to belong leads to a plethora of positive and/or prosocial out-comes such as achievement, engagement, wellbeing, happiness, and optimal functioning in a particular context or domain, to name a few. For instance, sense of belonging in college has been shown to influ-ence persistence intentions (Hausmann, Schofield, & Woods et al., 2007). Therefore, the goal is to develop campus environments that foster sense of belonging so students feel "stuck to" and supported by others on campus, to such a degree that severance of those bonds not only seems difficult and unpopular but impossible.

The truth is, *all* people try to preserve relationships and avoid end-ing them, particularly those in which they have invested a significant deal of time and energy (Hazan & Shaver, 1994a, 1994b). Threats to social attachments are primary sources of concern for most individu-als, especially those for whom peer relations are critically important such as adolescent youth or young adults who, according to human lifespan theory, are confronting core questions like "Who Am I?" People feel anxious about the prospect of losing important, meaning-ful relationships, and typically such loss results in depression, grief, and loneliness when connections with certain people are severed (Baumeister & Leary, 1995). To avoid these negative consequences, "the mass of men [and women] lead lives of quiet desperation," quot-ing Henry David Thoreau (1971), while many others satisfy their need to belong by devoting the time and energy needed to a particular task that allows previously established relationships to continue whether that's talking to a marriage counselor to avoid divorce or studying to do better in college to avoid dismissal.

7. *Sense of belonging must be satisfied on a continual basis and likely changes as circumstances, conditions, and contexts change.* Recall that sense of belonging is a basic human need and motivation. The drive to belong can be satisfied by a few meaningful attachments that engen-der the feelings that fuel belongingness: feeling appreciated, respected, and valued. Alternatively, sense of belonging can be satisfied by many bonds of support that cue attention, dependence, and importance. Over time and through various experiences, students' sense of belong-ing, of personal acceptance, or having a rightful, valued place in a par-ticular social context tends to stabilize and consistently influence one's commitments and behaviors. However, sense of belonging is "largely malleable and susceptible to influence in both positive and negative directions" at all times (Goodenow, 1993b, p. 81). In fact, Walton and

Cohen (2011) found that even a single instance of isolation or rejection can undermine sense of belonging. Disruption of one's need to belong can have immediate negative consequences and individuals must engage again in activities and interactions that foster belongingness to regain a sense of acceptance, support, or inclusion. Deprivation of belongingness needs often leads to diminished interest in activities, loneliness, self-hatred, disengagement from life (often through suicide), or, in the context of education, disengagement from college through attrition or disinvestment. Just because a student feels a sense of belonging today doesn't mean that they'll feel it tomorrow. Educators charged with building belonging and increasing student success should keep this in mind when formulating strategy plans.

THE MODEL

Now that we've discussed the core elements of sense of belonging, let me describe the shape and direction of the model proposed in this book. It's worth repeating that this model is just one way of explaining sense of belonging as it has evolved from my own research and review of the existing literature to date. I admit that the model may suffer from the paradox of theory (as do all models), which was aptly described by Parker (1977): any attempt at simplifying the complex gives up a degree of accuracy. So, while I strongly believe the model to be helpful and have used it many times in my consulting work with hundreds of campuses across the country, I recognize that my attempt to render sophistications as simple gives up a degree of accuracy in exchange for simplicity. Friends, we all make these concessions when writing but I assure you that what's offered is my best attempt at formulating a parsimonious model of sense of belonging that satisfies the expectations of theory and at the same time accounts for what's known from my research about this concept. The model offers something that is understandable for readers to apply to practice, employ when developing policy, and use (and test) in future research. These caveats behind us, let us proceed to discussion of the visual model, which is shown in Figure 3.3.

First, as Maslow (1954) explained, all humans have needs that are organized into a hierarchy from basic physiological needs (e.g., air, food, water, sleep, shelter) to higher needs such as belonging, esteem, and self-actualization. "If both the physiological and the safety needs are fairly well gratified, there will emerge the love and affection and belongingness needs, and the whole cycle already described will repeat itself with this new center" (Maslow, 1954, p. 20). The "whole cycle" to which Maslow refers is the process through which individuals satisfy their needs. Consider the

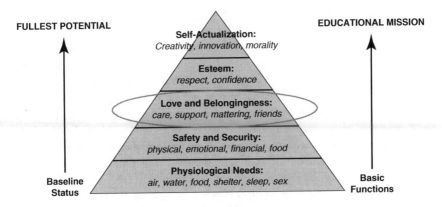

Figure 3.3 Revised model of college students' sense of belonging.

physiological need for food. If the body lacks some nutrient or vitamin provided by food, the individual will tend to develop an appetite or hunger for that missing element. In this condition, the individual is now motivated to do something—like hunt or beg—by the unsatisfied hunger for food. Every response, urge, behavior, and thought at this point—at least theoretically—is motivated by the need for food. Remember, "if basic needs are unsatisfied ... all other needs may become simply non-existent or be pushed to the background" (p. 16). Waking up, going out, getting a job, every twist and turn can be understood as the individual's striving to satisfy his or her need for food at that point.

So it is for college students' need to belong. As depicted in Figure 3.3, they enter various spaces or contexts during the college years, sometimes on-campus (like the classroom) and sometimes off-campus (like the family, community), where their fundamental needs emerge in the same order or hierarchy articulated by Maslow (1954) many years ago. Gratification of physiological needs permits emergence of other and higher social motives or goals such as the need to belong, or what I've called *college students' sense of belonging*. The emergence of that need in various college contexts drives students' behaviors and perceptions. Once enrolled, this need may drive a students' choice of academic major. It is why some choose to live on campus, while others "bunk up" with five or six others off-campus. It is why some seek shelter from racial battle fatigue in the campus cultural center, and while others like Justin create community elsewhere. It is why some join the campus gospel choir or young Republicans. Sense of belonging is critical for student success in college.

Some students attempt to whet their "belonging appetite" by becoming involved in campus clubs and organizations (see Chapter 10), establishing relationships with supportive others, learning the values of the profession to which they aspire (see Chapter 9), or engaging in any number of anti-social, unhealthy behaviors (e.g., drugs, alcohol, gangs), as shared in short vignettes throughout the book. Nevertheless, sense of belonging serves as a determinant of students' behaviors, recruiting all capacities of the individual in service to achieving belonging in college. Should the student succeed in this endeavor, he or she is rewarded by positive outcomes such as achievement, growth, persistence, and happiness. Those who cannot satisfy their need to belong tend to report negative outcomes such as frustration, arrested development, unhappiness, and a number of mental health issues such as depression, suicidal ideation, and even death (Kissane & McLaren, 2006; Weiss, 1973). In fact, in my research, I have found that college students from all walks of life—White, Black, Latino, Asian, Native American, mixed race, tall/short, straight/gay, Christian/atheist, Muslim, and even musician—who struggle to satisfy their need to belong describe that feeling as "failure" and often internalize such feelings to the point that the *incident becomes identity*; the experience of failure (or something that feels like it) creates thoughts that *one is* a failure. This connects sense of belonging theory to formulations about personal identity. See Figure 3.4 to explore linkages with Erick Erickson's stages.

The model calls attention to another important aspect of college students' sense of belonging, which was described in the previous section on

"Just because you struggle doesn't mean you don't belong." —*Abdul, Fisk University*

In **Stage Four** of Erickson's psychosocial model, youth (age 5-13) mature and become more self-aware. They put forth the effort to perform tasks, just like similarly-situated youth. They develop self-confidence when they succeed. If they fail or even struggle much, they tend to feel inferior to others oftentimes assuming that "they're the only one" experiencing difficulty; this is what psychologists refer to as "pluralistic ignorance."

This stage is also when/where students learn early lessons about failure and help-seeking. Without intervention, it is easy to believe that only "weak," "unready," or "lost" people seek help--think about this in the context of sense of belonging! Of course, this may be an appropriate belief pattern in some contexts like when one is "lost" driving a car in an unfamiliar area or neighborhood; surely, *good* lost drivers stop and ask for directions. College, however, is designed and structured intentionally so that students will likely face challenges, frustrations, perhaps a few setbacks, and maybe even some trouble while there. College, done well, compels students to ask for help at some point in time. For this to happen, students must see failure as inevitable, normal, ordinary, and part of the hallway to success; Carol Dweck frames this as adopting a "growth mindset."

Stage 4 of Erickon's model posits that experiencing failure can lead to feelings of inferiority and resentment which in turn can disrupt personal relations, prevent social connections or stymie development of community and belonging. College student educators would do well to alter how students interpret ordinary events like waking up late, failing a quiz, missing out on fraternity "rush," or asking for help.

Figure 3.4 Sense of belonging and Erickson's Stage Four.

core elements of the model. Recall that sense of belonging takes on heightened importance in certain spaces and contexts (e.g., classrooms, residence halls), at certain times (e.g., [later] adolescence), and among certain populations. As I have argued to this point in the book, students have to navigate, negotiate, and traverse many and multiple spaces and contexts during their college career. In each of these, their fundamental needs and motivations emerge, rising and falling over time and space in terms of salience. If a two-dimensional book could accommodate a three-dimensional model with multiple circles, I would have included it here. Rather, envision an individual student working within a number of the circles shown in the model at different times in his or her college career. The same logic holds: satisfaction of emergent needs leads to positive outcomes and permits emergence of higher motives, while deprivation of such needs leads to negative outcomes and frustration.

A final point about the model that hasn't been shared in other sections of the book. Some may wonder why I decided to include all of Maslow's (1954) theorized needs in my own model of college students' sense of belonging, especially when the focus of my work is on the middle belongingness needs. Well, even Maslow pointed out that human needs are not completely independent of each other or other motives. For example, physiological needs give rise to all sorts of other needs. And "the person who thinks he or she is hungry may actually be seeking more for comfort, or dependence, than for vitamins or proteins" (Maslow, 1954, p. 16). The same would be true for some college students seeking physiological or esteem needs. They may find in their strivings for esteem (or confidence) that what they really need is a sense of belonging, connection, and acceptance by others. There may also be times when some students are working under productive campus conditions to establish a sense of belonging, but out of nowhere, the threat of danger is triggered by a stimulus in the environment and therefore they regress to more basic safety needs. Consider the stories shared by gay students of color in Chapter 5, for instance, or information on Black male collegians in Chapter 8.

CONCLUSION

In sum, this chapter presents a descriptive overview of the theoretical model of college students' sense of belonging advanced in this volume. Core elements of the model were delineated and explained in relation to college students' experiences and a few of our most basic needs (e.g., food). Using this information, college student educators can augment existing knowledge about educational success, employ the model in their work with students, and refine the model based on new information or insights.

NOTES

1 With inspiration from Aristotle.
2 The idea that vulnerable students may manage college transitions and college-induced stress by yearning for the love and support of parents resonates with findings from Hirt (2006) and her colleagues (Hirt, Amelink, Bennett, & Strayhorn, 2008) about the ways in which student affairs professionals at historically black colleges and universities (HBCUs) act as "surrogate parents" to students, going beyond the call of duty to enact an ethic of care. For more, go to the source.

Chapter 4

Sentido de Pertenencia
[Sense of Belonging] and
Latino College Students

Latina/o students' perceptions of a hostile climate directly affect their sense of belonging in their colleges.

(Castellanos & Jones, 2003, p. 8)

Several years ago, during a midday luncheon sponsored by the higher education program at the university where I worked, I enjoyed a casual one-on-one sidebar conversation with the university's Provost about student retention rates in general and at our institution in particular. With a background in Germanic languages and history, the Provost spoke about "student success" factors without explicit references to the literature or logic upon which most of his arguments stood. Still, it was clear that he had a very keen understanding of the campus culture, institutional data, and how work gets done within various academic units across the campus.

With expertise in student retention research and theory, I seasoned my spoken words with parenthetical-like references to Bean (1982), Tinto (1993), Astin (1993), Braxton (2000), Kuh and Associates (2005), and scholarship produced by myself (Strayhorn, 2006) and other student success researchers. That body of work provided empirical support for many of my assertions about "what works" generally in college contexts, but I lacked the necessary experience with our campus to know the degree to which these theory-based programs and interventions would be successful at "Tennessee," if properly implemented. What he may have lacked in terms of familiarity with the literature, he certainly made up for in administrative experience. And I vice versa. Indeed, we made a likely team—the consummate practitioner–scholar duo. A few weeks later, the Provost invited me to serve as his special assistant and I happily agreed. In that role, I would conduct campus-wide research studies and assessments of students' experiences, author and disseminate findings to campus constituencies, ranging from deans to heads, faculty to students, and use the campus as my own "laboratory" of sorts (R. Holub, personal communication, January 30, 2007).

As Special Assistant to the Provost, I used my "laboratory" to study the experiences of first-year students at a large, public research university in hope of learning about barriers to their success and ways the institution could be more supportive during the first year of college. There were other studies too—one examining African American males at a predominantly White institution (PWI) and another on high-achieving, low-income ethnic minority students who, according to research, would be considered "at risk" of failure in education (US Department of Education, National Center for Education Statistics, 2000). I had countless opportunities to meet and get to know many students who continue to be an important source of inspiration for my work—students like Vincent. Consider Vincent's narrative when asked: "How often do you think about your race at [said] university?" He replied:

> I think about my race all the time; it's constantly there ... mostly because there are so few Latino students and faculty on campus. Usually when you hear the word diversity, you're not talking about Latina/os. We're rarely talked about, I think. I do all I can to fit in ... I'm like involved in a couple of groups on campus and we're trying to get a new Latino fraternity started up on campus. But that's hard and it can distract from other stuff like studying, writing your long-ass papers [laughing], and focusing on your work to graduate and get the hell out of here. I really do try but at the end of the day I know it's not for me ... like it's not my campus. [Interviewer: What do you mean by "not your campus?"] Well, like I just don't fit in and don't always feel like I belong here.

After (re-)reading through transcripts from that project, I became even more interested in *sense of belonging* as a theoretical construct, an antecedent to student retention, and its relation to the experiences of racially and ethnically diverse students attending PWIs. Scouring the literature for references to sense of belonging, I ran across multiple citations to Hurtado and Carter (1997). Thus, I thought that would be a promising point of departure for investigating deeper what sense of belonging is (or might be) and understanding better how it operates in the lives of Latinx college students. According to Hurtado and Carter (1997), sense of belonging "contains both cognitive and affective elements in that the individual's cognitive evaluation of his or her role in relation to the group results in an affective response" (p. 328). That is, they argued that students think about their place, position, and purpose in relation to a group to which they belong (or hope to belong) and those *thoughts* shape how they *feel*. It is cognitive processing that enables them to make meaning of certain

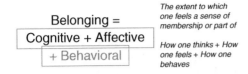

Figure 4.1   Components of sense of belonging.

Source: Hurtado, S., & Carter, D.F. (1997). Effects of college transition and perceptions of campus racial climate on Latino college student's sense of belonging. *Sociology of Education*, 70(4), 324–345.

experiences—such as positive feedback from a professor about their academic ability or a poster/sign that reads "You Belong Here"—and that leads to certain beliefs and feelings that align with the thoughts they have in mind. Consequently, individuals typically act in ways that are consistent with their thoughts and feelings, which is the "behavioral" part of the equation (See Figure 4.1 for more). Specifically, Hurtado and Carter were interested in understanding how social interactions enhanced Latino students' affiliation with college, but their findings have implications for all students.

Armed with a general understanding of sense of belonging and its theoretical underpinnings (for more, see Chapters 2 and 3 of this volume), I returned to "Vincent's story" that opened this chapter. Vincent's words left me curious about Latinx students' sense of belonging and its relation to other critical issues in higher education. I wondered: What influence do interactions with diverse peers have on sense of belonging for Latino students? And, was that influence stronger or weaker when compared with their White counterparts? How might culture relate to students' sense of belonging and their hunt to satisfy it in college? These questions led to a study that provided insights relevant to this chapter.

PURPOSE OF THE CHAPTER

The purpose of this chapter is to examine the role of sense of belonging in the lives of Latinx college students at PWIs. Specifically, I draw upon data from three studies to demonstrate the importance of sense of belonging to Latino collegians, factors that influence their level of belonging on campus and the role that belonging plays in their educational success. Additional insights are offered for discussion and new directions for educational practice and research are recommended at the chapter's end. Let us first talk about what we know, from research, about Latino collegians and then turn attention to the three studies that served as the chapter's basis.

WHAT WE KNOW

To determine what is known about Latino students' sense of belonging in college, I conducted a comprehensive literature review of all recently published studies—that is, those conducted within the last ten years—on sense of belonging, using a myriad of electronic databases, ranging from ERIC to EBSCO. Focusing on studies where sense of belonging appeared in the title, abstract, or body only, I uncovered over 100 books, chapters, journal articles, reports, and conference papers. Then, I narrowed the list by excluding those that did not fit the sampling criteria and all conference papers because they are rarely available for public use. Several major conclusions were drawn from this review.

I have said this elsewhere (Strayhorn, 2008d), but it bears repeating: "College participation rates have increased for all groups over the past 30 years. However, significant gaps across racial/ethnic groups persist" (p. 301). For instance, Latinos may well represent the largest ethnic minority group in the country, yet only represent 12 percent of total postsecondary enrollment (*estimate includes graduate and professional students*). Not only are Latino students disproportionately represented among college enrollees, but they also are (a) largely concentrated at Hispanic-serving, less-selective, or two-year institutions (Nora, Rendón, & Cuadraz, 1999; Thomas & Perna, 2004), (b) less likely to complete their college degree compared with their White and Asian peers, and the rest (c) take longer than four years to complete their degree, on average (Swail, Cabrera, & Lee, 2004). Research further suggests that some Latino students are disproportionately represented among those who are unprepared or underprepared for the rigor of college courses or may lack the requisite English-speaking skills (e.g., Warburton, Bugarin, & Nunez, 2001).

There are other challenges that may affect Latinx students' educational success. For instance, I argue that differences in the amount and nature of sociocultural capital inherited by Latino students may limit or expand their opportunity for success in academic settings (Strayhorn, 2008d). That is, students of color may inherit different forms of sociocultural capital than that which is valued and rewarded in school settings (Carter, 2005; Villalpando & Solórzano, 2005). Consequently, they are forced to acquire the form of capital necessary to succeed in such settings, representing a "second curriculum" that they must master (Fleming, 1981), quite often at the expense of their own need to belong. I have argued elsewhere (Strayhorn, 2015) that higher education is a culture marked by its own codes of conduct, rules governing expectations of members, and a lexicon chock-full of acronyms and somewhat misleading terms like "credit hour" that has little to nothing to do with one's creditworthiness and/or FICO score. But of course, this may be less clear to newcomers who know very little about college life and, thus, depend on the words and labels when making interpretations.

Other social factors support my argument for the studies described in the next section. As much of this appears in the article (Strayhorn, 2008d), I will resist the inclination to be repetitive and merely cite a few examples. Additional social factors that influence Latino students' educational success include strong familial obligations; feelings of isolation (particularly at PWIs); marginalization; and self-defeating stereotypes (Castellanos & Jones, 2003; Ortiz, 2004). Stereotypes, I argue, have a social dimension that is important to note when studying the influence of students' interactions with diverse others—namely, stereotypes are formed in the absence of face-to-face interactions (Sigelman & Tuch, 1997). It may be the case that Latino students' who encounter diverse peers frequently and in various ways are less likely to subscribe to and be negatively affected by racial stereotypes.

Countless studies have shown consistently that Latino students often experience social isolation, discrimination, and racism at PWIs (Gloria & Robinson Kurpius, 1996). Latino collegians face additional barriers that may compromise their educational success such as limited English proficiency and being first in their family to attend college (Castellanos & Jones, 2003; Justiz & Rendón, 1989). To overcome feelings of social isolation and marginalization, students must be validated and feel welcomed, valued, and connected—all core elements of belonging—which is a key aspect of the validation process (Locks, Hurtado, Bowman, & Oseguera, 2008). For instance, Valasquez underscored how positive interactions with White peers affected 687 Chicano students' sense of belonging in college. Sharing social affiliations with White students, having knowledge of Mexican history, and a strong sense of ethnic pride were positively correlated with Chicano students' sense of belonging. Others have found support for the role of peer interactions, faculty support, campus climate, and sports participation in fostering a sense of belonging (Hoffman, Richmond, Morrow, & Salomone, 2002–2003).

Many of these factors relate to issues raised by the results of the three studies that inform this chapter. With some understanding of what's known from research about Latino collegians, we are now ready to talk about the general scope and nature of the studies.

THE STUDIES

Given the chapter's focus on Latino collegians, I found it necessary to draw upon data from three studies that I conducted with students who identify as "Latinx" or "Hispanic."

The first of these studies is a quantitative analysis of secondary data from a national administration of the College Student Experiences Questionnaire

(CSEQ), which was published in the *Journal of Hispanic Higher Education* (Strayhorn, 2008d). The student sample consisted of 589 Latino and White college students who responded to the CSEQ; the sample was restricted to students who attended four-year institutions only. The final analytic sample consisted of 289 Latino students (54% female) and 300 randomly selected White students (63% female) as a comparison group. Additional information about the instrument, measures, and analysis procedures is available in the journal article.

The second study consists of one-on-one, in-depth interviews with 31 Latino undergraduates attending PWIs in the north- and southeastern regions of the country. Data were collected using a semi-structured interview protocol with additional probes for issues related to sense of belonging. With few exceptions, interviews lasted approximately 50 minutes, ranging from 35 to 75 minutes. All interviews were digitally recorded and transcribed by a professional (or one of my "willing" graduate students, if necessary). While the survey data (from Study #1) were analyzed using hierarchical linear regression techniques, these data (Study #2) were analyzed using the constant comparison method by Strauss and Corbin (1998).

A third study yielded useful insights for this second edition of the book. In this study, students participated in one of 15 different summer bridge or early outreach programs at a large, public research university in the Midwest region of the country. The overall sample was delimited to include Latinx students only. Data were collected using electronic surveys and interviews. Data analysis followed closely the approach described in the previous paragraph.

Before presenting several major findings that emanate from these studies, I recall information about the theoretical framework that influenced my thinking about the topic at the time of study. This may be helpful to readers as a way of demonstrating how my thinking about sense of belonging has evolved over time.

THE THEORETICAL FRAMEWORK

To understand the relationship between academic and social experiences and Latino students' sense of belonging, it was necessary to identify sources that provided information for talking about these constructs. For the reasons noted earlier in the chapter, it made sense to employ Hurtado and Carter's (1997) explanation of sense of belonging as one of the guiding frameworks for the studies. Their frame provided a lens through which to "see" aspects of sense of belonging that might otherwise be unclear or remain hidden. For instance, they point out that sense of belonging consists of both cognitive and affective elements, which not only called my attention to the academic, social, and environmental (e.g., campus climate) determinants of sense of belonging but helped me to (a) justify inclusion of certain variables from these domains in the survey analysis and (b) determine initial analytic codes or categories for the interview studies.

As one of my very first studies on sense of belonging, particularly for Latino students, I tended to collate information from various, and separate, sources to assemble a list of definitions about sense of belonging, which ultimately outlined the contours of the theoretical framework. Consider the following from the 2008 article in the *Journal of Hispanic Higher Education*:

> Sense of belonging reflects the social support that students perceive on campus; it is a feeling of connectedness, that one is important to others, that one matters (Jacoby & Garland, 2004–2005; Rosenberg & McCullough, 1981; Taylor, Turner, Noymer, Beckett, & Elliott, 2001). Sense of belonging may be particularly important for understanding the experiences of students who perceive themselves as marginal to campus life, such as Latino students (Hurtado & Carter, 1997).
>
> *(Strayhorn, 2008d, p. 305)*

Building upon the idea of marginality, I make a theoretical leap, if you will, connecting belonging and marginality to the issue of validation: "Students of color can experience simultaneous marginality that often results from an unwelcoming environment that fails to appreciate, embrace, and engage diversity" (p. 305). To overcome feelings of marginality and to adjust to the new social and cultural contexts of college, students want to be validated and positive, meaningful interactions with others on campus are a key aspect of the validation process.

To augment my understanding of the potentially unique interplay between academic and social experiences in college, I also leaned upon Tinto's (1993) interactionalist theory of college student departure as a guiding framework. Briefly stated, Tinto theorized that student traits form individual degree goals and institutional commitments, which interact over time with collegiate experiences (both informal and formal) to influence one's decision to leave college. His theory emphasizes the role that involvement in the academic and social systems of college life plays in predicting students' departure decisions. Melding these two perspectives together, it seemed reasonable to assume that involvement with others on campus, especially interactions with diverse peers and faculty, may influence Latinx students' sense of affiliation, membership, or sense of belonging on campus, which, in turn, could influence one's subsequent *goals* and *commitments*, offer the validation that some seek, and, thus, one's decision to "stay in" or leave college.

There were several advantages to using this conceptualization of belonging and retention theory. First, theory allowed me to "see" in new and different ways what might otherwise appear blindly abstract or unambiguously familiar. In other words, without the aid of theory, I could have puzzled over sense of belonging to no end. On the one hand, it appears too complex to distill its constituent elements (e.g., cognitive and affective evaluations). On the other, sense of belonging could be erroneously equated with mere satisfaction or involvement. Indeed, it is different (for more, see Chapters 3 or 10). Theory allowed me to see these differences, though subtle at times, and provided language for talking about them.

Second, using multiple theories resonated with my own identity as a critical scholar. I'm a scholar of color. The primary goal of my research is to improve the material conditions of education for the benefit of *all* college students in a variety of contexts; I have an unapologetic focus on improving conditions for historically underrepresented groups in higher education (e.g., racial/ethnic minorities) and this abiding commitment is, in part, due to my own experiences in college. Through my work I attempt to interrogate some of my own college experiences from a critical stance typically using quantitative methods [what Stage (2007, p. 1) calls a "quantitative criticalist"], although my use of qualitative methods has grown over the years as I have moved to studying marginalized subgroups that are difficult to access or relatively few in number.

My biography as a critical scholar empowered me to consider a number of prevailing theories with the healthy dose of skepticism that each deserves. For instance, I was aware that Tinto's (1993) theory enjoys near-paradigmatic stature (Braxton, 2000) but seems to have limited applicability to the decisions of students of color, such as African Americans and Latinos. In fact, some scholars (e.g., Rendón, Jalomo, & Nora, 2000) have criticized Tinto's conceptualization for its assimilationist language and assumptions—that students must break ties with former communities to become integrated into the academic and social communities of campus. For some students, especially students of color attending PWIs, severing supportive relationships with members of one's culture of origin can lead to serious psychological issues, dissatisfaction, a loss of cultural connectivity (what I would consider as "cultural suicide"), and, consequently, academic failure (Guiffrida, 2004, 2005; Strayhorn, 2008c; Thomas, 2000). I knew from the beginning that I was uncomfortable with this element of retention theory, and thus sought additional theoretical information to address this limitation.

As a result, I consciously melded an alternative conceptualization that connected retention with sense of belonging by focusing on perceived membership and "fit" rather than integration. Additionally, I consciously chose questions that sought to challenge the dominant paradigm. Rather than focusing on factors associated with Latino collegians' *integration* into college environments, I asked, "What is the relationship between academic and social experiences in college and *sense of belonging* for Latino students attending four-year colleges and universities?" A second question focused on differences or inequities that may exist between Latino students and their White peers. My epistemological stance compelled me to call into question the existing theory and assumptions about Latino students' success; I was drawn to ask the typical *answer* (e.g., Latinos lack what's necessary to succeed in education; they're to blame) a different *question* (i.e., What can be done to enable Latinos success; what's the role of others on campus?). In the end, I was satisfied—at least for the moment—with combining these two frames in my studies. Now, let's talk about the major findings and conclusions.

MAJOR FINDINGS

After conducting analyses of data drawn from the College Student Experiences Questionnaire, I was left to interpret these findings in light of the overarching theoretical framework and prior research. Generally speaking, results suggest a number of important findings that also were affirmed in the interview study. Here's a brief summary (for more, see Strayhorn, 2008d):

1. Latino students tended to report less of a sense of belonging at PWIs than their White peers.
2. Positive and frequent interactions with diverse peers predicted Latino students' sense of belonging in college.
3. The statistical model accounted for slightly more of the variance in Latino students' sense of belonging than their White peers.

There were several other findings that emanated from the interviews, some that were untapped by the survey study as the CSEQ did not include items measuring one's socioeconomic status or family connections. The following is a brief summary:

1. Latino student participants were disproportionately represented among those who were first in their family to attend college; for instance, 58 percent of Latinos (compared with 25 percent Whites) were first-generation in the CSEQ analysis.
2. Latino student participants were more likely to hail from low-income family backgrounds than White peers and a larger proportion of Latino students worked on- or off-campus for pay while attending college.
3. Latino student participants reported having to develop coping abilities or "navigational" skills to negotiate college environments that, on average, were remarkably different from their cultures of origin.

4. Latino student participants struggled to manage "ties back home," particularly with parents and younger siblings, while adjusting to a new and unfamiliar college environment, which tended to include making friends, joining clubs, and choosing majors.

Comments shared during the interviews revealed how students experienced the challenges mentioned above, the meaning they made of such experiences, and, specifically, the various ways in which these factors affected their sense of belonging on campus. Here are a few extended examples that illustrate the depth and meaning of comments shared by others in the interviews. For instance, Adrián described what being a first-generation Latino college student was like for him at a large, southern PWI:

> Me and my friends were actually just talking about this the other day [laughing]. It's like here [at this college], you really get by because you know someone who know [sic] someone, you know. It's not like other people are really smarter than you ... they just know shit that you can't know if you ain't from here or been here before. [Interviewer: Can you say more about this?] Yeah, like I'm Mexican and Puerto-Rican. I'm the first in my family to go to college ... even including my older cousins. My parents don't really speak English that good. So, I don't know nothing about like financial aid, scholarships, internships ... you name it and I probably didn't know about it. Even test banks ... you know what those are? [Interviewer: You can tell me.] Yeah, it's like old tests that some students have or can get through friends or their contacts. Well like I don't have any contacts that can help me. And my mom and dad don't either and they can't help me with college stuff because they can't really speak English. I remember stressing out my first year and thinking everybody was smarter than me because they were kicking my ass in the biology tests. But come to find out, they had friends, copies of old tests, parents who told them "this is what you study," some knew they had to go to mid-week small group or knew they could just ask the professor. I didn't know any of that and to top it all off, I'm Latino so I'm already working against that perception of me and I don't have the extras that they have. Without that, I'm left on my own ... to do it all alone and when I started failing it made me start to doubt myself and whether I should be in college.

So while we've known for years that first-generation college students face challenges in collegiate environments due to the fact that they enter college without the academic resources and "academic know-how" that continuing-generation students are privileged to inherit from or access through their parents, we've understood relatively little about how intersecting systems of power and oppression (e.g., privilege) coalesce and simultaneously influence the multidimensional experiences of Latino collegians. Adrián's story, along with many others that appear in my published works, reveal that limited financial resources, lack of academic "know-how," limited English proficiency, and unfamiliarity with one's surroundings can create formidable challenges for Latino collegians, which, in turn, can diminish their self-confidence and lessen their sense of belonging in college. Interestingly, I believe the job of all college student educators is to help provide all students with the "extras" that Adrian mentions.

Other participants shared perspectives that shed light on what it means to be a Latino college student who hailed from a working-class or low-income family. For most, this lived reality presented at least two immediate concerns. First, virtually all of these students worked on- or off-campus for pay; in some cases, participants worked in excess of 25 hours per week, which significantly limited the amount of time available for classes, homework, and extracurricular involvement, all of which relate to sense of belonging. Second, financial challenges produced an (over)reliance on student aid in the form of federal grants and loans; reliance on loans ran the risk of undermining academic goals as pressure to repay loans often intensified the need to work, which "crowded out" opportunities to establish a sense of belonging through personal interactions, involvement, and formal services such as orientation, living-learning communities, study abroad, and bridge programs. Fabían, Vían, and Mateo offer particularly compelling comments that echo the sentiments of their Latino peers; consider these before moving on to the discussion that follows:

I don't know about the other students in your study but I'm sort of torn between college and being back home, especially since I know my parents really need me to help them out money-wise. I mean, I work here on campus and stuff, but I really can't make as much as I would if I left college and went back home to work at like Advanced Auto Parts or the hardware store where I used to work. They [his parents] aren't really able to help me much with paying for school so I have financial aid for that but I still have to pay some of that back. It's stressful at times because most kids my age don't have to worry about bills and paychecks and stuff. Then, there's school [laughing] which I guess should be first, but family's first and that's related to work so I have to make all of it just work out. I ain't complaining but sometimes I just wish it were a little easier or that I had some help.

(Fabían, second year)

It's complicated because I'm basically like the breadwinner in my family. Clearly, I'm not the only one because my dad works but my mom doesn't. When I was back home, I would work and help pay bills. My dad really only agreed to me going to college if I would continue helping out with the bills. So, I work at the [deli] on campus. Usually I'm working there about five to six hours a day so I can send my check back home. A lot of my friends don't have to work but I tell them I *have* [emphasis added] to work or I can't stay in school. [Interviewer: Is that how you pay for college?] You'd think, right! No, I took out loans and I think I got a couple of grants too. I work to help pay for the rent on my parent's place, to keep the phone on back home so we can talk time to time, so they can get food. Sometimes my mom will send me $50 in the mail and say "keep this for yourself." But that's about it. I don't even tell my friends about it because I don't want them to judge me and think she's so poor. It's too embarrassing, I think.

(Vían, third year)

I don't think it's hard to explain [laughing]. We're broke so I work. And I have to work a lot. I can't work more than like 15 hours on campus, so I have an extra job at Subway off-campus. It gives me an additional 10 to 15 hours per week. I also tutor in Spanish. That's another two to three hours per week. [Interviewer: How do you manage that?] I basically go to class when I am not working. That might mean missing a lab, or a lecture, or a test ... I missed a pop quiz once. But what else am I supposed to do? A man's gotta [*sic*] work.

(Mateo, second year)

So much can be said about the lived experiences alluded to in the quotes from these three Latino students. They reveal through their words how one's socioeconomic condition can intensify the need to work for pay to support family (i.e., parents, younger siblings), as well as produce a reliance on student aid as the only way to pay for college. Working under such pressures, college students are inclined to make decisions that may undermine their academic success (i.e., skipping class, missing study sessions) or reduce, if not inhibit, their sense of belonging in college. Perhaps most importantly, they point to areas where college student educators can assist them in ways that enable their educational success.

DISCUSSION

Findings from these analyses indicate that Latino students feel a lower sense of belonging at PWIs than their White peers. This lends support to previous research about disparities in educational outcomes among White and Latino college students (Arbona & Nora, 2007; Massey, Charles, Lundy, & Fischer, 2003). It may be the case that academic, social, and financial struggles such as limited English proficiency, negative interactions, social isolation, and racism limit the extent to which Latino students can engage in educationally purposeful activities such as bridge programs or interpersonal interactions, which, in turn, removes opportunities to develop a sense of belonging on campus (Justiz & Rendón, 1989; Oliver, Rodriguez, & Mickelson, 1985). Additional supports are needed that help Latino collegians manage these pressures deftly.

In addition, positive and frequent interactions with diverse peers accounted for more of the variance in sense of belonging for Latino students than White students. This provides support for several theoretical arguments posited in this volume. For instance, these results add supportive evidence to the idea that sense of belonging may be a more culturally relevant way to measure minority students' "connectedness," "attachment," or "membership" to campus, thus accounting for more of their educational outcomes than other factors.

Information in this chapter also calls into question pre-existing theories that focus on integration while supporting alternative explanations such as sense of belonging that can be nurtured even while students maintain and negotiate ties to other important communities such as family and friends.

The applications of this chapter to practice are many. For example, participants shared new information about the belonging experiences of first-generation Latino college students. Diversity educators, multicultural affairs staff, and academic support advisors might consider this information when working with such students. Talking with them about the realities of college life, including the financial burdens they may assume, as well as offering tips about "academic know-how" (e.g., how to apply for aid, visiting professors' office hours, using study guides) may be effective in enabling Latinx students' success.

Students spoke, in detail, about the difficulty of balancing academic demands with work responsibilities, particularly when one hails from a low-income family and shoulders financial responsibility for the family. Financial aid advisors, recruitment specialists, and academic advisors might consider these results when advising students. Indeed, this is a rather unique situation for students enrolled at most PWIs; not all students are faced with this amount of pressure to work and, even when they are, it's rarely to support their parents or pay bills back home. That some Latino students are expected to do this deserves targeted attention. Working extensive hours on- or off-campus can be difficult to manage with 12 to 15 credit hours of college-level work; academic advisors and faculty can help students acquire strategies and skills (e.g., note-taking, studying, reading, and planning) that make this easier for them. Working long hours may also force a student—rightly or wrongly—to skip class or miss a test. Student affairs professionals, resident hall assistants, and student government leaders might address this issue by offering periodic workshops and seminars on balancing multiple commitments, making sound academic decisions, and focusing on achieving one's main college goal, which, I believe, is to earn a college degree.

In terms of future research, the analyses upon which the present chapter is based provide empirical support for analyzing survey data using a comparative group approach, where appropriate (Carter & Hurtado, 2007); that is, a "method of conducting statistical analyses separately by group" (p. 29). Future researchers should consider this recommendation when designing future studies, especially those based on applying critical approaches to conventional questions. This approach is appropriate only when testing whether the influence of independent factors, Xs, on a dependent variable, Y, in Group A is more or less than that observed in Group B. If this is not the purpose of the study, there is no reason to make a comparison group (e.g., typically Whites) the norm by which all others are measured. I offer this comment not only as a guide to future researchers but as a word of caution to reviewers and editors who *insist* on such techniques when scholars, like myself, attempt to "give voice" (and numbers) to those who are rarely heard in the literature or those who are often perceived as "too few" to *matter*.

CLOSING THOUGHTS

In closing, both Tinto's (1993) interactionalist theory of college student departure and Hurtado and Carter's (1997) definition of sense of belonging were gainfully employed in my research on Latino students' academic and social experiences in college. Theory allowed me to see in new and different ways what might otherwise be seen as ordinary and familiar (Anfara & Mertz, 2006). I have started to say that theory is a way of exoticizing the ordinary (Besnier, 1995) or making the familiar strange (Jakobson, 1987). And while useful, all theories have limitations. This led me to combine retention theory and notions of sense of belonging in these studies. It's my hope that the theoretical information contained in this volume (see Chapter 3) may be helpful to researchers and offer promising directions for expanding this line of inquiry.

Turning back to Vincent's story, information presented in this chapter should provide clues to levers that can be used to increase Latino students' sense of belonging on campus. Feeling a sense of belonging, feeling validated, supported, cared about, valued, and even just listened to may help Latino collegians feel like they matter (i.e., what Vincent calls "talked about"), like they "fit in," which, in turn, may raise retention rates and increase the number of Latino students who complete their college degree. The weight of evidence clearly suggests that *Sentido de pertenencia* (translated "sense of belonging") is a key element of Latino students' educational success.

Chapter 5

Sense of Belonging and Ethnic
Gay Male College Students

Positive feelings come from being honest about yourself and accepting your personality, and physical characteristics, warts and all; and, from belonging to a family that accepts you without question.

(Willard Scott)

That's a hard question because belonging is so important in my mind. Feelings of not belonging eat at your core. They can lead to feeling as if you're not worthy, not accepted, not special to anyone. And those feelings speak to me on a personal level.

(Angela, third-year marketing major, openly gay Black/Haitian lesbian)

Jokingly, I tell people that if I learned anything at all, I learned that I don't matter and I may not even exist [laughing]. I mean, of course, I exist in a physical sense; I breathe, I move, I take up space. Depending on where I am, that may be all I do or not much else. Among Blacks, I'm an automatic "delete" because I'm a gay man. Among gays, I stick out like a sore thumb because I'm Black. Before I even open my mouth, people make all sorts of assumptions about me because Black is straight for a lot of people and gay is White. So, where do I fit in the puzzle? Not many places [laughing], at least not easily or without trying hard to fit. That's the truth … it's sad, but like they say, the truth hurts.

(Reuben, third-year social work major at Midwest college)

INTRODUCTION

After much consideration and hours (well, okay, maybe more like many long minutes) of blank stares at the computer screen, I decided to open this chapter with the opening excerpt from Reuben, an openly gay Black male undergraduate who participated in my national study of gay men of color in accredited colleges and universities. Reuben, like so many other participants, spoke eloquently and at length about the achievements and challenges of gay men of color in college. Their words reflect their search for community, humanity, acceptance, and even visibility, all core elements of sense of belonging, as set forth in this book. They reveal through their tone and language the angst that some students experience when the fundamental need to belong is unfulfilled. Their words also signal the meaning they make of such uncertainties and longings, and how they strive to fashion healthy senses of self amidst unwelcoming campus environments and frequently contradictory values and perspectives while journeying to establish a sense of belonging in "places" where they feel accepted, valued, and understood. In this way, Reuben and the other students represent exemplars among historically silenced voices—exemplary in that they offer so much from which we can learn. So while this chapter is designed to offer useful insights about sense of belonging for LGB(TQ) college students, I draw upon research findings from my national study of gay and bisexual men of color to anchor my thoughts and recommendations in an empirical base; I firmly believe these insights have intellectual merit and broader impacts beyond communities of color. Before detailing the realities of the experiences my participants shared, I review some extant literature on gay men of color in higher education and society and prevailing gay identity development models.

WHAT WE KNOW

Literature on gay men of color in higher education and society can be conceptualized in any number of ways. Here I have organized the literature into three major categories: (a) popular press texts and expository essays on aspects of the lives of gay men of color; (b) empirical studies about gay men of color in educational and social settings, namely, schools, families, and social spaces; and (c) theoretical models on gay identity development. Literature in each of these areas is reviewed in the sections below.

Considerable attention has been directed to understanding—dare I say, exposing—aspects of the lives of gay men of color in America. For instance, authors of popular press books and essays have addressed topics such as gay men's sexual practices (both safe and unsafe sex), their use of illicit drugs and alcohol, their encounters with and engagement in violence in same-sex relationships, and, most recently, the ways in which they negotiate their public and private lives as gay men (e.g., Agronick et al., 2004; Brown, 2005; King, 2004). In reference to the latter, some authors, such as J. L. King, have coined the phrase "living on the down low" or "DL" to refer to men who lead public lives as heterosexual or "straight" men while engaging in same-sex, gay, or homosexual intercourse privately—that is, without telling significant others (e.g., wives, girlfriends, children)—in clandestine locations (e.g., men's clubs, gay bookstores, gyms), or without ever disclosing their "real" identity (e.g., name, job, marital status). Personally, I found King's treatment of the subject unexciting, atheoretical (perhaps by design), and unnecessarily reckless. His confessions about the down-low life he led (along with many of his friends) seemed to blame gay or same-gender-loving men of color for their own oppression, profile them all as selfish, shiftless, and vindictive lovers who set out to hurt everyone in their way to self-fulfillment and pleasure. Not one time in the 190-page volume did King expose the forces that conspire to keep men of color "in the closet," nor did he present a counterpoint to his narrative, perhaps a man living on the down-low who's not married, not lying to his kids, but merely living quietly in the face of society's racist, homophobic rage that plays itself out in the microaggressions of everyday life—in my research, I've met many more students who fit that profile than those similar to his characterization. And while this could be conceived as *personal criticism* of J. L. King himself, it's simultaneously none of that and more than that; it's a *literary critique* of his book that provoked near-national hysteria (especially among Black women) without even a passing glance at the ways in which we're all complicit in the "DL problem" in America. Black women who are suspicious of well-dressed Black men who comfortably wear pink or hug their same-sex brothers are complicit in the problem. Black men who tease, threaten, or bully other men who are energetic, charismatic, playful, or manicured—knowing nothing about their sexuality—are complicit in the problem. But, I digress.

Some of what's known about gay men of color in education and society can be placed in a second category that represents empirical studies about their experiences in educational and social settings. At least three major conclusions emanate from this stream of scholarship. First, gay men of color in society experience poorer health outcomes than their non-gay counterparts (Battle & Bennett, 2000; Icard, 1996; Zea, Reisen, & Poppen, 1999). Second, gay men of color still experience homophobia, harassment, and physical assault from peers on college campuses today (Díaz, Ayala, Bein, Henne, & Marin, 2001; Herek, 1993; Huebner, Rebchook, & Kegeles, 2004) and the causes of such harm are complex, rising from issues of masculinity, patriarchy, and racism. Third, gay men of color experience "coming out" in different ways, markedly different from what has been written about the "coming out" experience(s) of gays in general (Icard & Nurius, 1996; Strayhorn, Blakewood, & DeVita, 2010). For instance, Diaz and colleagues analyzed data from 912 gay and bisexual Latino men in three US cities to assess their experiences with social discrimination. They found high incidence rates of homophobia, racism, and financial hardship, which, in turn, led to high prevalence rates of three forms of psychological distress: suicidal ideation, anxiety, and depression. Suicidal ideation among LGBTQ youth is alarmingly high in the country.

In that vein, a third major category of literature consists of theoretical models of gay identity development. For instance, several prevailing models have been applied to the experiences of gay men of color (Cass, 1984; D'Augelli, 1991; Fassinger, 1991). For instance, D'Augelli posited a six-process model that explains the process through which men negotiate and assume a gay identity as movement from "exiting heterosexual identity" to "becoming a gay offspring" onward to "entering a gay community." Cass, on the other hand, outlined a six-stage model that describes how an individual struggles to resolve conflicts or tensions between perceptions of self and others. Her model begins with "identity confusion" and ends with "identity synthesis." Fassinger's model attempts to capture LGBT and ethnic identity development as they unfold simultaneously.

Interestingly enough, the most widely circulated models of gay identity development have been applied to students of color although the models themselves lack the necessary constructs and language for theorizing racialized experiences in gay identity development. For instance, D'Augelli's (1991) model holds that individuals move from "exiting heterosexual identity" to "developing personal [and then social] gay identity status," but fails to acknowledge that race is a powerful dimension of personal identity for people of color and it likely plays a critical role in the process of understanding one's self as LGB(TQ). Prevailing models also adhere to a number of assumptions that fly in the face of cultural commitments that characterize some communities of color. For instance, D'Augelli's theory posits that *all individuals* must "becoming an LGB(TQ) offspring" by disclosing their sexual orientation to their parents. While generally accepted by dominant scholars, my research on vulnerable populations—LGB(TQ) youth, formerly incarcerated adults, and youth emancipated from foster care—reveals the variability that exists across families and family-like arrangements where some students feel very connected to parents, guardians, foster parents, adopted parents, fictive kin, and the like. The notion of becoming a gay offspring rests upon the implied belief that one's relationship with parents is *so significant* that disclosing a gay identity to them represents growth and developmental maturity. But this is not always the case—consider gay foster youth of color who may not have strong ties to their biological or foster parents; disclosing their gay identity would be a relatively easy process or it might not happen at all. Indeed, culturally relevant models of gay identity development are sorely needed to address such nuances for specific populations.

There is one other observation that deserves mention as it relates to prevailing gay identity development models and core elements of sense of belonging. Consider that D'Augelli (1991) and Cass (1984) suggest that the process of assuming a gay identity starts with "exiting heterosexual identity" or recognizing the one does not "fit" traits associated with "straight people," to use everyday language. Exiting one identity—an identity that one has occupied, knowingly or unknowingly, up until the point of departure—can be frightening, intimidating, or scary as one sheds what they "used to be" and *where they used to be* to take on a new, unknown sense of self. That shift is likely punctuated with moments of anomie, confusion, and uncertainty where the individual is unsure *where they belong* or even *what group they belong to*, if any. This demonstrates how questions about sense of belonging likely emerge for LGB(TQ) individuals as they start to come to know themselves.

With the major threads of extant literature on the table, I turn attention to the details of the national study that informs this chapter, including a description of participants and data collection techniques. Then, I move to identify several major findings that flow from the study related to LGB(TQ) students' sense of belonging. Let's talk about what I did, with whom, and how I made sense of their comments.

THE STUDY

To explore the topic addressed in this chapter, I drew upon data from my on-going national study of gay men of color at predominantly White and historically Black colleges and universities in the United States. The study employed a constructivist qualitative approach (Merriam, 1998), which was congruent with my own epistemic beliefs about the very nature of knowledge regarding this topic as well as my positioning as a researcher.

Data were collected via semi-structured, in-depth, one-on-one interviews with willing participants. Participants were recruited via a number of methods over several years. Initially, members of my research team and I worked with presidents of the gay student alliances at each participating campus to identify and recruit a pool of prospective participants. Individuals who met the sampling criteria were contacted by the president of the respective gay student alliance, who relayed information about the study to them and encouraged them to share their email address with the principal investigator (Strayhorn). Over time, however, we employed additional steps to recruit participants. For instance, some participants were recruited through online gay networking sites and web advertisements; in each case, they received information about the study, its scope and purpose, and how to contact a member of our team. The interview questionnaire also was available on the internet for those who wanted to participate without face-to-face contact, which can be an absolute requirement for some gay men of color who prefer to keep their identity concealed or unknown (Icard, 2008). (For more information about the study, see Strayhorn, Blakewood, & DeVita [2008].)

Data were analyzed in three stages using the constant comparison method, as described by Strauss and his colleagues (Strauss & Corbin, 1998). First, transcripts were read and re-read to generate initial categories of information or codes that represented a general summary of preliminary patterns. This is known as open coding. Next, codes were collapsed by grouping categories that seemed to relate to each other while leaving intact those that stood independent from all others. This smaller list of categories was used to generate what I call "supercodes" or preliminary themes. Lastly, preliminary themes were compared and contrasted to understand the degree to which they were similar; closely related themes were collapsed, while those that stood independent were retained. In this chapter, I present three discrete themes as major findings.

MAJOR FINDINGS

Data from the national study were analyzed to identify three major themes related to the sense of belonging of gay men of color in college. The first of these is the emergence of a compelling need to belong, especially as they started to explore their sexual orientation or "come to know" themselves as gay, bisexual, or "something other than straight," as one put it. Participants also identified campus contexts in which their need to belong felt intensified, of greater importance, than in other settings. Second, participants described in vivid details the ways in which they sought to satisfy their need to belong in college as gay men of color. They also shared how their quest for belonging led, at times, to seemingly anti-social and unhealthy behaviors such as drugs (some intravenous), excessive alcohol, and unsafe, unprotected sex with same-sex partners. Another clear pattern was the association of these behaviors with negative psychological distress, including sadness, depression, and suicidal ideation at times. Of course, participants also shared how they engaged in prosocial activities to find a sense of belonging in college and these represent possible pathways for others like them. Lastly, gay men of color in the study talked about how they strived to fashion healthy senses of "self" and esteem once their belonging needs were gratified, in keeping with the book's theoretical model. Each of these themes is discussed below using verbatim quotes from participants to illuminate the context from which themes came, as well as to unpack the meaning and significance of each finding.

Emergent Need to Belong

Consistent with the argument advanced in this book, gay men of color in the national study shared that they often found themselves in situations where they felt they did not belong or did not matter to others on campus. For instance, virtually all participants explained that they enrolled in college with the expectation to "come out," although over half resisted the urge to use that language; instead, they talked about a more complicated process of making intentional decisions about disclosing and concealing their sexual identity to family, peers, roommates, and friends. Still, this process of coming out or being "more open," as several said, about their sexual identity stimulated a feeling or need to belong as they began to experience displacement in existing communities and/or relationships—displacement caused by growing discomfort with hiding "who they *really are*" or enduring "offensive gay comments and jokes" aired by friends and loved ones. Growing discomfort created displacement that left them feeling alienated, "out on their own," out of place and those feelings catalyzed their quest for a new place or sense of belonging. This period of disequilibrium was marked by a number of experiences including formation of new relationships with new gay or accepting/affirming friends, negotiation of previously established relationships, and even resolution of tensions associated with the termination of meaningful relationships with individuals such as parents, siblings, pastors, or mentors who may have rejected their sexuality. Facing rejection from close friends and family, while managing the uncertainty of newly established friendships, provoked strong feelings about mattering and belonging for gay men of color, which then served as a motive for behaviors to satisfy that need.

A significant number of participants talked about encountering peers (including gay or same-race) and faculty members who held negative beliefs and perceptions about gays and lesbians. These homophobic beliefs led to actions as well, such as proselytizing gay men in the study to consider Christian beliefs about homosexuality and, thus, revert to heterosexuality as a way of "saving one's self." There were other incidents where participants had negative encounters with campus administrators who treated them unfairly or aired offensive thoughts once they knew the students' sexual orientation—one who disclosed his identity to the Dean of Students spoke at length about how offended he was by the Dean's reaction: "See, I just knew you were gay ... you dress so nice and always be [*sic*] flying around here switching [referring to how he walks] with your cute self." Most participants found these spaces—whether dorm rooms, classrooms, restrooms, or office hours— very uncomfortable, unwelcoming, unsupportive, not to mention personally offensive. As a result, they felt threatened, unsafe, and insecure, which, consistent with belonging theory, seemed to place them back at the level of basic needs and far from feeling a sense of belonging in college. Once they got away from the moment or awkward conversation, they felt a bit safer but longed to be accepted, respected, affirmed for who they are (just as they are), or to feel a sense of belonging. Consider the following excerpts:

> I guess ... it's like I came here expecting college to be this life-changing experience ... and it was or it is. I expected to get away from [my hometown] and thought I would be around more open-minded people and feel free to be myself. But I don't really feel like I fit in here. I mean, I do in some places but then it's like really homophobic sometimes too. Well, for starters, the people here are not necessarily more open-minded.
>
> *(Desmond, 19-year-old African American male,*
> *psychology and public relations major)*

> For me, I think it's mostly name-calling and teasing and bullying kind of stuff, but not so much life-threatening stuff like. [Interviewer: Can you say more about that?] Sure, probably name-calling is like most often. You know, stuff like sissy, fag, punk, faggot, b*tch [asterisk added], flame and stuff ... punto ... I've had other stuff to happen too, but not as much as put-downs. Like last year, my roommate found out that I was gay and I had had a picture of my boyfriend on my desk ... but I told him it was my best friend, not because I was like embarrassed but because he didn't need to know ... and when he found out that I was gay, he acted crazy and broke my picture of my ex.
>
> *(Hugo, Latino male, marketing major)*

Hugo's story really captures the essence of my earlier points about disclosure of one's identity and the emergent need to belong. It was not that Hugo "came out" to his roommate—in fact, he didn't think it was any of his roommate's business to know his sexual orientation, especially as they didn't enjoy a meaningful friendship at all. But, over time, Hugo grew frustrated and uncomfortable "putting on" for his roommate or pretending to be straight when that wasn't his "real, true self." Discomfort with the situation created dissatisfaction that caused him to change his behaviors and "stop trying so hard to hide the fact that [he] was gay." This shift catapulted him from the "comfort zone" that was increasingly less comfortable to a new place that he had not known previously. Hugo sought out new friendships or (re)negotiated existing relations, all in hope of resolving his need to belong to others.

Comments like that shared by Hugo led to another important finding in this area: participants identified in detail several campus settings in which they experienced feelings of isolation or alienation, often due to explicit and implicit forms of anti-gay discrimination, homophobia, and/or racism. These settings included, but are not limited to: residence halls/dorm rooms;

cultural centers; restrooms; fraternities; classrooms; and local bars and clubs. Explicit actions included things like physical threats or name-calling; implicit actions ranged from offensive signs and symbols to racist or homophobic jokes. Whether threat of physical attack or innocuous name-calling, participants tended to make similar meaning of such experiences, which is best reflected in the words of Jorge: "I think the message's pretty clear. I'm not good here. I'm not to be accepted here. I'm not even protected as gay male [sic]." Experiences of this kind registered a single message to gay men of color: you don't matter and you do not belong here in college.

Despite encounters with unwelcoming spaces or negative perceptions of peers and faculty, some gay men of color took steps to satisfy their need to belong in college. These are discussed in the next section.

Satisfaction of Belongingness

Participants described in vivid detail the ways in which they sought to satisfy their need to belong in college as gay men of color. Careful analysis of interview and questionnaire data reveals the proportion of gay men of color, across all studies, who reported engagement in various activities as a way of satisfying their need to belong (see Table 5.1).

Certainly, the involvement data make logical sense; gay men of color devoted time and energy to certain groups and experiences (e.g., Asian American Student Association, partying at nightclubs) as a way of working out their sense of belonging in college. By involvement, I mean Astin's

Table 5.1 The belonging activities of gay men of color

Category/activity	Percent sample reporting "yes"
Involvement in salient communities	
Hanging out in ethnic nightclubs	48
Hanging out in gay nightclubs	41
Attending gay pride event(s)	77
Joining ethnic student organization(s)	62
Joining LGBT student organization(s)	35
Spirituality and religion	
Prayer	66
Church attendance	34
Yoga or related expression(s)	14
Journaling	25
Relationships	
Fictive kin	55
Monogamous dating	41
"Hooking up" with other gay men	31

Note: LGBT = lesbian, gay, bisexual, and transgender.

(1999) formulation of the concept that refers to the amount of physical and psychological energy that college students devote to the college experience, whether on- or off-campus. As I've said in other sections of the book, students who are more involved in college life also tend to feel more confident in their ability to "do college well," and a stronger connection with others on- (or off-) campus than those who are less involved, or not at all. The same holds true for gay men of color. It is important to note that the vast majority of gay men of color in this set of studies reported being involved in or attending ethnic student organizations (e.g., Black student association) over LGBT student organizations, although its less clear exactly why this is the case. Some participants shared that they found LGBT student organizations "too political" as members sought visibility of campus, acknowledgement of gay rights, and opportunities to champion gay causes before campus administration. Some participants were uncomfortable engaging in such movements and also struggled to see how the organization could "be so forward in pursuing gay rights without mention of race too." One guy from the study put it simply: "It's like you have to pick ... gay or Black ... and if I'm forced, I guess I will pick Black since it's the most obvious."

Engaging in spirituality and other religious activities also was reported by gay men of color across the studies. For instance, a large majority reported "praying" as a way of making sense of their experiences and trying to establish a sense of belonging while in college. While over 60 percent reported praying as a way of satisfying their need to belong, less than half of them (34 percent) reported attending church for such purposes. Indeed, a large majority of gay men of color in college reported negative perceptions and feelings toward organized religion; several went out of their way to clarify that their anger was directed toward "the church" (typically defined as the *individuals* who attend services) but not God or their respective deity. Approximately 60 percent of the samples—Black, Latino, and Asian—reported being ridiculed, chastised, or offended by a fellow parishioner or member of their church (sometimes even the pastor or spiritual leader) because of their sexual orientation. Ridicule or rejection of this kind interrupted existing feelings of connection or membership, thereby triggering feelings of alienation, loneliness, or isolation, which in turn catalyze the need to belong.

Relationships played an important role in the attempts of gay men of color to satisfy their need to belong. For instance, some men talked about establishing supportive family-like relationships with meaningful individuals (e.g., boyfriends, community members, older women), who I refer to as "fictive kin," in keeping with sociological literature. Karner (1998) defines fictive kin as individuals "who are not related by blood, but by imaginary ties of choice—they are 'adopted' family members who accept the affection, obligations, and duties of 'real' kin" (p. 72). Fictive kin also included gay faculty members of color, older gay students, and straight women or "allies" upon whom they could rely for support. Fictive kin provided much-needed social, spiritual, financial, and psychological support for gay men of color in the study. Hearing stories about the important role that fictive kin played illuminated the ways in which these relationships affirmed the identity of men in our study, connected them with individuals who either shared aspects of their identity or accepted them "for who they are," and facilitated their incorporation into college life on- or off-campus. For instance, one student shared how his biological family "didn't know about [his] love for other dudes" or sexual orientation and, therefore, he avoided going home during school breaks and limited communication with most of his family members. There was a lesbian Black faculty member who he met through mutual contacts who "became like an 'auntie' to [him]" and she would invite him to her family gatherings and check on him from time to time, in terms of grades and school progress. Through his "Doctor Auntie," as he called her, he met other gay students, other gay faculty, and found "a place that felt like home" while he was in college. Ultimately, all of this fueled his sense of belonging.

Finally, gay men of color also shared how their quest for belonging led, at times, to anti-social and unhealthy behaviors such as taking drugs (some intravenous), excessive alcohol, and unsafe, unprotected sex with multiple same-sex partners. In fact, 31 percent of participants, reported "hooking up" with different unknown partners on a regular basis to satisfy their need for acceptance, intimacy, love, and belongingness. "Hooking up" was defined as sexual relations with a same-sex partner in whom the student had no long-term interest; essentially, sex for a night. In most cases, students did not even know the other guy's name, his age, or his HIV serostatus. In an attempt to feel valued, needed, or loved (if only momentarily), some guys in the study hooked up with other men using online dating sites (e.g., gay. com) or at local gay bookstores. Another clear pattern was the association of these behaviors with negative psychological distress, including sadness, depression, suicidal ideation, and even attempts at suicide largely attributed to feelings of alienation, loneliness, and social isolation. I discuss this finding in detail elsewhere (Strayhorn, in press a).

Sense of Self and Esteem

In support of the model outlined in Chapter 3, gay men of color in the study talked extensively about how they strived to fashion healthy senses of "self" and esteem once their belonging needs were gratified, even if only partially fulfilled. For example, countless participants shared how they felt better about themselves, their experiences in college, and their identity as a gay male once they felt a sense of mattering to others or space of belonging, regardless of whether the "others" were family members, boyfriends, fictive kin, confidants, or even "hook-up" partners. Consider the following comment that illustrates this point:

> Damn right I felt better. I was feeling really bad before and very, very lonely. I can only remember feeling alone all the time and it didn't help that it was dead of winter. Hooking up with guys online made me feel like I had someone with me so I felt better, at least at the time. Then when Tareek (my boyfriend) and I started dating, I felt like a lasting, sort of support. Does that make sense? I didn't feel lonely anymore and that helped me feel better ... so I felt happy about being me, I guess.
>
> *(Yui, Asian male, fourth-year education major)*

Not only does this information lend persuasive support to the model outlined in this book, but it also affirms Maslow's (1954) original hierarchy of needs by extending it to gay men of color in college. As I've said a number of times, the need to belong is not a new idea. Information presented in this chapter stresses the important role that belonging plays in the lives of college students, particularly those who perceive themselves as marginal to campus life such as gay men of color.

DISCUSSION AND IMPLICATIONS

Recall that the purpose of this chapter was to illuminate the role that sense of belonging plays in the experiences of a particular group of college students, namely gay men of color. Analysis of data from my previous studies reveals three major findings. Gay men of color often found themselves in situations or contexts that emphasized their need to belong to others on- or off-campus. This led them on a path—constituted by a variety of behaviors and thoughts—to satisfy their need to belong. Attempts at gratifying their need to belong ranged from prayer to church attendance, from yoga to uninhibited sexual relations with strangers, at times. Once they gratified or at least reduced their need to belong, gay men of color talked about feeling better about themselves, their experiences in college, and their identity as a gay male.

Before discussing the implications of these findings, let me share one curious pattern that was observed in these data as well. Gay men of color who reported a sense of belonging were more likely to be high-achievers, involved student leaders, and very likely to "intend to stay" in college. And several participants talked, through tears, about how their grades improved, their involvement increased, and their aspirations changed once they felt valued, respected, and needed by others on campus; recall that all of these are core elements of sense of belonging (see Chapter 3). In terms of involvement, most of the gay men with whom I spoke reported feeling a sense of membership in small enclaves on campus (e.g., cliques, fraternities, musical groups), which later gave rise to active involvement in larger campus groups (e.g., student government, classrooms).

Findings from this chapter have many implications. In terms of theory, these three themes lend persuasive support to the model outlined earlier in the book. Gay men of color described belongingness as a need. They also talked about how their need to belong took on heightened significance in certain contexts (e.g., church), among certain populations (e.g., family), and at certain times such as when they were considering big identity questions surrounding "coming out," which they typically referred to as a more complicated process of decisions about disclosing and concealing one's identity. Future researchers might continue this line of work, advancing theory in a number of directions.

Also consistent with Maslow's (1954) original hypothesis and the model advanced in this book, gay men of color articulated—rather skillfully in my opinion—how the threat of danger, perceived or realized, produced a regression from higher needs (e.g., belonging, esteem) to more basic physiological and safety needs. This lends support to the proposed model and suggests that it may be applicable to the experiences of gay men of color, who may perceive themselves as marginal to campus life. Future theory work might be designed to test the timing and duration of such regressions and to assess the impact of regression on identity development across multiple dimensions of self, including race/ethnicity, sexual orientation, or vice versa.

Because a significant number of men in my studies reported losing contact or communication with biological parents and siblings as a result of disclosing their sexual orientation, they stressed the importance of friendships and meaningful "family-like" relationships with those who I call "fictive kin." Fictive kin are individuals "who are not related by blood, but by imaginary ties of choice—they are 'adopted' family members who accept the affection, obligations, and duties of 'real' kin" (Karner, 1998, p. 72). Fictive kin also seemed to constitute a band of resources upon which gay men of color could rely for support. I found their use of non-biological kin fascinating! Unfortunately, the scope of my work, to date, has not included examining *how* such relationships are formed; this might be a good step for future researchers. Learning more about how these relationships are formed, established, and maintained may yield helpful insights that can be used to bring other caregivers, counselors, and allies into familial-like relations with gay male collegians of color.

Information in this chapter may prove useful to a number of groups. For instance, parents and guardians of young gay men might consider this information when sorting through their own issues about sexual orientation. I am dismayed by the number of men in my studies who have been "cut off," ostracized, or rejected by their parents, guardians, or siblings as a result of disclosing their sexual orientation. And while I can't stop this from happening entirely, I can call attention to it through my research, this book, and my own advocacy for acceptance for all. I sport a bag that I purchased from the Human Rights Campaign that says simply: *Love conquers hate.* I hope that parents, guardians, pastors, parishioners, and educators will remember this phrase and information shared in this chapter when working with current and future generations of gay men of color.

Counselors and psychologists might find this information helpful when working with students and clients. What I provide here is a description of the need of gay men of color to belong, how they attempt to satisfy that need, and what happens when their need is satisfied, even if only partially. As I have mentioned earlier, until the need to belong is gratified, all behaviors and responses should be interpreted as the individual's attempt to meet a need. So, why do some gay men of color pray, attend church, journal, engage in yoga, pursue monogamous relationships, have sex with perfect strangers, use drugs, or drink alcohol excessively? They are motivated by one of our most fundamental needs, a need to belong.

CONCLUSION

Turning again to Reuben's comments that opened this chapter. I am indebted to the guys who have participated in my national study. Through them, I have learned something about something from "special someones" who know something about that which we've known very little or nothing at all about. These men matter, they belong, and their words (and consequent lives) are valuable to us all. Thanks guys. You've helped us tremendously.

Chapter 6

"A Bridge to Belonging"
Insights from First-Year College Students

Sometimes I really feel guilty for being in college. I know that it's hard out here for my folks [i.e., parents] and I sort of just left them to come to college. It has a purpose—I know it does—but sometimes it's hard to remember that when you're looking at all these people who have so many different lives from yours. Their moms and dads are calling to wake them up for class and to send money every weekend so they can party [laughing]. My folks call to tell me how much they *need me* [emphasis added] to send them and that I should be there helping out on the weekends. I just keep telling myself that it'll pay off, you know ... because it does, I guess.

(Jermaine, first-year African American male,
summer bridge student)

INTRODUCTION

Before I begin, let me share a bit of context about the program that is featured in this chapter. In Chapter 4, I explained how I came to be Special Assistant to the Provost at the University of Tennessee, Knoxville (UTK), where I worked as a professor for the first five years of my career. Basically, I was at a luncheon sponsored by the graduate program in which I taught, sat next to a very tall gentleman with rather impeccable taste who wore wool-blend business suits and felt top hats (fedoras, his favorite!), and invited him into a conversation about campus life.

We talked about the causes and cures of student retention, particularly musing about the factors that give rise to racialized gaps in student retention rates at UTK. I enjoy telling graduate students about this experience because I think it's one of many examples where "knowing your stuff"—that is, the literature and theory that inform one's work—paid off. I etched on the back

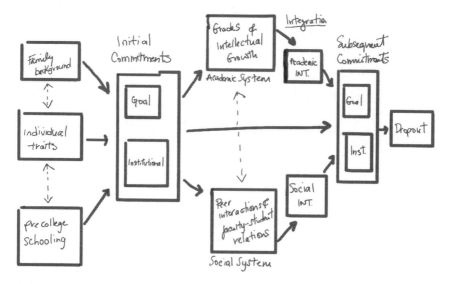

Figure 6.1   Replica of hand-drawn college student retention model, reflecting core elements of Tinto's (1993) attrition theory.

of a paper napkin the broad contours of college student retention theory, largely reflecting the elements posited by Tinto (1993). With a few lines and arrows, I briefly explained how background traits influence students' initial goal and institutional commitments, which, in turn, shape the degree to which they become involved in the academic and social life of campus—what Tinto referred to as academic and social integration. Integration, in most cases, leads students to reconsider those initial commitments over time. This whole process unfolds and shapes students' intentions, leading to subjective evaluations of college, all of which influence their retention decisions—that is, should I stay or should I go? See Figure 6.1 for a representation of my sketch.

Impressed by the little visual that I drew on the napkin, the "very tall gentlemen," who I later learned was the university's new Provost, asked if he could keep it as a souvenir of sorts. I agreed and turned my attention to the most important matter of the luncheon ... dessert (and coffee, for those of you who know me). The event ended, we parted ways, and I went back to my office or "cave" (as I called it) where I worked with my graduate students to carry out research studies that yielded the kind of information shared in this chapter. Two days passed and I received an email from the Provost. It read:

Dear Terrell,

I would like to meet with you very soon to discuss an opportunity. Thank you for sharing your knowledge with me the other day. I found your points excellent and recognize that you can help the university in many ways.

P.S.—THANKS FOR YOUR COMMENT ABOUT MY HAT. I NOTICED YOUR BLAZER AND TIE AS WELL. AND IF I'M NOT MISTAKEN, DID YOUR GLASSES MATCH? ☺

You can imagine my surprise, as a relatively new assistant professor at a major research university, when I read this personal note from the Provost. First, I was impressed that he remembered my name and spelled it correctly—this is important to mention in a book on belonging. For whatever reason, his note signaled that I mattered to someone important on campus—and by now you can understand how that message was conveyed. Look again at his note for cues about mattering: "I ... recognize ... you" (attention, visibility) and "you can help the university" (dependence). After that moment of bliss, I was overcome with worry about whether I had the time or resources to do anything more on top of my other commitments. Despite these doubts, I agreed to meet with him and greatly appreciated his mention of my own sense of fashion, blazer, tie, glasses, and all.

Long story short, we met, we talked, we laughed, and he invited me to serve as special assistant to him, specifically in the area of student retention and success. As I've shared on many occasions in public talks and lectures, the Provost invited me to "make the campus my laboratory." What a novel way to think about this assignment. At the end of the meeting, I realized that the Provost was right about at least two things. Number one, yes, my glasses were designed to match my suit and tie precisely. And, two, this was, in fact, a *great* opportunity!

INVESTIGATION OF THE PROBLEM

As special assistant, I commissioned university data on student retention and achievement rates for a few years. Close examination of institutional research data revealed that racialized gaps in student retention at UTK emerged early on in one's college career. By the end of the first year, we could already detect significant differences in the achievement and retention rates among Whites, Blacks, Latinos, Asians, and Native Americans, although the latter group was too small to disaggregate. My discovery led me to "look back" to see if I could detect differences anywhere else in students' paths to their college degree.

Up first was academic preparation, based on all that we know about the importance of academic readiness for college. Research has consistently shown that academic preparation is an important predictor of enrollment and success in college (e.g., Adelman, 1999; Perna & Titus, 2005; Strayhorn, 2010). Analyses of national, state, and local data all converge on a single take-home message: preparation matters. Specifically, scholars have shown that the intensity and quality of courses, the type and frequency of assignments, the nature and structure of instruction (especially in critical subject areas like math and science), as well as the prevailing school conditions that have a significant influence on the college-going culture and students' readiness for postsecondary education. Similarly, I found some evidence to suggest that students of color at UTK were, on average, less prepared than Whites and Asians for college academics, based on high school transcripts, grade point average, test scores, and a brief review of application essays.

Related to preparation, some scholars have found that a disproportionate number of students of color enter college academically underprepared for higher education—that is, lacking the basic skills necessary for success. For instance, approximately one-third of all entering freshmen require remedial or developmental work (Bettinger & Long, 2005). Other reports indicate that racial/ethnic minorities, first-generation, and/or low-income students are disproportionately represented among those who require remedial coursework (Breneman, 1998). Similar trends were apparent among minorities at UTK.

I found it interesting that although there is considerable debate about the value that remediation adds (Glenn, 2005), state policymakers and college administrators continue to invest resources in such programs. For instance, Bettinger and Long (2009) report that colleges and universities spend more than $1 billion annually on remedial education. Others estimate that businesses and institutions of higher education spend approximately $17 billion annually to teach students skills that they should have learned in high school.

Not only have sizeable investments been made to remedial education programs, but a range of compensatory programs have been established to help students acquire or enhance knowledge, skills, and abilities that they should have upon graduation from high school. Summer bridge programs are one type of compensatory program. Most of these operate under the assumption that students who participate in the program are better prepared for college than their peers without such experiences (Villalpando & Solórzano, 2005). And while somewhat limited, the weight of empirical evidence suggests that summer bridge programs can be effective interventions for improving students' readiness for college (for more about such programs, see Strayhorn, 2011a).

My investigation into the racialized achievement and retention gaps at UTK had turned up at least three factors. First, students of color differed from their White peers in terms of academic preparation, based on traditional measures of students' readiness for college. Second, racial/ethnic minority, first-generation, and low-income students were more likely than their peers to graduate from low-resource, urban high schools and to enter college in need of remedial education. Third, research had shown the effectiveness of compensatory programs, especially summer bridge programs. And while there were certainly academically underprepared students at UTK, there was no formal, university-sponsored summer bridge program ... or, at least, not yet.

THE SUMMER BRIDGE PROGRAM

In response to the trends described in the previous section, we worked to establish a new summer bridge program at the university. As summer bridge programs can vary widely (Swail & Perna, 2002) in purpose and structure, I think it is necessary to describe the general nature of the program discussed in this chapter. Specifically, the five-week residential summer bridge program was designed to increase students' college readiness by promoting critical skills development, acclimatizing them to the campus environment, and nurturing their sense of belonging in college. Participants were enrolled in two courses for credit: an academic skills/career planning seminar and English Composition I (or Psychology 101, if English credit was granted upon placement). In addition, all participants were offered weekly math supplemental instruction sessions.

Summer bridge participants spent most of the day (from 8 am to 3 pm) in academic classes such as those listed above. They also participated in evening activities that aimed to achieve program objectives. For instance, students participated in diversity workshops, movie nights, outdoor athletic events (e.g., whitewater rafting), and seminars on leadership and money management, to name a few. Extracurricular activities were chosen to facilitate transition to college life, encourage peer engagement, and make a big campus smaller for students who were likely to feel overwhelmed, intimidated, disconnected, or marginal to the campus community (sounds like sense of belonging, right?). Despite our good intentions, I knew that we needed to collect data to measure the extent to which we achieved our desired outcomes; the next section describes the study in brief.

THE STUDY

The larger study employed a two-phase, sequential mixed-methods design to obtain pre-test and post-test survey data from a sample of summer bridge students and then follow-up with willing individuals to probe the survey results in more detail using in-depth interviews and personal narratives. In addition to survey and interview data, the evaluation team worked closely with program administrators and instructors to collect data through other means, including class activities, assignments, reflection journals, and performance date. Figure 6.2 highlights the levels and types of data collected.

Participants were drawn from the population of at-risk or academically underprepared students who were *selected* to participate in the newly established summer bridge program. Here I present findings from the first cohort of students ($N = 55$). Women comprised a large majority of the sample (69.8%) and the participants' mean age was 18 years ($SD = 1.83$).

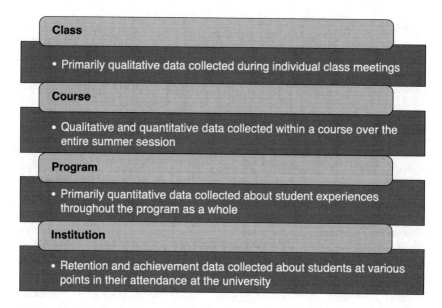

Class
- Primarily qualitative data collected during individual class meetings

Course
- Qualitative and quantitative data collected within a course over the entire summer session

Program
- Primarily quantitative data collected about student experiences throughout the program as a whole

Institution
- Retention and achievement data collected about students at various points in their attendance at the university

Figure 6.2   Levels and type of data collected for longitudinal assessment of summer bridge program.

All participants were students of color, most of whom were African American/Black (63%) and Latino (27%). Academic performance varied; the cohort's mean grade point average (GPA) in high school was 3.61 (*SD* = 0.39). At the end of the program, the mean college GPA was 3.53 (*SD* = 0.39) and grades dropped lower at the end of the first fall term in college (*M* = 2.35, *SD* = 0.94).

Using a combination of survey and interview data, I assessed the influence of the summer bridge program on participants' readiness for success in college, as defined by the program's major objectives. Here I draw upon information from the study to demonstrate the impact of the summer bridge program on first-year students' sense of belonging, which is the focus of this book.

FIRST-YEAR STUDENTS' BELONGING IN COLLEGE

I don't want to sound like a broken record, but I think it's important to recall a few key components of sense of belonging in college. Throughout this book, I posit sense of belonging as a basic human need and motivation, sufficient to influence behavior. In college, it refers to students' perceived social support on campus, a feeling or sensation of connectedness, the experience of mattering or feeling cared about, accepted, respected, valued by, and important to the group or others on campus (like I did to my "very tall gentleman" provost). It's a cognitive evaluation (i.e., "I think these are my people") that typically leads to an affective response (i.e., consequently, one feels good) and oftentimes behavioral manifestations (i.e., does things like build personal connections or join clubs). Sense of belonging is context-dependent, takes on heightened significance in settings perceived as unfamiliar or foreign, and likely changes over time and place. All of these seem to be important considerations, given the precarious situation of first-time entering freshmen who may tend to perceive college as a new or foreign culture, especially historically underrepresented groups like first-generation, low-income, or foster youth. For more, see Figure 6.3.

Given the importance of belonging to the experiences of first-year students in college, we thought it appropriate to include sense of belonging as one of the primary goals of the summer bridge program. In the next section, I present data to illuminate the extent to which the summer program achieved its goal in this area.

MAJOR FINDINGS

A paired-samples t-test was conducted to evaluate whether students' sense of belonging changed after participating in the summer bridge program, as measured by comparing pre-test and post-test scores. Results indicated that students' mean sense of belonging at the end of the program ($M = 13.02$, $SD = 2.21$) was slightly higher than that before the program ($M = 12.75$, $SD = 2.12$), although these differences were not statistically significant, $t(52) = 1.15$, $p = 0.25$. The standardized effect size, d, was small ($d = 0.16$). The 95 percent confidence interval for the mean difference from the two ratings was –0.20 to 0.72. Figure 6.4 presents this finding visually.

Interview data provide clues regarding the factors and experiences that likely explain the change in sense of belonging over the course of the program. First, the program consisted of a fairly elaborate opening ceremony where select administrators (two of us from the Provost's Office), a few admissions counselors (plus their director), and members of the implementation team welcome students to campus, celebrate their selection for the program (e.g., "Congratulations! This is a great opportunity for which you've been selected. We're so glad you're here"), and encourage them with motivating words (e.g., "You're here on purpose and we believe you will succeed"). Several faculty members don their "caps and gowns" (academic regalia) and march into the room with the "graduation song" (pomp and circumstance) playing. After a few words about the importance of college, the most senior-ranking official in the room proclaims, "We look forward to seeing you right here in a few years when we confer your degree." It's actually quite moving! And students talk about it, at length, during their

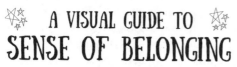

A VISUAL GUIDE TO
SENSE OF BELONGING
CORE ELEMENTS OF THE THEORY

1. IT'S A FUNDAMENTAL NEED OF ALL PEOPLE.

The need for belongingness is universal and applies to all people. Whether "fitting in" or "standing out," everyone wants to belong and know they matter. It's a basic human need, expressed or latent.

2. IT HAS THREE CORE DIMENSIONS.

Sense of belonging has three core dimensions: cognitive, affective, and behavioral. Key questions respectively include: Do I belong? How do I feel? What will I do?

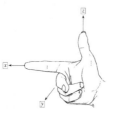

3. IT'S RELATED TO MATTERING.

Belonging is closely related to mattering, feeling significant and visible. Mattering has 4 elements: attention, dependence, ego-extension, and importance.

4. IT TAKES ON HEIGHTENED IMPORTANCE AT VARYING TIMES, SPACES.

Everybody needs to belong but one's desire to satisfy that feeling can be heightened or intensified at certain ages and places, like going to college.

5. IT LEADS TO WELLBEING AND SUCCESS.

Dozens of studies clearly show that sense of belonging, feeling like one matters, not only reduces suicidal ideation but positively promotes well-being and success.

NOTE: Infographic made by Author. Images are either self-created or available in the public domain.

Figure 6.3   A visual guide to college students' sense of belonging, created by author.

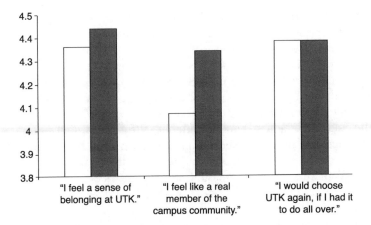

Figure 6.4   Pre- and post-test mean differences in summer bridge students' responses to "sense of belonging" at the university. o, pre-test; n, post-test.

end-of-summer interviews. It made them feel special, smart, valued, and worthy, all of which are reflective of the essence of sense of belonging.

There were at least three other ways in which students' sense of belonging was promoted over the course of the five-week program. Summer bridge instructors reportedly went out of their way to assist bridge students wherever possible (with the exception of a few folks, of course). Students shared how faculty members knew their name, asked about their childhoods and high school experiences, and went beyond "the call of duty" to make sure they had a successful summer. The meaning that students made of these experiences was that they mattered to someone on campus, someone was concerned about their success, and someone would miss them if they didn't show up for class or left college entirely. Sound familiar? You've got it— sense of belonging.

Recall my argument that sense of belonging changes and takes on heightened significance in certain contexts, at certain times, and with certain populations. Evidence from the interviews speaks to this issue as well. For instance, summer bridge students stressed that the campus was very large, much larger than any of their previous schools or neighborhoods. Gerald said it best: "It's easy to be just one in the number here because it's so huge. [Summer bridge] helped me feel like it [i.e., the campus] was smaller than it was because I got to know people." In short, sense of belonging may be more important to summer bridge students whose academic and social profile might be qualitatively different from that of their non-bridge peers who may score higher on exams, have better high school grades, and project greater confidence about themselves academically. Without such resources, students may be placed at risk for academic failure at the university or made to feel marginalized in such a "huge place," to use their words. By engaging their purpose-driven peers, meeting with caring faculty members, and participating in educationally meaningful activities and ceremonies, summer bridge students developed a stronger sense of belonging on campus during the five weeks.

Other data from the project reveal an interesting—and troubling—trend, however, when it comes to building sense of belonging over time. Gains in sense of belonging resulting from the five-week program were not maintained over the course of the first semester in college (by end of Fall term). Specifically, the increases in sense of belonging witnessed from time 1 (pre-test) to time 2 (post-test I) are reduced at time 3 (post-test II). In other words, at the end of the first full semester, students started to feel a bit of alienation, isolation, and lack of support, which diminished feelings of belonging. Figure 6.5 presents a visual summary.

Of course, the natural follow-up question is "Why?" For clues, I turned to the reams of transcripts from the student interviews. There are probably many reasons for this reduction (or regression) in sense of belonging over time, but at least three primary reasons were identified across multiple interviews. First, using their own words, students longed for the "structure," "sense of community," "togetherness feelings," or "connections" that the summer bridge program afforded, even after the program had ended and the Fall semester began. Almost half shared that they felt "on their own" or unsupported after the summer ended. They struggled to navigate the campus environment a bit once other, non-bridge students arrived. And even though they felt connected to each other at the end of the summer, they rarely saw other summer bridge students once the semester began. (See the end of this chapter for useful exercises that may enhance readers' understanding of these points.)

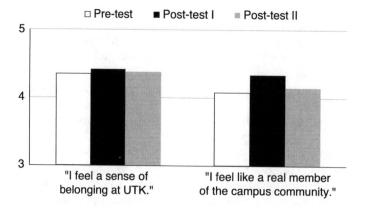

Figure 6.5 Summer bridge students' responses to "sense of belonging" survey items at pre-test (o), post-test I (n), an post-test II (n).

Recall that one of my arguments is that sense of belonging is variable; it changes with situation, circumstance, and time. This relates to this issue precisely. The longer students are enrolled in college, the more sensitive their sense of belonging to various factors and the greater the likelihood that sense of belonging has shifted a bit. Summer bridge students with whom we spoke talked at length about encountering negative experiences during the first year that affected their sense of belonging. For instance, a Black male shared (through tears) how he was refused membership in a (White) fraternity, presumably on the basis of his race. Like all students, he longed for acceptance and belonging. Another Latina uttered an emotional story about responding to a faculty member who refused to grade her term paper because "it was too good for her to have written it." No matter what influence the summer bridge program plays on students' sense of belonging, it's unlikely that those gains will be maintained in the face of experiences such as those described here. And while summer bridge programs can't save students from the pain of biased incidents, programs can be designed to equip students with strategies and tools for properly reporting and amicably resolving such encounters in productive ways.

Students' sense of belonging may be reduced, if not compromised, by "pulls and tugs" back home. To illustrate this point, I call upon Maria, a first-year Latina summer bridge student who stands at 5 feet 5 inches. Maria was born and raised in Memphis, Tennessee; second generation to this country. Maria left her parents to enroll in the university, which was "a big jump" for her socially and culturally. "In Latino families, it's really important to be obedient, to listen to your parents, and for girls, particularly, to listen to all that their father says." Her dad didn't want her to go to college because it would leave her parents on their own, with limited resources in terms of finances and literacy. Maria shared how her mother would call almost daily, "making it easy for her to leave." Her mother complained that they couldn't function without Maria in the house; English was a second language to them so they did not answer the phone, greet people at the door, or respond when neighbors came knocking. Semester rolls on and Maria feels caught "betwixt and between." "Do I go back home to take care of my family? Or, stay here and help my family in the long term?" Eventually, Maria decides to leave and go back home—not because she can't perform academically but because she failed to establish a sense of belonging on campus that kept her "stuck to" campus while negotiating the ties back home.

Consistent with the overarching framework set forth in this book (see Chapter 3), I identified at least three other factors that were positively correlated with summer bridge students' sense of belonging at time 3 (post-test II): involvement in social/leadership activities, positive interactions with diverse peers, and academic achievement. For instance, summer bridge students

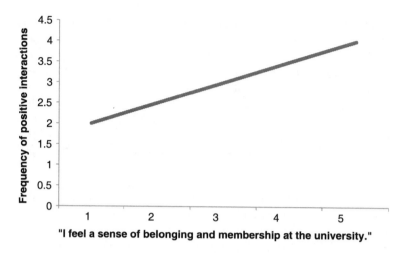

Figure 6.6   Summer bridge participants' sense of belonging at the university (post-test II) and the frequency of positive interactions with peers.

who were involved in a campus club or organization, served in a student leadership capacity, or reported being engaged in a service organization on campus tended to feel a stronger sense of belonging than their non-involved peers at the end of the first semester. Figure 6.6 illustrates this trend.

DISCUSSION

The purpose of this chapter was to set the stage for discussion of a summer bridge program that was designed to achieve several purposes, one of which was to facilitate students' sense of belonging on campus. Specifically, I reviewed the literature on summer bridge programs briefly, identified the factors that I considered when working with others to design the program, and then analyzed data from multiple sources to examine the influence of the intervention on belonging. With this information in mind, I offer several major recommendations.

First, summer bridge programs must be designed intentionally. Intentionality generally refers to something done or completed by design, a conscious or deliberate act. To be effective, summer bridge programs must reflect our very best effort to provide what students need to succeed in college, those strategies that hold great promise for enhancing students' skills, and a number of other logistical considerations (e.g., Will it be residential? What courses will students take? What activities, if any?). See Appendix A at the end of this book for a set of guiding questions that may be helpful for program development.

Although some evidence presented in this chapter underscores the importance of sense of belonging in educational contexts and the influence of summer bridge programs on students' belonging, it is less clear which aspects of the program likely yield the desired outcomes. Interview data from students in the bridge program suggest a number of possible suspects. These include whitewater rafting, ceremonies, block scheduling (e.g., where all summer bridge participants take the same courses), and educationally purposeful engagement with faculty and peers in-and-out the classroom. For instance, students raved about having fun with peers at the movies, creating memories while rock-climbing, and strengthening ties with staff who seemed to care about their success; feeling special, making friends, knowing that you matter, and that others care are core elements of *sense of belonging*. Still much more information is needed to mine the concept generally, just as we need more information about the components listed in this paragraph. Future program directors and researchers might consider these results when designing appropriate assessment and evaluation plans.

For all they're worth, summer bridge programs are not the panacea for all belongingness needs, and neither should they be. In most of my studies, summer bridge participation accounts for 2 percent to 7 percent of the variance in outcomes, a fairly modest percentage, thereby making at least two important points about belonging. First, it may be unreasonable to expect measurable or "sizeable" shifts in belonging over the course of a five-week program. It simply might take longer to change the extent to which students feel a sense of belonging. Second, results may suggest that other factors influence outcomes such as sense of belonging. Other such factors might include level and frequency of involvement in campus organizations; nature of relationships with faculty and staff; and the degree to which students feel that they matter to others on campus. Implied are the less direct impacts of race/ethnicity, gender, social class, and other identity markers that structure students' opportunities to find belonging; for example, I learned from student participants in my studies that "hanging out" can be powerfully effective in helping students find belonging but hanging out costs. Even a simple "Friday Funday with Friends" might involve paying Uber or Lyft (ridesharing apps) for transportation, dining out at a restaurant, buying tickets to a movie, and paying a "tab" at a local bar (for first-year students who are over legal age, of course!). How does a newly recruited, low-income, first-generation freshman shoulder the financial burden of "hanging out" with peers and who helps? Future researchers might take up this issue by designing studies that investigate the relation between such factors and sense of belonging, controlling for confounding differences, partialling out the effect of other variables, or estimating the simultaneous influences of "Xs on Y" using multi-institutional samples of college students. Qualitative studies (e.g., ethnographies, narratives) that capture the lived experiences of students *on the margin* as they strive to find a sense of belonging would be powerfully instructive.

Recall the story of Maria. She was an academically capable Latina who, according to most, stood much to gain from the supports provided by a summer bridge program. The program, however, was never designed to help her manage the very issues that affected her college experience the most—negotiating and renegotiating ties with her family (i.e., parents) back home. Some have interpreted Tinto's (1993) work as requiring students to sever ties back home, which, in my book (and experience), is the equivalent of academic suicide, especially for students whose backgrounds differ significantly from the dominant culture on campus, and thus those for whom belonging is critically important. Rather than sever ties, I think students often have to negotiate, renegotiate, and maintain (in new and different ways) their previously existing ties to family and friends back home so that pulls in that direction don't compel them to leave college before completing their degree. Without such support, we'll likely lose other "Marias in the world," so to speak; they'll drop out of college and feel like they never belonged there in the first place. Seems to me that teaching students how to rework or negotiate existing social ties could be an important addition to the curriculum of any summer bridge program; see Appendix B for a tool that could serve as a "starting point" for achieving this goal.

Armed with the information included in this chapter, along with any current or forthcoming studies on topics related to those recommended here, we can work together more effectively to build bridges to belonging for first-year college students.

REFLECTIVE THOUGHTS

1. What may cause regression in students' sense of belonging during the first-year of college for students who had participated in a summer bridge program? How can this be addressed and remedied?
2. What do you think would have been helpful in retaining Maria in college?
3. What are your main take-aways from this chapter?

Chapter 7

Sense of Belonging and STEM Students of Color in College

I just never seemed to adjust to the place ... like from the very beginning I was an automatic outsider because I didn't look like the other guys, they had exposure to the very things that I didn't when I was growing up and it all made me feel jealous and like very alone at times.

(A. J., third-year mechanical engineering major)

The politics made it hard for me. The longer I stayed in the major, I realized that I had to play the game according to their rules. And I wasn't very good at playing their games [laughing]. Like I wasn't even willing to play it sometimes because it started to mean that I couldn't do what I wanted to do ... what I came to college for. So, I'm changing my major to social work.

(Tiffany, second-year biochemistry major)

INTRODUCTION

In 2008, I won a prestigious CAREER grant from the National Science Foundation (NSF) for my five-year project titled, "Investigating the Critical Junctures: Strategies that Broaden Minority Male Participation in STEM Fields." The purpose of the project, which was still underway at the time of first writing, was to conduct a systematic and empirical study of the factors that influence students' decisions at critical junctures in the educational pipeline so as to (a) broaden participation in science, technology, engineering, and math (STEM) fields, and (b) improve the recruitment, retention, and success of minority undergraduate men in STEM and STEM-related fields across colleges and universities in the United States. The larger study was designed to scaffold several smaller projects in such a way that knowledge about this topic accumulated over the life of the multi-year federal grant. Indeed, it did.

The larger program for research consisted of six studies. The first was a survey study of the social psychological determinants of college students' success in STEM and non-STEM fields. The second was a multi-institutional mixed-methods study of undergraduates participating in formal under-graduate research programs with a particular focus on those engaged in research experiences for undergraduates (REU) funded by federal agencies and the Ronald E. McNair Postbaccalaureate Scholars Program. Building upon findings from my previous studies, I also developed and tested a multi-item instrument for measuring sense of belonging in STEM; the third study focused on reliability and validity of the proposed scale.

There were several other components to my NSF CAREER research pro-gram. For instance, a fourth study consisted of face-to-face and telephone interviews with willing participants to understand the nature of their aca-demic and social experiences in STEM learning environments (e.g., class-rooms, labs, departments). In 2009, I launched a national study of racial/ ethnic minority men in STEM graduate programs; a large majority of respondents were African American male master's and doctoral students. Finally, I collected survey and interview data from undergraduates who left STEM (voluntarily or involuntarily) as their academic major of choice. Voluntary departure refers to students who opted to change majors on their own volition often because they determined the major was incongru-ent with their own interests, unwelcoming or unsupportive, or that another major matched more closely (Tinto, 1993). Involuntary departure refers to students who were encouraged to leave by their institution or department due to poor academic performance (Tinto, 1993); Figure 7.1 also describes another force of *involuntary departure* that I learned about in my research studies. While all student departures should be cause for initial concern, I was particularly interested in understanding the factors that gave rise to stu-dents leaving STEM voluntarily—on their own volition—as such students were assumed to be in "good standing" academically, and consequently eli-gible to continue their studies. Keep in mind, gentle reader, that this dichot-omy—voluntary or involuntary—is a bit arbitrary when it comes to student departure from college (at least in my opinion). Fairly consistent research has shown that some students, particularly women and/or members of eth-nic minorities, encounter negative experiences in STEM fields and are far more likely than White men to describe STEM environments as unfriendly, unsupportive, or hostile. It's worth debating whether an individual who is being treated unfavorably or with hostility has a true "choice" in the mat-ter of leaving; some might argue they were forced, coerced, chided, pushed, even advised out of the major. Figure 7.1 goes into more detail.

Previous studies have explored the reasons given by students for leaving college (Tinto, 1993), as well as the reasons for leaving STEM fields gen-erally (Seymour, 1992; Seymour & Hewitt, 1997). For instance, Seymour

"Don't beat yourself up ... a lot of [fill in the blank] students don't do well in STEM. Ever think of business?"

Many will be familiar with the NSF's quality criteria—intellectual merit and broader impacts. As part of my original CAREER proposal, I promised to develop and host a "mini-conference" for underrepresented STEM students in the final year of grant activity. This proved to be a great way of leveraging findings from the grant to benefit students.

The STEM X-Change, a one-day conference was organized into several segments with different sessions led by campus professionals. For instance, I learned from the CAREER studies that many women and ethnic minorities reported limited opportunities to apply or compete for prestigious internships and co-ops, especially those that required nomination by a professor who would often think of students "most like them" when rushed to pass along potential names. Another session was facilitated by staff from the Counseling Center and it focused on tactics for "help-seeking" and effective strategies for "self-care," based on findings from my work that STEM students reported high levels of stress, little sleep, and anxiety about doing well.

During the luncheon keynote, I asked the large crowd of diverse STEM students: "How many of you have ever been told that you don't belong in STEM?" I expected a few hands based on our work. Much to my dismay, every single hand went up! Students shared vivid stories like the quote shown at the top of this figure. I realized this is yet another way in which some students depart involuntarily—that is, at the implicit advice or request of those who teach. Careful...our words matter.

Figure 7.1   Lesson learned from STEM X-Change.

and colleagues conducted several studies and found that women leave STEM fields because they do not feel welcomed, valued, or respected by others. Some women are also dissatisfied with the work-life conditions of those in STEM fields, reporting a general unwillingness to work long hours, forgo starting a family or child-rearing just for their occupation. There has been a fairly consistent line of research that points out how difficult it is for women and ethnic minorities to "see themselves" in STEM fields without role models who are like them. All in all, this points to the importance of sense of belonging in STEM environments, which will be addressed in the present chapter.

PURPOSE

The purpose of this chapter is to examine the role of sense of belonging among students of color in STEM fields. Specifically, I draw upon data from previous studies to demonstrate the importance of sense of belonging to STEM students of color and the role it plays in their academic and social success in STEM contexts. Additional insights are offered for discussion and new directions for future research are recommended. Before discussing details of the studies that informed this chapter, I briefly review literature related to sense of belonging generally.

SENSE OF BELONGING

Sense of belonging is not only an important aspect of college student life but as I have argued to this point in the book, it is also a motivation (Baumeister & Leary, 1995) and a basic human need (Maslow, 1962). Psychologically, sense of belonging refers to the "experience of personal involvement and integration within a system or environment to the extent that a person feels they play a special role in that system or environment" (McLaren, 2009, p. 3) and, conversely, that the system or environment plays a special role for them; imagine the STEM student who rushes to get to class on-time because they feel like their comments are valued by instructors and peers and doing well in the class will help them earn a degree and enter their profession or STEM field of choice. Sense of belonging takes on heightened significance in environments that individuals experience as different, unfamiliar, or foreign, as well as in contexts where some individuals are likely to feel marginalized, unsupported, or unwelcomed (Anderman & Freeman, 2004). For instance, women and students of color may experience STEM fields in this way, given that relatively few enter such fields and, even when they do, they often report feeling invisible, unsupported, or "out of place," as many students have described (Strayhorn, 2009a). Women and minorities also face stereotypes about their ability to excel in STEM subjects—stereotypes can hijack their abilities, erode their confidence, and suffocate their esteem to a point that failure becomes inevitable or a *self-fulfilling prophecy*.

Previous scholars have stressed the important role that sense of belonging plays in the success of students in schools and colleges generally (e.g., Anderman, 2003; Hausmann, Schofield, & Woods, 2007; Strayhorn, 2008d). Additional evidence suggests that sense of belonging is particularly relevant to the experiences and behaviors of those who "perceive themselves as marginal to the mainstream life [of college]" (Hurtado & Carter, 1997, p. 324). Yet, very few scholars have brought these lines of inquiry together with an intersectional approach to the study of sense of belonging, paying close attention to the influence of sense of belonging on racially and ethnically diverse students' experiences in STEM fields. The select few who have examined this topic have tended to adopt an additive approach, assuming that a student's experience is the sum of individual parts, as represented by this simple mathematical equation: *student experience* = gender + race + major + ... Reducing the complexity of students' intersectional experiences to a simple computation is not only wrong but also guaranteed to lead to singular solutions that fail to account for the complexity—the nuances—of students' diverse experiences, which, in the end, are doomed to fail. As broadening minority participation in STEM fields is a national policy priority (National Research Council, 2006), nuanced information—like what works for first-generation engineers at urban campuses versus computer scientists at community colleges—is sorely needed, as it may provide clues to strategies that, if properly mounted, hold promise for effectively increasing the number of minorities in our nation's most critical fields.

Turning attention to understanding the influence of sense of belonging in STEM fields is important for at least three reasons. First, as I've said before, sense of belonging is a basic psychological need. Satisfaction of the need to belong affects individuals' perceptions, behaviors, and ultimate success; environments that are vibrant, close-knit, collaborative, and supportive tend to engender belonging while competitive, hostile environments do not. And, aspects of the social context influence how well needs, such as belongingness, are met. So, it's reasonable to assume that characteristics of STEM environments may influence, directly or indirectly, the extent to which college students' need to belong is satisfied. We need to know more about those characteristics and conditions that promote community or prevent belonging. Many will be familiar with Boyer's (1990) *Principles of Community;* see Figure 7.2 for a quick review and think about them in the context of building community and belonging in STEM departments.

Second, students' experience of acceptance or belonging influences multiple dimensions of cognition and behavior, including their perceptions, well-being, involvement, academic performance, and mental health (Baumeister & Leary, 1995). Students who feel securely connected with others in an environment or group, who feel that the group is important to them, and they are important to the group, tend to have higher self-concepts, greater confidence in their academic skills, and rate their college experiences as satisfactory

Figure 7.2 Boyer's six principles.

(Hausmann, Schofield, & Woods, 2007; Strayhorn, 2008a). When students' need to belong is left unfulfilled in educational settings, they experience diminished motivation, impaired psychosocial development, alienation, and poor academic achievement (Anderman & Freeman, 2004; Deci, Vallerand, Pelletier, & Ryan, 1991). Failure to satisfy the need to belong can produce other pathological and long-lasting negative consequences such as deflated self-esteem, substance abuse, depression, suicidal ideation, violence, and physical or psychological death (Choenarom, Williams, & Hagerty, 2005; Hagerty, Lynch-Bauer, Patusky, Bouwsema, & Collier, 1992; Kissane & McLaren, 2006). Indeed, we need additional information about sense of belonging in STEM fields so that we can marshal our resources to reduce, if not prevent, such negative outcomes among all students, particularly those in STEM fields who are most likely to occupy highly skilled positions of technical leadership in the future.

Third, as Brazzell (2001, p. 31) aptly said, lack of a sense of belonging may "prompt some [students] to abandon either their institutions or—worse—their education." Indeed, as I argue in this volume, there is substantial evidence to support the idea that sense of belonging is related to college student retention. Feeling accepted, included, valued, welcomed, and cared about leads to positive cognitive, affective, and behavioral responses such as greater confidence, stronger achievement motivation, making college friends, studying hard, joining clubs, studying abroad, seeking help, all of which, in turn, influence retention, whereas lack of belonging remains a primary cause of student departure from college. The same seems to hold true in STEM fields, although this hypothesis requires additional empirical testing. If we hope to increase student retention in STEM fields, we need to know what inspires or inhibits students' sense of belonging in that context; then, we use what we know to connect students to what they need to excel. This is the expressed purpose of the studies that are described in the next section.

THE STUDIES

To craft a chapter on undergraduate students' sense of belonging in STEM fields, I found it necessary to draw upon data from my recent studies in this area. Specifically, I employ data from four projects: the social psychological determinants of student success study; the REU multi-institutional study; the experiences of minority males in STEM study; and the STEM leavers study. The first two studies consist of electronic surveys, using pre-existing or locally developed questionnaires. The latter two are mixed-methods and qualitative studies, respectively, consisting of one-on-one, in-depth interviews, although there are still plans to use that information to construct a questionnaire for future use on larger samples.

Speaking of samples, they varied across studies as you might imagine. For instance, there were nearly 700 respondents to the social psychological determinants of student success survey. There are approximately 125 respondents, from 3 different universities, to the REU survey. My research team and I have conducted over 60 interviews with minority men in STEM fields, across more than 12 universities. And while the STEM leavers study was conducted at two large, public universities, the sample size grew to be 40. Given the difficulties researchers face when locating students once they leave a department or institution, we were encouraged by this sample size. Despite differences in the size or *quantity* of each study's sample, the *quality* of information gained from these studies is consistently high and perfectly aligned with the focus of this chapter.

To make sense of the data, I employed a variety of techniques for analyzing survey and interview data. For instance, survey data were analyzed using descriptive and multivariate statistics. Qualitative data were analyzed using the constant comparison method recommended by Strauss (1995). I present several major findings that emanate from these studies in the next section before discussing the importance of these results in light of previous findings and their implications for future policy, practice, and research.

MAJOR FINDINGS

Results from the four studies featured in this chapter converge on four major findings related to undergraduate students' sense of belonging in STEM. First, sense of belonging in STEM is important and students place significant meaning on "belonging experiences." Second, mattering seems to facilitate students' sense of belonging in STEM. Third, not all students experience sense of belonging in STEM equally; social identities intersect and affect students' experiences and their subsequent belongingness evaluation in STEM. Fourth, sense of belonging, as hypothesized in earlier chapters, begets success even in STEM fields. Below, I present selected results to support these conclusions. Where possible, I provide verbatim quotes from the interview participants to animate my points, to color my conclusions with students' lived experiences, and, most importantly, to give voice to experiences that are rarely presented in the published literature or are done so far too infrequently.

Importance of Sense of Belonging in STEM

One conclusion is unequivocal: sense of belonging in STEM fields is important for undergraduate students, particularly historically underrepresented racial/ethnic minorities who face unique challenges in establishing meaningful connections in fields where they are "one of very few," to quote a student. The *Oxford English Dictionary* defines importance as the fact or quality of being important, importing or signifying much; gravity, weight, or bearing consequence. Similarly, the *Merriam-Webster Dictionary* defines importance as the quality or state of being important, significant, or a weighty matter. Applied to my point here, the main takeaway is that sense of belonging in STEM fields, according to my research, is a significant, weighty matter that bears certain consequences for college students, especially students of color who are prone to feel "out of place" or invisible in STEM classrooms. I will identify a few consequences later in the chapter.

The importance of sense of belonging in STEM fields is demonstrated in at least two ways. First, the frequency of its emergence as a significant factor in students' experiences across multiple studies suggests the gravity of its importance. In terms of frequency, sense of belonging in STEM was identified as significant in each of the four studies that inform this chapter. For example, sense of belonging in STEM was *significantly* (and statistically) related to students' self-esteem and the frequency of their interactions with diverse peers. Figures 7.3 and 7.4 illustrate this positive relationship.

Sense of belonging in STEM was also important for racial/ethnic minority students participating in summer or short-term research experiences for undergraduates. End-of-program sense of belonging in STEM was *significantly* higher than sense of belonging in STEM measured before the program began. STEM leavers also underscored the importance of sense of belonging, or lack thereof, when discussing reasons for changing majors, changing

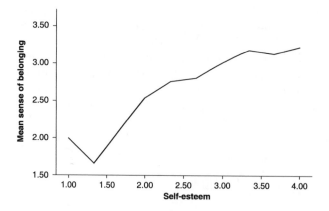

Figure 7.3   Students' sense of belonging in STEM as a function of their self-esteem score, derived from the social psychological determinants study.

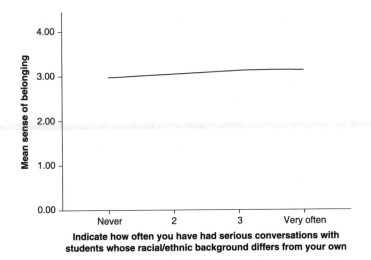

Figure 7.4   Students' sense of belonging in STEM as a function of the frequency of their interactions with racially diverse peers, derived from the social psychological determinants study.

institutions, or leaving higher education altogether. Consider the following quotes from two STEM leavers that reflect the sentiments of others:

> I couldn't ever really lay my hands on it, but I just didn't adjust to being in that major (referring to chemistry). I didn't really connect, I guess. [Interviewer: Can you say more about that?] Well, like I didn't really have friends who were in chemistry and I never really related to the other guys in my classes. They were all smart, but super-nerdy. I wasn't like that so I would study hard to get good grades but I wasn't feeling how they felt. What interest [*sic*] them really don't interest me and I guess the same is true for them. So, I switched to something that I felt right in, you know.
>
> *(Marquis, third-year communication studies major)*

> Can you imagine going to class every day and feeling like you're not supposed to be there? No one looks like you. Nothing sounds like you. And, on top of all of that, you don't give a f*ck about what they're teaching. I just really wasn't interested like that … in that much math. That's why I switched majors and I knew that I would start to do better. And if there ain't nobody [*sic*] else like me in there … 'cuz, I didn't have any friends in there, I guess I won't miss it much. And I'm pretty sure they won't miss me.
>
> *(Kylee, fourth-year Africana Studies major, formerly math major)*

A second way that sense of belonging in STEM is important is reflected in the meaning that students attached to it. For instance, comments from students like Marquis and Kylee, A. J. and Tiffany (that began the chapter) illustrate that sense of belonging is significant, because it relates to a basic human need—that is, the need to belong, to matter (to someone), to feel valued, respected, and a part of. Students spoke, at length, about connections between sense of belonging and their identity, self-esteem, or confidence to pursue STEM degrees, as well as their self-worth. Note how Marquis (above) ties sense of belonging, or lack thereof, to feeling disconnected from others. Kylee, too, connects sense of alienation, versus belonging, to feeling unwelcomed in class, unheard (or invisible), forgotten, and uninterested in the subject matter. Together, findings from these studies demonstrate that sense of belonging in STEM is important generally and to racially/ethnically diverse students specifically. Students could not function optimally or adjust to the academic environment when their basic need for belonging was unsatisfied. In many cases, they *felt* like they did not belong (affective), which led them to *think* that they did not belong (cognitive), and, consequently, they left the major, minor, or education altogether (behavioral). This all making sense now?

Mattering and Sense of Belonging in STEM

Schlossberg (1985) was one of the first counseling psychologists whose scholarship was adopted by higher education scholars to make sense of the term "mattering," which typically refers to the feeling, right or wrong, that one belongs or commands the attention of others. Research to date has identified five major dimensions of mattering, as discussed in earlier chapters: (a) attention; (b) importance; (c) dependence; (d) ego-extension; and (e) appreciation (Rosenberg & McCullough, 1981), each revealing a specific aspect of feeling appreciated or respected by others. Using this analytical frame, I argue that mattering is a critical part of sense of belonging, both generally and in STEM fields.

A number of data points suggest a positive relationship between mattering to others and sense of belonging in STEM. For instance, students who perceived a stronger sense of belonging in STEM were more likely to report having friends in the major, socializing with peers and faculty in the department, and feeling like "friends would miss [them]" if they left the major. Figure 7.5 illustrates this relationship using survey data.

Mattering, according to Rosenberg and McCullough (1981), is a motive: "the feeling that others depend on us, are interested in us, are concerned with our fate, or experience us as an ego-extension" (p. 165); the same holds true for belonging in STEM. For instance, some participants described in detail how faculty members' behaviors helped to make them feel they matter. Faculty members knew their name (and pronounced it correctly), demonstrated an interest in their degree or professional goals, seemed to care about their mastery of STEM course content, and showed concern for

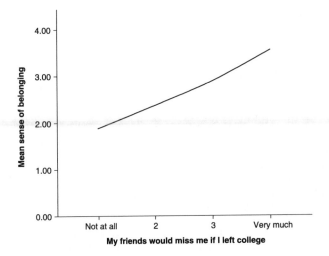

Figure 7.5 Students' sense of belonging in STEM as a function of their perceived mattering to others in college, derived from the social psychological determinants study.

their personal wellbeing. Participants also revealed *how* faculty members conveyed this message. Some professors went out of their way to remember students' names to get to know them by inviting all students, no matter the class size, to their homes for a social or asking to meet with each student personally at least once in the first few weeks of school. These "teachers who cared," as one student put it, recalled from memory (or notes) individual students' career goals during class or contacted students by phone or email to inquire about their attendance, absence, and/or progress in the class. One student at Carthage College shared how impressed he was that his biology professor would "shoot [students] a long email if they were absent from class ... like two or three *whole sentences* [emphasis added] talking about how much he *missed them* and their *important contributions* to class that day." What students took away from these encounters—whether virtual or face-to-face—was a sense that they mattered, they were appreciated for what they brought to class (i.e., their ideas, questions), and they felt significant, cared about, and perhaps special in some way. Belonging experiences seemed particularly meaningful for students who might otherwise have felt marginalized, unprepared for, or "out of place" in STEM fields such as people of color.

Several other data points across my studies illuminate how the nature of STEM undergraduate education provides numerous opportunities for students to feel as if they matter. Darren, an African American male who stands at 6 feet 2 inches with large brown eyes and a hint of a mustache, spoke in detail about the nature of STEM undergraduate education at his university:

> A lot of what you do is projects ... team-based projects mostly. You have to work with other people to do something, like make something usually. In my first-year lab, we had to build a bridge. Everyone know [*sic*] that the most important part of a bridge is its legs. If you got weak legs, then the bridge is going to fall down. Well, I had some good ideas about building these asymmetric posts for legs, but the other guys ... they all White, of course ... in my group didn't like it or didn't understand my idea so basically I got out-voted. They wanted to do something else and didn't really care what I wanted to do. I knew it was down hill from there. We built it, the professor tested it, and it crashed in just a few seconds. Yeah, I didn't really like that class because I couldn't be involved in the stuff much because I didn't think they were good ideas. [Interviewer: What would have made it better for you?] For people to listen to me ... at least once group members who appreciated my ideas and thoughts, you know ... who treated me like my ideas were decent, not stupid [laughing] ... by actually including them in the assignment.

As a number of STEM undergraduate courses are designed to engage students in team-based projects, there seems to be plenty of room to help students feel as if they matter, which, in turn, strengthens their sense of belonging in STEM. Of course, this means that STEM educators—faculty and teaching assistants—would do well to set guidelines or "ground rules" for how groups should function in ways that are far more inclusive than what Darren experienced. I'll expand upon this a bit in the next major section (and the last chapter of the book), but faculty might consider these results when setting course objectives, writing course syllabi, and even organizing students into work groups. Talking overtly about the importance of true teamwork, appreciating differences, and valuing the contributions of all team members is one way to set classroom conditions that likely engender students' sense of belonging in STEM. Since the first edition of this book, I have received emails from STEM educators across the country who read the book and started placing students in workgroups based on personal traits and interests (e.g., favorite color, desired occupation, favorite candy) versus numbering off "1-2-3-4," as a way of getting to know students better and building bonds of belonging.

Intersectionality and Sense of Belonging in STEM

Fairly consistent evidence across the studies suggests that not all students experience sense of belonging in STEM equally; social identities intersect and affect students' experiences with belonging in STEM fields. To expound upon this point, let me offer an operational definition of intersectionality.

Intersectionality, as a theoretical framework, resists essentialist notions of identity categories and assumes that social conditions are structured by multiple forces interacting with intersecting social locations, thereby producing relatively unique circumstances for individuals and groups (Crenshaw, 1991; Dill & Zambrana, 2009; Strayhorn, 2013). Adopting intersectionality as a theoretical lens prevents us from making the fallacious assumption that a common threat or problem requires a common response or that a similar response necessarily results in similar change or relief.

Applied to STEM, what I have found is that not all students experience sense of belonging in STEM equally. Said differently, *who you are* determines, in part, *what it* takes to feel and find a sense of belonging in STEM fields. For instance, some results from my studies suggest that men feel a greater sense of belonging in STEM fields than women. Yet, that's less true for men of color, first-generation (to college) men, and even men of color who are former foster youth, homeless, or hail from low-income families or backgrounds. For example, college men were more likely than women to report having same-sex friends in their major, spending time socializing with peers in their major, and feeling satisfied with their choice of STEM major. Black and Latino men, on the other hand, reported significantly lower scores on each of these outcomes compared with their White and Asian male counterparts. And Todd, an African American male third-year biology major who transferred from a community college to his four-year university shared how social identities can intersect and create relatively distinct social realities for minority men in STEM:

> You definitely need to establish yourself first because you're going to need a support system ... a set of friends that you can depend on and study with from time to time. But who you fit in with depends on a lot of different aspects. It's wild how many different cliques there are in my lab. The rich kids all know each other and they use their fancy equipment and tools to out-do everybody else. The non-majors all stick together too because they don't really know that many other people ... they're just taking the class to fill a requirement, you know. Then there's people like me who are majors but not White ... I'm a guy, but not rich ... I'm Black, but kind of nerdy [laughing] ... so I find myself wiggling around to really find a place to fit in somewhere among different groups because no one group is exactly like me ... does that make sense?

Indeed, Todd's point makes perfect sense and supports findings drawn from my other studies. Not all students experience sense of belonging in STEM equally. They don't find it the same way or using the same path. They don't satisfy their need to belong in the same amount of time and, importantly, what works for helping one to belong may not work for someone else. This makes the work of belonging complicated, messy, and yet central to our best efforts for student success. Quite often social identities intersect in new and different ways to form relatively unique social realities for some students, which, in turn, may require very different tactics for encouraging students' belonging in STEM fields. Just as we've opened up the door of college access to many different groups, we'll need a menagerie of tactics to help today's diverse learners. We return to this point again later in the chapter and at the end of the book. Keep on reading ...

Sense of Belonging and Student Success in STEM

Last, but certainly not least, I have found persuasive evidence that sense of belonging in STEM is related to college students' success in such fields. Here success is defined in one of three ways: satisfaction, academic achievement (as measured by grades), and intent to stay in the academic major. Below I present evidence to support conclusions in each of these three areas.

College students who feel they belong in STEM fields, who report a sense of feeling valued by others in their STEM major department, and who feel a sense of connection or relatedness to their peers and faculty tend to be more highly satisfied with the academic and social life of college generally. Student satisfaction reflects the "favorability of a student's subjective evaluation of the various outcomes and experiences associated with [college]" (Elliott & Shin, 2002, p. 198), consistent with my previous work (Strayhorn, 2008c). For instance, correlations between sense of belonging in STEM and overall satisfaction with college ranged from 0.18 to 0.35. Figure 7.6 illustrates the

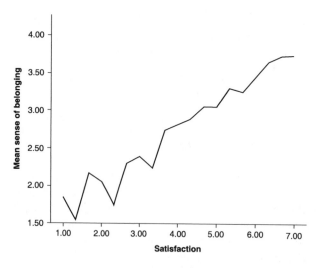

Figure 7.6 Students' sense of belonging in STEM compared with their overall satisfaction with college, derived from the social psychological determinants study.

positive relationship between sense of belonging in STEM and satisfaction with college as well.

As might be expected, college students who feel they belong in STEM fields also earn better grades in college generally and STEM specifically. Approximately 70 percent of students who feel a sense of connection or support in STEM fields earn grades of "B or better, on average," whereas almost half of the students who do not feel a sense of belonging in STEM have failed or repeated "at least one" class since declaring their major. As others have explained, "feelings of belonging help students connect with their peers and the institution [including faculty and student services personnel], relationships that, in turn, are associated with persistence and satisfaction ... including the value placed on academic achievement" by students (Kuh, Kinzie, Schuh, Whitt, & Associates, 2005, p. 119).

Finally, I have put forth, along with others, that sense of belonging refers to the "feeling that others depend on us, are interested in us, are concerned with our fate, or experience us as an ego-extension" (Rosenberg & McCullough, 1981, p. 165). Sense of belonging in STEM reflects feeling that others depend on an individual in STEM contexts and that he or she is a valued member of the STEM community in college. This is usually experienced in several ways. First, students working in groups fulfill specific roles and pick up cues from their classmates that their contributions are meaningful and valued. Second, students spoke eloquently about how some faculty stressed not just class attendance but the value that students add to the learning environment; one professor told students at the beginning of the semester: "I have a lot to offer through teaching, but I can't do any of it without you ... I need you here in class, each of you play a critical role here." Feeling needed, integral, or indispensable to others, like professors and peers, in STEM departments likely affirms one's "place" in the system and reinforces one's decision to enter the major and field, all of which seem to strengthen students' commitment to STEM degree completion and reduce, if not totally eliminate, any intentions of leaving the field or institution prematurely. Figure 7.7 illustrates this latter point graphically.

DISCUSSION

Recall that the purpose of this chapter was to examine the role of sense of belonging among students of color in STEM fields. Specifically, I reported findings from my recent studies to demonstrate the importance of sense of belonging to STEM students of color and the role it plays in their academic and social success in STEM contexts. Four major findings were identified. First, sense of belonging in STEM is important and students place significant meaning on "belonging experiences." Second, mattering seems to

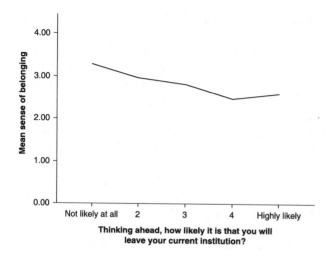

Figure 7.7   Students' sense of belonging in STEM compared with the likelihood of premature departure from college, derived from the social psychological determinants study.

facilitate students' sense of belonging in STEM, especially among women and students of color, who are the focus of this chapter. Third, not all students experience sense of belonging in STEM equally; social identities often intersect and affect students' experiences and their subsequent belonging in STEM. Fourth, sense of belonging in STEM is positively related with achievement outcomes such as satisfaction, grades, and intent to remain in versus leaving one's major or college altogether.

This chapter makes several important contributions to our collective understanding of college students' sense of belonging. It adds additional support to the growing body of research that posits belonging as a basic human need and fundamental motivation (Baumeister & Leary, 1995; Maslow, 1962). Sense of belonging develops in response to the extent to which an individual feels respected, valued, accepted, and needed by a defined group. In STEM contexts, students have a basic psychological need or longing for belonging as a bona fide member of the STEM classroom, laboratory, or department, as well as a shared emotional connection with others like faculty, peers, and lab assistants.

Data from this chapter also lend support to conclusions that sense of belonging is context- or domain-dependent. Said differently, individuals have specific psychological needs that must be satisfied for optimal conditioning, such as the need to belong in terms of STEM students' academic achievement. Characteristics of the social context—in this case STEM environments—influence the extent to which psychological needs are met. Satisfaction of such needs affects perceptions and behaviors.

When belongingness needs are met, optimal functioning is possible and STEM students thrive; however, when such basic needs are unfulfilled, negative consequences result such as dissatisfaction with college, poor grades, and attrition from the major (Kissane & McLaren, 2006).

There's at least one other aspect of sense of belonging that deserves mention. Social psychologists have explained for years that basic human needs are dynamic and ongoing. Thus, they must be met on a continual basis. Changes in context, climate, or character over time can (and likely will) affect satisfaction of one's need to belong. For instance, just because Tiffany—whose quote opened the chapter—might currently feel a sense of belonging in social work as a major, does not mean that she will necessarily always feel that way. Her need to belong must be negotiated regularly and satisfied on a continual basis. Should the conditions that foster her sense of belonging in social work change, so too might her feelings of support and connectedness. The same holds true for students in STEM fields. For instance, I once visited a large, public research university to deliver a keynote on STEM topics. I met a student who simply did not feel like she belonged, although that was not always the case. When I asked her what had changed, she was fluent in describing how the departure of her advisor set in motion of number of cascading events (e.g., new advisor assigned, research focus shifted, class schedule changed) that left her feeling alone, irrelevant, unsupported, and "not very special at all," which clearly maps onto feelings of alienation, not belonging. When things change, sense of belonging can too. Institutional leaders would do well to continually assess STEM students' sense of belonging and implement programs or activities (e.g., picnic socials, awards) that nurture sense of belonging regularly.

The potential applications of this chapter to practice are many. The chapter's content should be of particular interest to campus constituencies who have a vested interest in nurturing students' success in STEM fields, especially among historically underrepresented racial/ethnic minorities. For example, department heads and faculty members might adopt practices, such as new student orientation programs, as a way of introducing new students to others in the department and the norms or rules that govern their actions as a member of the group. Facilitating new students' engagement with others and the values of the department could likely provide much-needed support, all of which contribute to students' sense of belonging in STEM. Other practices hold promise for cultivating a sense of belonging in STEM: living-learning communities, collaborative learning experiences or team-based projects, faculty- or peer-mentoring programs, summer research opportunities, and even frequent interactions with diverse peers. Elsewhere, I demonstrate that sense of belonging increases when racial/ethnic minority students hear about the contributions of minorities to science and society through reading assignments and lectures (Strayhorn, 2011b).

Counseling and academic advisors may benefit from information included in this chapter. For instance, unsatisfied needs such as the need to belong, to "fit in," or "stand out" in one's major department may lead students to resign from their academics silently, change from a STEM major abruptly, or drop out of college prematurely. Professional staff might use information from this volume to help students develop meaningful relationships with others in STEM departments. Encouraging use of office hours seems to be an effective way for STEM students to get help and build rapport with faculty members and teaching assistants. STEM students also can engage in meaningful ways with STEM faculty through research collaborations or lab experiments, internships, and co-ops. In terms of peer relations, it is important for STEM students to identify interests they share in common with others as a way of fostering a sense of belonging in such majors— discipline-specific student groups like National Society of Black Engineers (NSBE) operate under this assumption. Indeed, being accepted, included, and welcomed in STEM environments leads to positive emotions such as happiness, contentment, and satisfaction, as well as positive outcomes like achievement, optimal learning, mastery, and success.

Findings presented here also suggest the need for policies that facilitate students' sense of belonging in STEM fields. For instance, provosts and deans might consider this chapter when making decisions about strategic goals of academic units. Helping all students feel like they belong is an appropriate *strategic goal* of a campus or college/department. Using information from this book, academic leaders can identify a set of promising strategies for achieving that goal that can be organized over time, in light of available resources. That's what makes it strategic. It follows, then, that other policies might be formulated to allocate resources to activities that engender belonging such as orientation programs, networking socials, and faculty–student collaborations. Academic leaders can make decisions to establish campus-wide efforts or campaigns that "tell" students they belong on campus, much like Kent State University has done; see Figure 7.8.

Institutional policies might also be constructed that introduce new ways of collecting data about students' decisions and departures. As mentioned earlier in the volume, colleges and universities might elicit information about why students change their major or leave college altogether. Rather than assuming that all leavers depart because they simply couldn't "keep up" academically, provosts and institutional research officers should administer surveys to capture the myriad reasons for departure decisions, which likely includes a lack of sense of belonging for students of color in STEM majors.

Federal policymakers might also consider information about the important role that sense of belonging plays in STEM students' success when making decisions about federal research and development initiatives; grants awarded by federal agencies such as the National Science Foundation might

Figure 7.8 Campus sign at Kent State University.

support research and interventions that instigate students' sense of belonging in STEM. A few years ago, agencies like the National Science Foundation (NSF) devoted resources to funding basic research and those dollars have since dried up. More money toward this goal is needed.

As with all studies, there are a number of implications for future research. First, researchers should continue to test for differences in the importance of sense of belonging in STEM by race, social class, sex, and even year in college. That sense of belonging in STEM was positively associated with self-esteem, satisfaction with college, and grades in my studies is consistent with previous research (Hausmann, Schofield, & Woods, 2007; Hurtado & Carter, 1997; Rhee, 2008; Strayhorn, 2008d). Future research might expand this line of inquiry by testing the relationship between sense of belonging in STEM and other desired outcomes such as student learning, professional competency, and skills in specific STEM-related domains such as use of computerized design software and C+ programming language proficiency. In light of my previous point that sense of belonging is an ongoing need that must be satisfied regularly and on a continual basis, researchers might employ time-series techniques to examine changes in students' belonging-ness over time. All of these would add to our existing knowledge as well as take this line of inquiry in important new directions.

In closing, recall one of the book's main points—that sense of belonging reflects the social support that students perceive on campus; it's a feeling of connectedness, that one is important to others and one matters (Rosenberg & McCullough, 1981; Taylor, Turner, Noymer, Beckett, & Elliott, 2001). Sense of belonging may be particularly important for students who perceive themselves as marginal to campus life (Hurtado & Carter, 1997). And sense of belonging is domain- or situation-dependent; thus, STEM students long for establishing a sense of belonging in their department or major, which, in turn, affects their perceptions and behaviors in that context. To broaden participation in STEM fields, particularly among racial/ethnic minorities, we might do well to nurture their connectedness, relatedness, even their psy-chological need to belong; it's virtually impossible to *broaden participation* in STEM fields for people who don't feel like they belong there in the first place. We don't want STEM students of color, like A. J. at the beginning of the chapter, to continue feeling like "automatic outsiders" before they even begin their major studies. With our help and support, they won't.

Chapter 8

Sense of Belonging and Black Male Collegians
"Brothers 2 Bruthas"

I grew up in St. Louis but I spent a lot of time in Detroit and Chicago too. Where I'm from, I knew I had two options to survive: join a gang or go to college. I chose school; either way I knew I wanted to get in where I fit in, be valued and respected, you know. I guess I chose the right one.

(Tyson)

And my problem was that I always tried to go in everyone's way but my own. I have also been called one thing and then another while no one really wished to hear what I called myself. So after years of trying to adopt the opinions of others I finally rebelled. I am an invisible man.

(Ralph Ellison)

INTRODUCTION

As a new Assistant Professor at the University of Tennessee, Knoxville, I remember contemplating where I would launch my research program in terms of topic and expertise. Having completed a dissertation on testing an integrated model of graduate student persistence using information drawn from extant data sources, I thought that might be an appropriate site for my work. Yet, no matter how interested I was in graduate student persistence and the use of statistical modeling techniques in educational research, I was far more intrigued by issues of race/ethnicity, social class, and gender and the ways in which social identities simultaneously affect the collegiate experiences of certain student populations. I had an unapologetic interest in and *commitment to* understanding the experiences of Black men in higher education, in part reflecting curiosity about my own educational experiences. This, too, seemed a lucrative site for my research in light of an abundance of grant dollars directed toward the "Black male crisis" in postsecondary education (Cuyjet, 2006). Caught in a moment of indecision—immobilized by the strength of my competing interests—I settled on both and all. Here, I draw upon my previous research to describe the role of sense of belonging for Black men in college; in the next chapter, I move on to graduate students and their belonging experiences.

WHAT WE KNOW

Much of what is written about Black men in higher education (HIED) can be organized into four major categories: representation of Black men in HIED, the educational pipeline to college for Black men, challenges they face in HIED, as well as supportive factors that enable their educational success. Before describing the studies that informed this chapter, I offer a laconic review of the existing literature identifying several major threads that emerge from research.

Representation of Black Men in Higher Education

Black male representation in HIED can be illustrated in at least three ways. First, national enrollment data indicate significant gender disparities among Black collegians. For instance, recent data released from the US Department of Education, National Center for Education Statistics (2016) suggest that approximately 21 million students (both part- and full-time) are enrolled across more than 4300 colleges and universities in the country. Of those, approximately 2 million are Black[1] and Black women outnumber men by a margin of 2 to 1, one of the largest gender gaps among all racial/ethnic groups.

Gender disparities among Black collegians persist in terms of academic achievement, persistence, and degree attainment rates. For instance, several studies have shown that Black women earn higher grades than Black men in college (Cuyjet, 1997; Flowers, 2004). Achievement disparities are a function of differences in terms of academic preparation for college, time spent studying, help-seeking behaviors, and engagement in academically purposeful activities, to name a few correlates (Adelman, 1999; Harper, 2006; Strayhorn, 2010). It's no surprise, then, that more Black women than Black men complete their college degree; in fact, still today, about two-thirds of all Black men who enter college leave before completing their degree, the highest attrition rates among both sexes and all racial/ethnic groups (US Department of Education, National Center for Education Statistics, 2010, 2011).

The condition of Black men in higher education is reflected in another way: media representation through music, film, and print/news sources.

For example, some will be familiar with Spike Lee's smash-hit film, *School Daze*, from the late 1980s, which depicted an unpopular Black guy ("Half-Pint") who aspired to join a popular fraternity at a fictitious historically Black college and university (HBCU) located in rural Georgia. The film offers caricatures of Black male collegians as politically conscious and astute (e.g., "Dap"), unenlightened, threatening jocks (e.g., "Big Brother Almighty"), and even others as unintelligent, dangerous, and violent, images that have been documented in research as well (Majors & Billson, 1992; Mincy, 1994). Print and news sources also tend to portray Black men negatively. Headlines from leading higher education news sources—including but not limited to the *Journal of Blacks in Higher Education*, *Diverse Issues in Higher Education*, *Inside HigherEd*, and *Chronicle of Higher Education*—call attention to declining enrollment rates, dismal graduation outcomes, poor academic readiness, and what has been coined the "Black male crisis in higher education." In fact, Roach (2001) raised the question, "Where are all the Black men on campus?" If we learned anything at all from that line of inquiry, we now understand that Black men are sorely represented in higher education compared with their non-Black and/or female counterparts for many reasons. Experiences faced earlier in the educational pipeline give rise to these patterns of inequity in higher education.

Educational Pipeline to College for Black Men

Social scientists have devoted considerable attention to understanding the educational pipeline to college for Black men. And despite some disagreement among scholars about the appropriateness of the "pipeline metaphor" (some argue for the use of "pathway" or "funnel"), several major conclusions can be drawn from previous work. First, teachers' perceptions and expectations influence Black male students' achievement. For instance, Gilmore (1985) conducted a case study and found that African American boys were denied full access to literacy-based experiences because of teachers' expectations of students' attitudes; Lee (1994) and others found that educators' predetermined negative view of Black men limited their learning potential. Analyzing national data, I found that teacher's perceptions, and specifically whether they recommended "work not [college]," had a disproportionately negative influence of Black males' grades and enrollment in college (Strayhorn, 2008f). Quite simply, high expectations matter; students rise to the expectations set for them.

That so many teachers hold negative perceptions and low expectations of Black male youth is cause for concern; all too often, perceptions shape expectations, which, in turn, affects behaviors. Said plainly, what educators see or believe shapes what they look for in students and that, ultimately, influences what they find. Further, negative perceptions of teachers can be internalized by students, thereby hijacking students' abilities to a point where it all becomes a self-fulfilling prophecy (i.e., perception becomes reality). For instance, Steele (1997) described how negative stereotypes about Black students shape what educators expect of them; to the extent that Black students are aware of such stereotypes, they can become internalized and lead to negative "anti-self" beliefs, which diminish performance and compromise achievement. Furthermore, Ferguson (2000) explained that some educators (teachers and principals) often deny Black male youth the masculine dispensation that typically casts White boys as "just being boys," while labeling Black males as "bad boys" who are innately naughty, decidedly disruptive, and biologically bad or incorrigible. It's no surprise, then, that Black males represent a disproportionate number of school suspensions, expulsions, and drop-outs (Gregory, 1997), especially in urban and rural schools (Strayhorn, 2009d). It's not because they are "born bad" or inherently troublemakers—or that they even did anything wrong necessarily—it could also be that some educators are socialized to believe they're bad, which leads them to look for bad and to conclude that things are bad even in the face of evidence to the contrary. This is not just true in K-12 education, but related to the challenges that Black men may face in higher education; these are discussed in the next section.

Challenges of Black Men in Higher Education

Scholars have documented the academic and social challenges that Black men may face in higher education, at least three of which focus on issues related to sense of belonging in college. For example, Black males' underrepresentation in higher—what scholars refer to as lack of a critical mass—can lead to feelings of isolation, marginalization, and alienation both inside and outside the classroom (Fleming, 1984; Turner, 1994). Black males' experiences at predominantly White institutions (PWIs) can be compounded by the fact that PWIs tend to be less supportive, less sympathetic, and less welcoming than HBCUs for Black men (Gasman, 2008; Palmer & Gasman, 2008). Consequently, Black male undergraduates at PWIs tend to have less of a sense of belonging in college than their same-race male counterparts at HBCUs who enjoy racially affirming campus environments, supportive faculty who go beyond the call of duty, and same-race peers who tend to share pride in their ethnic history (Strayhorn, 2008f). That's not to say that Black males are guaranteed sense of belonging at HBCUs—circumstances, contexts, and identities conspire together to structure one's opportunity to feel a sense of belonging in a certain context.

Black male collegians' sense of belonging at PWIs hinges, in part, upon interacting positively with faculty members and peers; experiencing a welcoming, supportive campus racial climate; and engaging in educationally purposeful activities that foster a sense of mattering or community among various members (Strayhorn, 2008f). For instance, previous scholars have provided substantial evidence to support the role that positive peer interactions, nurturing environments, mentoring, and involvement in clubs and organizations play on Black male students' educational success (Harper, 2006; Strayhorn, 2008f; Strayhorn & Saddler, 2009). As another example, I recently found that self-efficacy, frequency of hearing about the contributions of minorities in one's field, mentoring, percent minority faculty in a department, and campus climate perceptions predict sense of belonging for African American male undergraduates in science, technology, engineering, and math (STEM) fields (Strayhorn, 2011b). Still, much more information is needed about the role of sense of belonging in Black males' educational success, factors related to their perception of belonging, and campus conditions or experiences that inhibit or promote their sense of belonging in college. To achieve this objective, I draw upon findings from my previous studies of Black male undergraduates, which are described in the next section.

THE STUDIES

As some of you know, I have conducted a number of studies on (and with) Black men in higher education. "Strayhorn studies" range from quantitative analyses of both nationally representative and locally collected survey data using multivariate statistics to qualitative investigations of students' meaning-making, identity constructions, and their experiences in Black Greek-lettered organizations (BGLOs). Table 8.1 presents a summary of a few of these studies.

Sample sizes varied across the studies as noted. For instance, over half of my published studies on Black men in higher education are based on nationally representative samples drawn from federal databases (available through the US Department of Education) or locally collected surveys that I have conducted with my graduate students. Qualitative studies, on the other hand, have been based on samples ranging from single digits (e.g., 4) to larger groups (e.g., 50). Despite differences in the size of samples or quantity of participants, the quality of information gleaned from these studies is consistently high.

To analyze data, I have employed a variety of techniques depending on the type of data collected in the study. For instance, most of the quantitative studies employ a smooth blend of descriptive and multivariate

Table 8.1 Strayhorn's studies of Black men in higher education

Topic	Sample	Key findings	Source
Retention	National sample of low-income Black men	Background, academic, and social factors are related to low-income Black males' retention	Strayhorn (2008e)
Academic achievement	National sample of Black (55%) and Latino male collegians	Social and cultural capital are related to college achievement; academic preparation was most significant for Latino males, while socioeconomic status was most significant for Black males; involvement and pre-college outreach programs important too	Strayhorn (2008a)
Educational aspirations	National sample of Black men in urban, suburban, and rural high schools	Socioeconomic status, achievement, and urbanicity are related to Black males' aspirations	Strayhorn (2009c)
Mentoring	554 Black CSEQ respondents, 35% male	Meaningful, research-focused mentoring relationships with faculty positively affect Black students' satisfaction with college	Strayhorn (2010)
Challenges and supports	Seven Black men who identify as gay or bisexual	Academic and social challenges ranged from lack of sense of belonging to coming out, from homophobia to racism	Strayhorn, Blakewood, & DeVita (2010)
Parental influences	Four African American faculty members	Three sources of parental influence were identified: polarity, occupation, and involvement	Holloman and Strayhorn (2010)
Sense of belonging	531 male collegians; 231 Black, 300 White	Cross-racial interactions with peers significantly predicted sense of belonging for Black men; those who frequently engage diverse peers have a higher sense of belonging than those who do not	Strayhorn and Terrell (2007)

Note: CSEQ = College Student Experiences Questionnaire.

analytical techniques such as frequencies, chi-square, *t*-test, analysis of variance, multiple regression, logistic regression, or advanced modeling techniques. Qualitative analysis, however, shifts from a step-wise process of coding to a more nuanced comparison of chunks and excerpts to existing theory as a way of testing existing theory, unearthing new theory "from the ground up," or describing the essence of phenomena about which we know something already. In the next section, I present several major findings that emanate from these studies, relating to Black males' sense of belonging in college. Then, I discuss the importance of such results in light of previous findings and their implications for future practice, theory, and research.

MAJOR FINDINGS

Given the large number of studies that I have conducted to date on the experiences of Black men in education, it would be unreasonable (not to mention overwhelming) to catalog all of the findings that relate to sense of belonging in this single chapter. Instead, I highlight several major threads that hold promise for informing future educational practice, theory, and research, which will be mentioned in the section that follows. Specifically, results from the "Strayhorn studies" suggest that sense of belonging is important for Black male collegians, that they place significance on their "belonging experiences," that mattering facilitates their belonging in college, that Black men may experience belonging differently based on various identity factors, and sense of belonging promotes educational success, in keeping with the core elements outlined in Chapter 3. See Figure 8.1 for a summary.

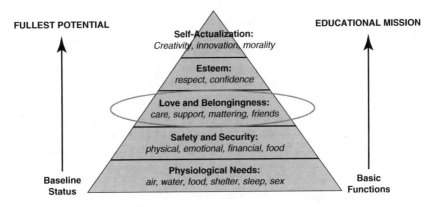

Figure 8.1   Revised model of college students' sense of belonging.

Sense of Belonging is Important

Sense of belonging in college is important for Black men. It is important in at least two ways. First, sense of belonging serves as a goal, a desired end, or optimal psychosocial condition. In survey studies, most Black men reported sense of belonging as an aim or ambition, while Black men who participated in qualitative studies of mine explained the importance of belonging as a goal. Consider the following examples:

> College can be so very different from anything else you've experienced that you need to sort of adjust to the place and there aren't that many "safe places" on campus where Black guys can go. You just have to try hard to fit in around here and make it work, you know.
>
> *(Tyson, second year)*

> Well, building on what [he] said, I think it's good advice for younger guys to know that you're going to have to acclimate to the campus. You can't just stick out like a sore thumb or else you'll never really fit in or become part of [the place]. I won't say you need to assimilate or nothing like that but you have to sort of work your way into the community here.
>
> *(Orlando, graduating senior)*

> My first year was horrible because I didn't have any friends, I didn't get to know anyone on campus, and no one got to know me [laughing]. It was terrible ... like my worst nightmare. But I made it my business to get through it and to earn my place here. It's made a world of differences [*sic*].
>
> *(Levi, third year, fraternity member)*

Not only has sense of belonging been identified as an important goal or desired end for Black male collegians, but it also acts as a motive for academic and social behaviors. For instance, some Black men aspire to establish a sense of belonging in college—that is, "to fit in" or stand out—and thus devote sufficient time to studying and class preparation in hopes of knowing enough to engage in class or answer questions correctly, which helps them feel more confident about their sense of belonging in college. Others talked about participating in study sessions and workshops that enhance their writing and thinking skills, or accessing help, where needed, by raising questions in class, visiting the writing center, or talking with professors during "office hours." This is particularly true for Black men enrolled at selective admissions universities or those majoring in academic fields where a premium is placed on high academic achievement. Read the electronic note that I received from a Black male undergraduate ago (see Figure 8.2). Then ask: Why was he compelled to do all of that? Answer: To belong.

Yearning for fulfilling of the important goal of belonging or "community" on campus drives some other Black men to engage in educationally

Figure 8.2   Email from Black male student about belonging.

purposeful activities such as mentoring programs, clubs and organizations, or leadership experiences. For example, I've met dozens of Black men at campuses across the nation who participate in mentoring programs (both peer and professional mentoring arrangements) as a way of adjusting to college or becoming part of the campus community. I've found that Black men who participate in formal mentoring relationships with faculty members are more satisfied with college, report a stronger sense of belonging on campus, and thus are expected to succeed at higher rates than their same-race male peers who do not engage in such experiences (Strayhorn & Saddler, 2009; Strayhorn & Terrell, 2007).

Participating in campus clubs and organizations is another way that some Black men negotiate their sense of belonging in college, which is an important ingredient in the recipe for college success. Joining a BGLO provides some Black male members with opportunities to interact with others who share similar perspectives—what some participants called "brothers helping bruthas"[2]—cultural values, and collegiate experiences. Such experiences ease Black males' adjustment to college, help them to make sense of their experiences in unfamiliar settings like PWIs, and foster a sense of belonging among members of BGLOs. A quick anecdote. Several years ago, I spoke at the National Conference on Race and Ethnicity (NCORE). When I arrived at the room where my talk was scheduled, I was surprised to find the room set up in "small group circles" rather than standard, conference style rows as expected. With a small handful of minutes before the start of my session,

I worried that I would not have time to reset the room and place a copy of my handout on each chair. Stressed but silent, I looked up and met three guys who said: "Hey brother, need any help? Just let us know." I immediately explained the situation and, within moments, my new three brothers and I were busy getting things ready for the audience. Later, I learned that my "angels disguised as brothers" were members of my fraternity and, indeed, their presence, support, and help eased my anxiety, reduced my stress, and enabled me to focus on delivering a solid presentation. The underlying causal mechanism is similar for Black male undergraduates involved in BGLOs and other strong ethnic enclaves such as Black student alliances and gospel choirs (Strayhorn, 2011c). Consider the following excerpts that illustrate this point:

> I'm a Black dude in nursing so there are no other first-year Black students, let alone males, who are in the nursing school. I decided to join [the gospel choir] as a way of meeting other Black students, making friends, [finding my group].
> *(Henry, first-year nursing major)*

> As a member of a fraternity and the BSA, I have made several meaningful friendships that will last me a lifetime. Some of these people have helped me even when I couldn't help myself ... I'm serious! Without them, I know I wouldn't feel like I should be here in school. They really make it comfortable for me.
> *(Olajuwon, third year)*

Across several studies, Black male participants used words or phrases that implied sense of belonging as important when describing their impetus for involvement in campus clubs and organizations. Examples of such words and phrases ranged from "acclimate myself to campus," "to get tied to this place," "to make it in," and "finding my niche." Other students talked about feeling like "one in the number," "invisible," a "stranger in an unknown land," or "the only Black face in a sea of Whiteness," although their involvement in campus clubs and organizations provided a way to reduce, if not eliminate, such feelings.

Sense of Belonging Is Significant

It's also true that Black men, in my previous studies, seemed to place considerable significance on their belonging experiences. For example, some participants stressed the importance of joining fraternities or engaging in peer mentoring programs (such as Student African American Brotherhood [SAAB]) as a way of aiding their social integration into college by providing a critical mass of "brothers" upon whom they could rely for support (Strayhorn, 2010); see Figure 8.3 to learn about peer mentoring and my notion of "academic spotters" and brainstorm ways to apply the concept

What Gym Time Taught Me About "Academic Spotters"

A few years ago, I decided to join a workout facility so I could "go the gym" like all my friends. I didn't really *want* to work out per se but it seemed like "the thing" to do (safe space, don't judge; you'd be surprised how many human behaviors are motivated by similar logic). I went to the gym and felt lost, confused. It was new territory for me and I didn't know where to stand, run, get water, or even ask for help. I remember feeling anxious, nervous, unsure, hypersensitive to judgment by others, and as if I did not belong there.

I noticed after 30 minutes or so another Black "brutha" who was lifting weights. He wore gloves, a tight shirt, grunted when he pushed to lift the bar and I noticed that he seemed to always squat twice before starting his "reps" of lifting. Striving to be a good student (not stalker LOL), I seized my cellphone and unknowingly snapped a few pictures and short videos of his workout routine. I knew that I could "be just like him," if I studied closely. That night I went to a sporting good store and purchased gloves, shoes, a tight shirt, and matching headband for my weight-lifting debut.

Next day, I arrived to the gym early. Placed just as many weights on my bar as my "brutha" lifted. Donned my gloves and did two squats. Surprisingly, no matter how I pushed and twisted, it took way more work to get the bar lifted; finally it was up but I could NOT ease it back down. I held it for what seemed like 20 minutes and just before my arm gave way to death-by-dumbbell, my "brutha" appeared and took the weight off of me. Trying to "save face," I yelled: "What are you doing? I was lifting that." He replied: "No, what are YOU doing, trying to kill yourself?" I learned later that you should lift with a spotter--someone who cares, cheers you along, helps when needed, and lifts the weight when you can't bear it. I immediately thought about the idea of "academic spotters" in higher education, especially for Black men who spend time in the gym but not so much in the lab.

Figure 8.3 Peer mentoring as "academic spotting" for Black men.

to your work with students in terms of providing support, holding them accountable, monitoring their progress, and giving feedback, to name a few. Again, words or phrases used during their interviews signaled the significance that Black men attach to their belonging experiences, often describing such incidents as "critical," "life-changing," "game-changing," "transformative," "necessary," and "wildly memorable."

Not all experiences identified as "significant" by Black males were positive in nature such as joining a club, being mentored, or playing a sport; some participants identified negative experiences that significantly influenced the degree to which they felt they belonged in college, at least at the moment. Consider the following quotations:

When I came to [said college], I firmly believed in stuff like that ... that all people were good, all people were fair, and all people were fairly honest. But going to school here has taught me a different story and, truth is, it has changed what I believe and think. One day at this damn school, a White parent started cheering in the parking lot when me and my parents got out the car. They was [*sic*] like, "Hooray, thanks for bringing us another basketball player. We're going to the championship this year." But I'm like 5-foot-7 and I don't play no damn ball. You know? It's just shit like that that I remember.

(*Chaz, second-year biology/Spanish major*)

I was taught as a little boy that you should not fight. When I got older, my pastor preached "Thou shalt not fight," but turn the other cheek. Then my mom and step-dad always told me that I better not fight as long as I'm in their house. But when I got here to [college], I met a lot of White kids who hadn't seen a Black guy before or at least that's what they say [laughing]. One of my dorm mates—I think I know who it was too—put this letter under my door that said, "Go back to Africa, Nigger." You know the history of that word, right? So, I was pissed, steaming … definitely ready to go the fuck off! You know, it's like I'm trying to be the "nice guy" but they push me to be "the mad angry Black guy" sometimes.

(Alvin, third-year history major)

Both Chaz and Alvin recall negative encounters with discrimination and racism—and what scholars have coined racial "microaggressions"—that catalyzed their re-examination of previously held beliefs about certain values, triggered a reconsideration of their position on campus, and thereby affected their sense of belonging in college. Microaggressions are subtle insults (verbal, non-verbal, and/or visual) or "mini-assaults" directed toward people, often automatically or unconsciously (Solorzano, Ceja, & Yosso, 2000). "[T]he cumulative burden of a lifetime of microaggressions can theoretically contribute to diminished mortality, augmented morbidity, and flattened confidence" (Pierce, 1995, p. 281). One of the most troublesome things that microaggressions and social pathologies like racism do is "other" groups and individuals as something different from the dominant or norm; they conspire to create boxes and categories in which *some* people are placed and that sets limits on where they can go, who they can be, or what they can do. Interestingly, most contemporary research suggests that students don't live in boxes—their lives are far more complex and complicated than that.

BELONGING EXPERIENCES ARE NOT EQUAL

At least two more points about Black male collegians' sense of belonging deserve mention. First, Black male collegians do not experience sense of belonging equally and the factors that give rise to their belonging also vary by social identities and locations. For instance, my previous work provides fairly persuasive evidence that Black men who hail from low-income and/or urban backgrounds face unique challenges in the college environment that directly or indirectly influence their belonging perceptions.

Taken a step further, different strategies may be needed to alleviate such burdens, which, in turn, may effectively promote their belonging on campus. For instance, a majority of low-income Black men identified college costs, the need to work for income, and ways in which their social interactions with same-race peers are shaped by one's socioeconomic status as barriers to their sense of belonging. To remedy this problem, many of them shared that they make conscious decisions about what to do (or not do) based on these issues. For instance, one first-year student shared why he didn't "hang out much with [his] friends on the weekend, although [he] want[ed] to." He simply could not afford eating out, a movie ticket, and "paying for Uber or Lyft everywhere." Generally speaking, samples of Black men from higher socioeconomic backgrounds rarely, if ever, discussed financial factors in terms of their sense of belonging. Similar differences were observed between Black male first-generation and continuing generation students, fraternity members and non-members, leaders and non-leaders, high-achievers and low-achievers.

Sense of Belonging Leads to Success

Yet and still, all of these studies bring evidence to bear on the fact that sense of belonging facilitates Black male collegians' educational success. Time and time again, research results have shown that Black male undergraduates who feel a sense of belonging in the classroom, department, residence hall (Strayhorn & Mullins, 2012), or broader campus adjust to college more easily, earn better grades, assume campus leadership positions, and rate their college experience satisfactory. In other words, many of these findings can be reduced to one major conclusion: without a sense of belonging, there can be no educational success for Black men in college. Recall the stories shared by Alvin, Chaz, Orlando, Olajuwon, Levi, Tyson, and many others whose stories animate my previous publications; as Kuh and colleagues (2005) posit, in keeping with my own thinking about this concept, "feelings of belonging help students connect with their peers and the institution, relationships that, in turn, are associated with persistence and satisfaction" (p. 119). The same wisdom holds true for Black men in higher education and thus can be aptly applied to our work with such students.

DISCUSSION

The purpose of this chapter was to extend our discussion of sense of belonging in college to include Black men in higher education, drawing on findings from my previous studies. In keeping with the book's theoretical framework, I have highlighted findings that underscore the **importance** of sense of belonging to Black men in college, the **significance** of their belonging experiences, the role that forms of engagement play in facilitating (or inhibiting) their belonging, and the fact that not all Black men experience it equally, although belonging seems to beget success for all.

Several pieces of information presented in the chapter relate to the literature reviewed earlier. For instance, the condition of Black men in higher education is represented through national statistics about enrollment, achievement patterns, and media such as music, film, and news sources (Roach, 2001; US Department of Education, National Center for Education Statistics, 2011). Representations shape individuals' perceptions, which, in turn, can influence behaviors even among educators such as teachers, principals, and professors. Black men in my previous studies have recalled direct encounters with such negative perceptions—confronting professors and peers who seem to believe that all Black men as dangerous or athletic— and explained how those incidents reduce, if not eliminate, their feelings of connectedness or belonging in college. Seems to call out that fact that many of us are complicit in creating the circumstances that challenge Black men's success in college—literally our beliefs and perceptions can hold them hostage from finding belonging and success. To promote their sense of belonging, then, we must work to correct the image of Black men in higher education by sharing more information about their successes, highlighting the structural factors that give rise to leveled aspirations and performance without blaming the victim, and changing the discourse about Black men from a directory of deficiencies to a volume of strengths. Messaging like "you belong here" should include images of Black men engaging with their college peers as a way of connecting with them authentically. Figure 8.4 gives an example from Springbrook in New York.

Not only do teacher perceptions and expectations shape the capacity for Black men to feel as if they belong and can succeed in education (Ferguson, 2000; Lee, 1994; Strayhorn, 2008f), but so does their engagement with faculty members and peers in college. Black men in my studies have pointed to a number of mechanisms that enable their educational success including, but not limited to: campus clubs and organizations, fraternities, gospel choirs, peer mentoring programs, and even positive in-class experiences.

Figure 8.4   Belonging message from Springbrook University.

In fact, Black male collegians' sense of belonging at PWIs hinges, in part, upon interacting positively with faculty members and peers; experiencing a welcoming, supportive campus racial climate; and engaging in educationally purposeful activities that foster a sense of mattering (i.e., "I matter, others care about me") in college. All of these findings add support to the theoretical argument that I am advancing in this volume—that belonging is a basic human need and fundamental motivation, that it drives student behaviors, and facilitates educational success. Sense of belonging develops in response to the degree to which Black men feel respected, valued, accepted, and needed by others on campus. This is the personal sensation or longing to which Tyson referred at the opening of the chapter when he considered his options—to join a gang or go to college. As a Black male, he decided to go to college in the hope of being accepted as a bona fide member of the campus community. He hoped to share an emotional connection with others at his school especially "his brothers,"[3] even though he was leaving behind strong personal connections with "his boys" (i.e., close friends) and members of his immediate family. He hoped he would enjoy college and feel respected and valued by others on campus. To the extent that this was true for him, Tyson *found* a sense of belonging in college.

The potential applications of this chapter to practice, theory, and future research are many. The chapter's content should be of particular interest to campus constituencies who have a vested interest in promoting the educational success of Black men. For instance, admission counselors and staff might consider stories like those shared by Tyson when reviewing student applications to college. For some students, college is a matter of life or death, a choice between "going to school" or joining a gang or some other anti-social behavior; see Winkle-Wagner's (2010) excellent work about Black women where she frames it as a matter of "life or death," for more. Information of this sort may be useful for understanding students' motivations for college, the circumstances in which they live, and the public and private benefits of college attendance. Just as I have said about sense of belonging throughout this volume, it's true that not all people benefit from a college education equally—for some it brings purpose, meaning, direction, and hope to an otherwise dire situation. Of course, not all Black men see college as a choice between "school or a gang," as Tyson did; higher education administrators should bear this in mind as they work with Black male students.

Encountering negative experiences such as discrimination and racism tended to reduce, if not eliminate, Black males' sense of connectedness on campus. A wide range of incidents were identified across my studies that inhibit the belonging of Black men in higher education. For instance, participants have talked about racist peers, judgmental faculty members, racial slurs and epithets, uninformed opinions about Black culture, burdens to prove one's academic ability (Strayhorn, 2009c), and even grossly generic crime alerts that cast all Black men (on campus) as suspect and danger-ous, thereby creating a hostile, unwelcoming environment for them at PWIs. Presidents, provosts, chief diversity officers, campus police, and administra-tors of support units can all play a critical role in addressing these issues using information gleaned from this chapter. First, there is sufficient rea-son to address each of these concerns; we must confront them head-on, name them for what they are; racism is racism and it shouldn't be tolerated on campus ... period. We should also establish policies and practices that align with our espoused values. Fostering *all* students' sense of belonging in college is an appropriate institutional goal or objective for academic units such as diversity offices, academic colleges, and support units or centers. Institutional leaders might enact policies to allocate resources to activities that engender belonging for Black men such as peer mentoring programs like SAAB, campus organizations, and fraternities. Workshops and semi-nars could be offered to faculty members, staff, and students on confronting racism, suspending racial stereotypes and implicit bias, and serving as allies to students of color on campus.

In almost all cases, Black men who fared well in higher education reported a strong(er) sense of belonging in college and those who performed less well tended to feel invisible, isolated, or alienated on campus. Academic advi-sors, program directors, and campus counselors may find this information useful when working with Black men. For instance, an academic advisor who meets with a Black male about his academic difficulties might inquire about his sense of belonging using conversation-like probes including: Do you feel connected to others on campus? Do you have a support system upon which you can rely? Are there others with whom you work or study? In your opinion, would friends miss you if you left college? Should these prove to be untapped areas of support, advisors and directors might sug-gest ways for students to meet and connect with others through counseling, mentoring programs, summer research experiences, clubs and organiza-tions, study abroad, fraternities, or more formal arrangements with faculty members. Multicultural specialists and diversity officers might formulate policies that establish new or revise existing campus-wide programs of this sort, where possible. For faculty to play a role here, they would have to know what campuses offer to students in the way of program and services. Rarely are faculty members educated on the wide range of services (e.g., writing center, counseling, career services, food pantries, recovery) available to students. I've always argued for "organization fairs" for faculty (similar to what's provided for new students) where campus services and supports are on display for faculty to learn about them and what they do best. Also never underestimate the power of a good 'ole list, if you want to keep it simple and efficient.

Findings presented in this chapter also inform future research. For instance, here I draw upon previous results to demonstrate the importance of belonging for Black men in higher education, to call attention to the significance of their belonging experiences, to identify differences among Black men in terms of belonging, and to underscore that belonging promotes educational success. Future research might test these theoretical suppositions using data from various samples of Black male collegians such as athletes, student leaders, high achievers, fraternity members, foster youth, justice-involved, and low-income students. Other research may examine this issue more closely by providing detailed information on the belonging experiences of Black men using qualitative methods such as one-on-one interviews, focus groups, journals, and in-depth observations. Comparative research on sense of belonging also is warranted; for instance, future research might compare Black men with Black women or Black men with other racial/ethnic minorities, or examine differences among Black male subgroups.

CONCLUSION

By encouraging participation in campus clubs and organizations, promoting engagement in educationally purposeful activities, challenging racism and discrimination on campus, and providing academic support among Black male students, we may effectively raise their sense of belonging in college, which satisfies a basic human need that may take on heightened importance during the college years and lead to educational success in college and beyond.

NOTES

1 Throughout this chapter, the terms "Black" and "African American" are used interchangeably to refer to individuals whose ancestral origins are traced back to the African diaspora (e.g., Haitian, West Indian, African) in consonance with federal guidelines (US Census Bureau, 2000).
2 Pronounced phonetically and while related to the term "brothers," it is often used to refer to Black buddies or fictive kin; that is, individuals who do not share biological ties with a person but are often considered equal in stature and importance to biological family member (Hirt, Amelink, Bennett, & Strayhorn, 2008).
3 Pronounced phonetically and while related to the term "brutha" (see #2 above) and the *biologically determined relationship* shared between two male off-spring of the same parent(s), it is used here to refer to fictive kin or individuals who do not share biological ties with a person but are often considered equal in stature and due all rights and privileges of actual kin.

Chapter 9

Sense of Belonging and Graduate Students

In my opinion, one of the strongest differences between graduate school and being an undergraduate is that when I was an undergraduate I was connected to the university is so many ways. I spent time hanging out with my friends, going to parties, going to football games, you know, "kegs and eggs" [laughing]. But now as a graduate student, I feel like I should connect with others in my program, my professors, my advisor, and maybe even the larger field where I'll work, but it's not the "university" per se.

(Edith, first-year PhD student,
human factors engineering)

INTRODUCTION

Much of what has been written about student success in higher education focuses on undergraduate students, their motivations for attending college, factors influencing their choice of a particular college, and conditions that promote or inhibit their academic and social success in college. Far less is known about the academic histories, motivations, and experiences of those seeking master's, doctoral, and first-professional degrees, hereafter referred to as graduate students. Yet, graduate students represent a significant proportion of all students enrolled in higher education and they play a major role in the nation's research and development production.

According to data from the US Department of Education, National Center for Education Statistics (2016), approximately 21 million students are enrolled across 4300 colleges and universities in the United States. Of these, a majority are women, a growing number are underrepresented racial/ethnic minorities, and about 16 million are undergraduates. Approximately

2 million are graduate students, with roughly 75 percent representing master's degree students and 25 percent doctoral and first-professional degree seekers. Figure 9.1 presents a graphical summary of these data.

Some research has examined students' motivations for attending graduate school, although studies of this kind are few in number. For instance, we know that some students go to graduate school to acquire the knowledge and skills necessary for working in a particular field that requires specialized or technical talents (Poock, 1999). It is also true that some students attend graduate school to engage in independent research as a way of advancing knowledge and theory in a particular field (Burgess, 1997; LaPidus, 1997).

Contrary to research on undergraduate students, very little information is available about factors that influence students' choice of a particular graduate school. While some scholars posit that the factors that influence undergraduate college choice are similar, if not identical, to the factors that shape graduate college choice (e.g., proximity to home, success of sport's team), others argue that the nature and function of graduate education forces students to consider a unique set of characteristics and options when making such decisions. For instance, some empirical evidence supports the importance of institutional ranking, reputation of a particular degree program,

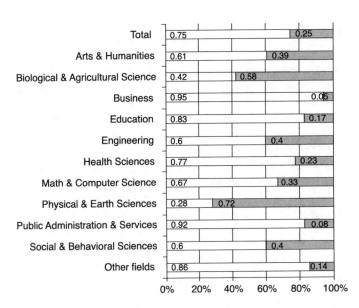

Figure 9.1 Total graduate enrollment by field and type of degree, Fall 2010. Master's/other (o), Doctoral (n).

Source: CGS/GRE Survey of Graduate Enrollment and Degrees. Image reproduced digitally by author.

availability of reputable faculty members, financial assistance, and time-to-degree in graduate school decision-making (Ellis, 2001).

Understanding how students come to choose a particular graduate school may provide clues to meeting their needs, which, in turn, is likely to increase their chances of success. This is particularly important because, still today, 50 percent of all graduate students leave their graduate program before completing their degree (Nerad & Cerny, 1993; Nettles & Millett, 2006), a phenomenon typically referred to as "attrition" or "dropping out." That 50 percent of all graduate students leave their degree program prematurely is a serious cause for concern given the exorbitant costs associated with recruiting new graduate students, teaching them highly technical skills such as lab preparation techniques, and providing them with meaningful interactions for collaboration with faculty members. Indeed, there are other non-monetary costs associated with graduate student attrition such as loss of confidence in one's abilities, diminished self-esteem, and loss of human capital (Berelson, 1960; Nerad & Miller, 1996). Altogether it is clear that increasing graduate student success would have many advantages.

Previous research has established that graduate student persistence (or, conversely, attrition) is a function of students' socialization to their role as a graduate student as well as their role as a bona fide member of the professional field in which they aspire to work (Weidman & Stein, 2003). Graduate student socialization is defined as the process through which students come to know and understand the values, norms, and behaviors enacted by members of a particular discipline or field (Boyle & Boice, 1998). Research has shown that socialization takes time, consumes significant resources, and unfolds differently for different students across different disciplines and fields.

A large number of scholars agree that successful socialization of graduate students to their new roles likely results in feelings of membership, community, relatedness, or a **sense of belonging** among others in the graduate department or professional field. Despite this agreement, much less is known about the underlying causal mechanism and ways in which sense of belonging plays out for today's graduate students. Again, most of what is known about sense of belonging has focused on undergraduate students, and existing research about graduate student socialization fails to link it to sense of belonging. I believe that Clark (1993, p. 356) had it right when he wrote:

> The first-degree level has historical primacy, predominates numerically and possesses a deep hold on traditional thought and practice. It comes first in budget determination, public attention and the concerns of governments. Graduate or advanced education is then prone to develop at the margin as an add-on of a few more years of unstructured work for a few students.

Given its importance to the production of knowledge and advancement of science and society, I want to contribute to changing this predicament by directing explicit attention to understanding sense of belonging in graduate education. More information is needed if graduate education is to assume primacy in public debates about education, if it is to move to the center of educational policy decisions, and if it is to be seen as more than "a few more years of unstructured work" for a select few. More information is needed to frame graduate school as a proper training ground of sorts for acquiring the knowledge, skills, and abilities needed for full active membership in a professional field. This chapter was designed with these purposes in mind.

The aims of this chapter are threefold. First, I draw upon existing literature and research to explain the relationship between graduate students' socialization and their sense of belonging. Second, I draw upon data from previous studies to demonstrate the link between aspects of students' socialization and their sense of belonging in graduate school. Third, I identify important implications for policy, theory, and future research, recommending specific strategies for promoting conditions that foster a sense of belonging among graduate students.

GRADUATE STUDENT SOCIALIZATION: THEORY IN BRIEF

Given the importance of socializing agents such as faculty members and peers and both informal and formal experiences (e.g., orientation, advising) to the success of graduate students, I drew upon socialization theory as a framework for guiding the development and implementation of my studies on graduate students. As Gardner (2010) rightly noted, "socialization has become the common theoretical framework used to better understand the complexity of the doctoral student experience" (p. 61).

Graduate student socialization generally refers to the process by which individuals acquire the knowledge, skills, dispositions, and behaviors that make them effective members of a particular department, school, and/ or professional field to which they belong (Brim, 1966). One of the most widely cited conceptualizations of graduate student socialization was that postulated by Weidman, Twale, and Stein (2001). They argue that graduate student socialization consists of several core elements: (a) knowledge acquisition; (b) investment; and (c) involvement. Figure 9.2 presents a graphical depiction of the model.

I settled on Weidman and colleagues' framework because it allowed me to examine the internal processes and external influences by which graduate students acquire the knowledge and skills needed to participate successfully in graduate school and a particular discipline or field. As such, data on a number of variables were collected through my studies to operationalize

Interactive Stages of Socialization: Anticipatory, Formal, Informal, Personal

Figure 9.2   Representation of Weidman, Twale, and Stein's (2001) socialization model. Image reproduced digitally by author.

the sources of influence, mechanisms of socialization, and external factors delineated in the conceptual framework.

Successful socialization yields a number of important outcomes. For example, well-socialized students understand the values, beliefs, and mores of the professional field to which they belong (Bragg, 1976). Individuals who are successfully socialized to a particular department or professional field also possess the skills and competencies required for working within a particular discipline, and thus may feel connected to others in the field and valued and respected by others as a competent member, all of which contribute to their sense of belonging (Strayhorn, in press b).

Belonging is a universal human characteristic and a basic need (Maslow, 1962). Belonging may also offer a shared sense of socially constructed meaning that provides a sense of security or relatedness among individuals—that relatedness becomes the glue that connects individuals in a group. Generally speaking, people strive to be accepted by others, valued, and respected as competent, qualified individuals worthy of membership in a defined group or particular social context. The experience of belonging, then, is context-dependent, such that sense of belonging in a particular context has the greatest influence on outcomes in that context. For example, sense of belonging in an academic department has the greatest influence on a graduate student's adjustment to the department life; sense of belonging in the classroom may have greatest influence on graduate students' participation in class activities.

With this understanding in mind, it is reasonable to assume that aspects of graduate students' socialization will positively influence their adjustment and achievement in graduate school. Adjustment to graduate school is defined as successful adaptation to the norms, values, and expectations that predominate the degree-granting department or field, which, in part, reflects one's sense of belonging. Achievement, in this chapter, is defined as the extent to which students meet the academic standards set by the graduate institution as reflected by their grade point average (GPA). Now, let us turn our attention to the studies that inform this chapter.

THE STUDIES

Since I was interested in understanding the relationship between aspects of graduate students' socialization and sense of belonging in graduate school, I drew upon data from several studies that I conducted from 2008 to 2011. Generally speaking, these studies can be divided into two major categories based on the methods employed to collect data: survey studies and interview studies.

The survey studies elicited information about graduate students' demographic characteristics, academic histories, motivations for attending graduate school, the frequency and nature of their academic and social experiences (e.g., time spent studying, engagement in research), and subjective evaluations of their skills and development, including measures of the extent to which they felt a sense of belonging in graduate school. For instance, graduate student surveys included items such as "I feel a sense of belonging in my graduate school," "Faculty in the graduate program care about me," and "My peers in graduate school would miss me if I were gone." Responses were made on a five-point Likert scale ranging from one ("strongly disagree") to five ("strongly agree"). Sense of belonging, as a composite, was measured as the average of these items.

The interview studies served at least two purposes. First, interviews were often used to make deeper meaning of the survey findings. For instance, in one study, I worked with members of my research team to conduct one-on-one and group interviews with willing graduate students to probe more closely their motivations for attending school, challenges faced in graduate school, and the diversity of experiences that fostered a sense of belonging in graduate school. Interview studies served a second purpose that focused more closely on the theoretical underpinnings of sense of belonging in graduate school. Specifically, interview questions were designed to elicit information about precursors to establishing a sense of belonging in graduate school, conditions that either promote or inhibit graduate students' sense of "fitting in" among others in their field, and whether belonging in graduate school facilitated belonging in larger social or professional contexts or vice versa.

Samples varied among the studies but generally can be compared across several important characteristics. The vast majority of participants are racial/ethnic minorities, reflecting the dominant hue of my research program. Most respondents to the graduate student survey are master's degree students or recent graduates. Altogether, approximately 250 survey respondents and 35 interviewees are ethnic minorities at the doctoral level.

Using appropriate techniques for analyzing survey and interview data, I present several major findings from these studies in the next section before discussing the importance of these results in light of previous studies and their implications for future policy, research, and practice. Without further ado, let's talk about three major findings.

MAJOR FINDINGS

Results from my survey and interview studies suggest that socialization matters for graduate students, regardless of academic field or discipline. Not only is socialization positively associated with graduate student outcomes such as confidence in one's ability to complete academic tasks typically expected of graduate students (e.g., writing term papers, conducting research), but evidence from multiple studies demonstrates a link between aspects of socialization and sense of belonging in graduate school. Establishing a sense of belonging in graduate school is important given its theoretical tie to persistence (see Chapters 2 and 3 of this volume) and results from the studies discussed in this chapter yield consistent support for sense of belonging's relationship with graduate school GPA and satisfaction. In the following subsections, I present selected results from my studies to substantiate these claims. Where possible, I provide verbatim quotes from the interview studies to illuminate the relationship in the words of graduate students themselves.

Socialization Matters

If findings are based on the frequency with which they appear across multiple studies or experiments, then one finding is crystal clear from my studies of graduate students: socialization does indeed matter. I have uncovered fairly consistent evidence that graduate students acquire much-needed information about the values, beliefs, and norms of a particular department and/or professional field through formal and informal experiences that introduce them to particular customs of a graduate department (e.g., preparation for the comprehensive exam) or field (e.g., presenting at conferences). Those experiences may also promote their involvement in socializing

Table 9.1   Graduate students involvement in socializing activities

Have you participated in:	% No	% Yes, once	% Yes, two or more times
Formal orientation program	15	75	10
Advising session(s) with faculty	10	42	48
Social gathering with faculty	25	46	29
Social gathering with peers	8	35	57
Research training activity	32	44	24
Internship(s)	35	42	23
Professional association	44	36	20

Note: Numbers may not sum to 100 due to rounding.

activities (e.g., faculty–student collaborations), and encourage students to carry out a self-directed regimen of professional activities. Graduate student socialization typically occurs through orientation programs, faculty–student advising, social gatherings among peers and staff, research training, and internships, to name a few. In a study of 360 graduate students enrolled across 15 institutions, I found that the majority reported involvement in formal orientation programs while relatively few had worked with a faculty member on a research project (excluding those in science fields, who typically spend a great deal of time in their advisor's laboratory). Table 9.1 presents a summary of these survey findings.

Graduate students spoke extensively about the importance of socialization in graduate school. Careful analysis of transcripts from these studies yielded a litany of terms that all seemed to coalesce around the theme of socialization. Words and phrases ranged from "transformation," "process," and "system" to "preparation for," "changing [one] into," and "making [oneself] ready for." Consider the following quotes from graduate students about the important role that socialization plays in their experience:

> I know that part of why I'm here is to get ready for what's next for me in my career. I mean, I know it's about getting good grades and doing well in graduate school but it's also about a process … a process that will prepare me for my career in education. I really can't get to what's next until I learn the ropes from those who have already been there, done that.
>
> *(Billy, third-year doctoral student)*

> Graduate school is about transformation to me. I didn't come here to just get a degree quick [*sic*] and get out. I want to be changed or transformed by my professors … by the whole experience. I'm here to learn what I need to know in order to be a psychologist one day. And it's clear to me that I have a lot to learn about counseling, the kinds of patients that I will have, and how to help them through their problems. So, I'm making the most of graduate school to get ready for that.
>
> *(Deirdra, second-year master's student)*

As mentioned earlier, interview participants tended to use words and phrases that suggest the importance of socialization as a "process" that prepares, even transforms, them for success in their desired career. Other evidence suggests that socialization facilitates a sense of belonging in graduate school. It is to this theme that we turn next.

Socialization Begets Sense of Belonging

Socialization matters because it produces certain outcomes that move individuals from being perpetual "outsiders" to valued "insiders"—that is, bona fide members of a group or society to which they belong. Meaningful engagement in purposeful socializing experiences (e.g., orientation, social gatherings, peer collaborations), in this case, introduces graduate students to the norms of an academic field or profession, puts them in touch with their peers and faculty members, and, ultimately, engenders a sense of belonging (or alienation) in graduate school and their professional field. Survey results from my studies suggest that socialization experiences are positively and moderately correlated with graduate students' sense of belonging.[1]

In interviews with graduate students, I learned a great deal more about *how* socialization engenders a sense of belonging in graduate school. Generally speaking, this occurred in one of three ways: developing competency, forming supportive relationships, or affirming one's professional identity. For example, students talked at length about the myriad ways in which they acquired information about the norms and practices of their graduate department (or professional field), which enabled them to act in accordance with such norms. Following the norms, practices, and expectations of one's department or field was a way of demonstrating competence— that is, possessing the required skills and capacities needed to perform well. Demonstrating competence led to acceptance by others (e.g., peers, faculty members), which, in turn, led to feeling valued, respected, and connected to the experience, all of which are core elements of sense of belonging.

Engaging in meaningful socializing experiences had other effects as well. Graduate students talked, at length, about the role that formal and informal experiences played in forming supportive relationships as well as affirming their professional identity. Consider the following long quotes that reflect the sentiments of many:

> One of the most important pieces in my mind is the support you receive from others in the program. I always try to tell people you can't make it on your own in graduate school. It might be easier for some master's students but I don't know. I KNOW [emphasis added] you can't do it for a PhD program. You have to go to new student week. You have to go to the library orientation workshops. You have to go to class [laughing]. If the professors invite you

to their house, you have to go. They won't say it necessarily, but you have to. Over time, you learn who they are, what makes them tick, and they learn whether or not they like you [laughing] ... whether you know how to play "the game" or not. Once you've proven yourself, they go out of their way to help you ... they can be really supportive.

(Joseph, second-year doctoral student)

I'm in my last year and working on my dissertation. I'd say all of my support has come through various activities. My advisor is head of the department. My committee members are from my academic department and one is from social work. Two of my [graduate] cohort buddies are trained facilitators for my group interviews as part of my dissertation. And I have an undergraduate who's helping me transcribe my interviews. I wouldn't know any of these people if it weren't for the activities offered by my department. I met my advisor—like really met him—at a Christmas social my first year. My cohort buddies and I spent a lot of time together studying, preparing for classes. And I met my undergraduate assistant through a summer research camp sponsored by my department. So I think you have to participate in these activities because you never know what you'll gain.

(Gladys, fifth-year doctoral student)

At times, I've thought about leaving graduate school because I don't know if I'm really cut out for this kind of work. But just then my advisor would say something positive to me or nominate me for some fellowship or award that I didn't even know about or one of my peers will ask for help with a subject that I'm really good at and that will make me feel confident again ... that I've made the right choice.

(Tomas, second-year master's student)

By engaging in educationally purposeful activities or social gatherings with their peers and faculty members, graduate students developed competence in their professional field or discipline; established meaningful, supportive relationships that enabled their success; and affirmed or reaffirmed their professional commitments, all of which fosters their sense of belonging. So, what's the relationship between sense of belonging and success in graduate school? Thought you'd never ask; keep reading to find out.

Sense of Belonging Begets Success

Conventional wisdom suggests that the way one feels determines one's success. Empirical evidence from my graduate student studies lends support to this conclusion. For instance, without exception, I've found a fairly consistent and positive association between sense of belonging and success in graduate school as measured by one's GPA.[2] In brief, graduate students who felt a stronger sense of belonging to their department, peers, and faculty members also tended to earn higher grades in graduate school. It is interesting to note that the average "effect size" of sense of belonging on graduate GPA was higher for doctoral ($d = 0.30$) than master's ($d = 0.11$) students, possibly indicating that sense of belonging matters most for doctoral students seeking the highest level of education afforded in this country (LaPidus, 1997).

While the survey findings yield fairly consistent evidence to support the statistical relationship between sense of belonging and success in graduate school, information from the interview studies seems to reveal just why this is the case. Overall, graduate students who felt they belonged reported feeling safe, respected, and comfortable when interacting with their peers, staff, and faculty members. Cynthia, Frank, Joyce, Derek, and Joseph offered powerful illustrations of how their academic success was predicated upon their sense of belonging. Joyce's comments reflect the tenor of many others:

> Once I started to fit in, I started to do better. I didn't start fitting in until I got to know people, opened up to them, worked with my professors on projects that I wasn't even that interested in. Still it helped me feel valued and respected in the program in the end.

Derek, too, offered words that reflect the essence of comments shared by others. He said quite simply, "I didn't do well my first semester because I wasn't really here ... I hadn't adjusted yet. When I started to fit in around here, I did better, I felt better, I mean, I was like better all way 'round'."

Under conditions that signal they matter and play a role, graduate students were motivated to learn, ready to participate in class discussions or lab demonstrations, and willing to seek help when needed. All of these are activities that positively influence one's grades, thereby linking sense of belonging to academic success in graduate school.

DISCUSSION AND IMPLICATIONS

Recall that this chapter was designed with three purposes in mind. First, I drew upon existing literature and research to explain the relationship between graduate students' socialization and their sense of belonging in school. Check! Second, I drew upon data from recent studies to demonstrate the link between aspects of students' socialization and their sense of belonging in graduate school. Check! Third, I promised to identify important implications for policy, theory, and future research, thereby recommending specific strategies for promoting conditions that foster a sense of belonging among graduate students. And it is to this third purpose that the remaining section will be devoted.

Three major findings emanate from my studies of graduate students, reviewed in the previous section. First, socialization matters. Graduate students acquire much-needed information about the values, beliefs, and norms of a particular department and/or professional field through formal and informal experiences that introduce them to particular customs of a graduate department or professional field. Those same experiences such as admission interviews, new student orientations, and career fairs promote their involvement in socializing activities and encourage graduate students to carry out a self-directed regimen of professional activities before and after graduation. Graduate student socialization typically occurs through activities such as orientation programs, faculty–student advising, social gatherings among peers and staff, research training, professional conferences, and internships, to name a few.

A second major conclusion from these studies is that socialization fosters a sense of belonging in graduate school. In some ways, this finding reflects those reported by previous researchers. For instance, Michael Nettles and Catherine Millett (2006) analyzed data from thousands of graduate students in their book *Three Magic Letters: Getting to Ph.D.* Among their many conclusions, Nettles and Millett state plainly, "The socialization process is important because student socialization contributes to students' performance, satisfaction, and success in doctoral programs" (p. 89). In my work, I have found additional evidence to support this claim even among students seeking master's degrees. Meaningful engagement in purposeful socializing experiences introduces graduate students to the norms of an academic field or profession, exposes them to peers and faculty members upon whom they can lean for support, and, ultimately, engenders a sense of belonging (or alienation) in graduate school. In short, socialization matters for graduate students because it produces certain outcomes that move students from being perpetual "outsiders" to valued "insiders"—that is, bona fide members of a graduate program or professional field to which they belong or aspire to belong one day.

Third, sense of belonging facilitates success in graduate school, as measured by one's GPA. Though far from perfect, survey results suggest a positive, albeit modest, correlation between sense of belonging and GPA in graduate school. Overall, graduate students who felt they belonged reported feeling safe, respected, and comfortable when interacting with their peers, staff, and faculty members both on-campus and generally within their larger profession. Under such conditions, they were motivated to learn, ready to participate in class discussions or lab demonstrations, and willing to seek help when needed. And there's a fair amount of evidence to support the link between these dispositions and academic success.

There are many implications of these findings for policy, theory, and future research. In terms of policy, findings suggest the importance of socializing experiences as ways of introducing students to the norms of a particular department or profession, as well as a vehicle through which meaningful, supportive relationships are formed among students, their peers, and faculty members. Graduate deans and department heads might consider these results to establish new or continue existing activities such as new student orientation, department-wide socials, and "brown bag" lecture series where students and faculty gather to discuss critical issues or recent research in their respective field(s). Knowing that time invested in these activities does more than build the intellectual life of the department but also increases graduate students' sense of belonging is crucial.

Findings presented in this chapter provide useful insights that might advance theory in this area too. For instance, statistical and qualitative data converge to support the relationship between socialization and sense of belonging, as well as sense of belonging and academic achievement. Scholars might use this information to enhance existing models of graduate student socialization such as the one posited by Weidman, Twale, and Stein (2001). Figure 9.3 provides an example based on information from the present chapter.

In this chapter, I have shared selected findings to demonstrate the importance of sense of belonging to graduate students' success. Specifically, I drew upon data from survey and interview studies that I have conducted with members of my research teams since 2008. While useful, the studies are limited in a number of ways. First, I operationalized sense of belonging similarly in all studies, using a multi-item composite as described earlier in the chapter. Indeed, there are other ways of measuring sense of belonging. Future researchers might develop and test new scales of belonging that assess students' subjective sense of membership. Second, I employed interview questions that encouraged students to share stories about their experiences in graduate school. Several of these were worded in accordance with

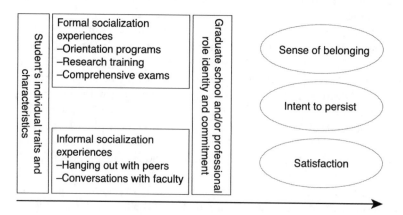

Figure 9.3 Hypothesized enhancement of socialization theory with sense of belonging.

the hypothesized direction between sense of belonging and related concepts (e.g., "How have these experiences fostered support for you in graduate school?"). It is possible, in some cases, that the relationship is reversed—the proverbial "chicken before the egg" scenario. So, does sense of belonging influence achievement, or vice versa? This question deserves more attention to which future researchers might turn.

In closing, I offer the following list of strategies for promoting conditions that seem to foster graduate students' sense of belonging:

1. Introduce graduate students to the prevailing norms, values, and expectations of the degree-granting department and/or professional field through promotional materials, orientation programs, and skill-building workshops. For instance, departments and fields that place significant value on knowledge production through independent research might signal that commitment through explicit statements on promotional materials and flyers (e.g., "We value research and prepare you for it"). Departments that value collaboration and teamwork might display pictures or images of people working together, structure classroom assignments in ways that require collaboration, or even offer students the option of completing milestone projects (e.g., thesis, dissertation) in groups. Understanding the norms and values of a department or profession allows a student to act in accordance with such expectations, which, in turn, generates a sense of belonging. Such information may be useful to students when making decisions about which graduate school to attend; it increases the likelihood that they will select a program that resonates with their own values and preferences. And it is symmetry between their values or preferences and the norms of the department that bring about sense of belonging.

2. Advise graduate students about what's required to complete their degree and to gain entry into their professional field of choice. Degree requirements can be shared through checklists and degree plans. Professional requirements can be shared through coursework, "brown bag" lectures, and involvement in activities such as presenting at professional conferences or internships. When graduate students know what's expected of them and they feel confident in their ability to meet those expectations, they also feel a sense of belonging that establishes and sustains their success professionally.

3. Provide meaningful opportunities for creating a community where graduate students can engage their peers, staff, and faculty members in informal social settings or collaborative arrangements outside the classroom. Shaping the culture of many graduate departments

(and institutions) are beliefs and practices that encourage individualism and fuel, even unknowingly, unfettered competition (e.g., highly competitive fellowships, awards, honors), rather than collaboration and community. Meaningful experiences that hold promise for promoting community include social gatherings, department-wide picnics, and common areas where students and faculty can mingle, as well as faculty–student research collaborations. Engaging others in meaningful activities of this sort nurtures graduate students' sense of belonging and ensures their success.

4. Celebrate students, their backgrounds, and achievements. Boyer (1990) identified several aspects of community, one of which is celebration. Communities are marked by celebration of its members, individually and collectively. Thus, I urge graduate educators to establish policies and practices that celebrate their students, their diverse backgrounds, and their achievements while in school. For instance, advisors might share "news" about their new advisees upon matriculation by posting information to their website, office door, or department newsletter. In other cases, department heads might announce the arrival of new graduate students in the department's website, newsletter, or main office. Acknowledging their presence, celebrating their past histories, and affirming their success in the current department all work together to engender their sense of belonging; and when they feel a sense of belonging, they excel. Here's a sample excerpt that could be adapted, modified, or used as a template to introduce new and/or continuing graduate students:

> Our department welcomes Ms. Pea H. Dee to the psychology program. Ms. Dee earned a master's degree from Folgers University and completed an impressive thesis on social cognitive conditioning of tenth-graders in a low-income school. She will work in Dr. Latte's laboratory and serve as his teaching assistant. We're delighted to have Ms. Dee as a member of our community.

As I have argued over the course of this book, sense of belonging is a basic human need. It takes on heightened importance in contexts where individuals are most unfamiliar or uncomfortable with the values, norms, and practices that predominate. Graduate school represents such an environment for many individuals. By exposing students to meaningful experiences, engaging students with their peers and faculty, and providing the support needed for them to overcome challenges, we can effectively foster their sense of belonging in graduate school, thereby effectively transforming them from "outsiders" into "insiders" with all rights and privileges thereof. Graduate students thrive and excel where they feel like they belong.

NOTES

1 In several studies, I calculated the correlation between aspects of graduate student socialization and sense of belonging in graduate school. Correlation coefficients ranged from $r = 0.20$ to $r = 0.52$.
2 Across various studies, the computed correlation coefficients ranged from $r = 0.33$ to $r = 0.55$.

Chapter 10

Clubs, Organizations, and Sense of Belonging

Crafts make us feel rooted, give us a sense of belonging and connect us with our history. Our ancestors used to create these crafts out of necessity, and now we do them for fun, to make money and to express ourselves.

(Phyllis George)

By building relations we create a source of love and personal pride and belonging that makes living in a chaotic world easier.

(Susan Lieberman)

Meet Myrna (pronounced "My-rah ... the 'n' is silent"). She's a brunette, who stands 5 foot 6 inches and prefers to "wear her hair in ponytails, depending on the day." Technically, she's a sophomore in college, although the credits registered on her transcript suggest junior ranking. Last year, she joined the student government association. Initially, she participated as a silent spectator at monthly association meetings, but later became an active—and in her words, "fairly popular"—member of several committees, including the student government steering committee, affectionately known as "the committee *of* committees." After a productive year serving the association, Myrna decided to run for student government president. Despite her promising campaign slogan, "Together, We Can," she was not elected. When asked to reflect on her experience during her interview with members of my research team, Myrna shared the following, while fighting back tears:

I'm not going to lie ... it really hurt my feelings. I was hurt deeply because I felt rejected. I felt like they [her peers] were basically saying that I wasn't good enough or I wasn't acceptable by them. By then, I had been a part of student government for like a year, but when the results were announced, I didn't feel like such a part anymore. I didn't feel like I fit in anymore. It took me forever to even start going to meetings again. I just didn't want to face them because I felt like we had built something together and, if they cared about me or appreciated me, they would have voted me into office. Do you know what I mean? I mean, I know it's an election and someone's got to lose but I never thought it would be me because I was a part of the group and the group was a part of me.

Now meet Adrienne. Last year, she attended an interest session for Delta Sigma Theta Sorority, Incorporated, hereafter "DST," indicating her strong desire to join the historically Black sorority as an undergraduate. She "came from a long line of Deltas ... [her] mother, grandmother, aunt, and sister ... all are Deltas." Despite symmetry between Adrienne's interests, convictions, and the values of DST, as well as her familial legacy with the sorority, she wasn't selected for membership. When asked to reflect on the experience during her interview with members of my research team, Adrienne shared the following, although her words were slow and broken with erratic emotion, mascara ruined by tears streaming down her cheek:

> I didn't feel like anybody ... worthless ... like rejected by the group of people I thought would accept me. I was embarrassed. I didn't think I'd even tell my family. What would they say? What would friends of mine say? They all knew how much I wanted to be a Delta. It took me by surprise and it was a good solid year ... no, probably a little longer to get myself together after that. I stopped talking to people, stopped going to Delta parties, and I didn't deal with a lot of Black students, especially girls on campus, because I felt like I wasn't part of them anymore.

INTRODUCTION

So, what do Phyllis George, Susan Lieberman, Myrna, and Adrienne all have in common? Yes, they were all born female. But, more than that, they all refer to the critical role that sense of belonging plays in educational contexts and general life settings. Some of them also reveal how college students' sense of belonging can be inspired or diminished by involvement experiences, such as running for student government office or pledging to join a sorority. Whether measured in terms of the quantity or quality of meaningful relationships that students develop with others on campus, or the frequency with which college students engage in their own learning, college students' sense of belonging is important and yields a statistically significant (and sizeable) influence on learning and development outcomes. Although faced with very different circumstances, Myrna and Adrienne fundamentally are wrestling with satisfying a basic psychological need: the need to belong. As discussed in previous chapters, individuals have psychological needs; satisfaction of these needs affects perception, behaviors, and likely leads to optimal functioning (Baumeister & Leary, 1995; Hausmann, Schofield, & Woods, 2007). Before extrapolating what Myrna and Adrienne offer to other contexts, let's turn attention to the involvement literature and the opportunities for learning and development that college student involvement affords.

INVOLVEMENT IN HIGHER EDUCATION

For years, scholars have argued that what happens *in* college matters most. And if that's true, then it follows that student involvement in college also matters (Astin, 1984). An impressive body of research has been produced to support this assertion for college students of all races and both sexes (Pascarella & Terenzini, 1991, 2005). For instance, college student involvement is associated with a set of prevailing learning outcomes in higher education including, but not limited to: artistic interests; civic responsibility (Astin & Sax, 1998); clarified values (Strayhorn, 2008b); critical thinking (Flowers, 2004); enhanced self-esteem or self-concept (Berger & Milem, 2002); leadership skills (Kimbrough & Hutcheson, 1998); multicultural competence (Einfeld & Collins, 2008); and even racial identity affirmation and expression (Harper & Quaye, 2007; Taylor & Howard-Hamilton, 1995).

There are other benefits to students' involvement in college. Here I argue that college student involvement is related to sense of belonging. Specifically, students who are more involved in college life also tend to feel a stronger connection with others on campus than those who are involved less, or not at all. Astin (1999) affirmed this idea by noting that student involvement in college can result in "a greater sense of attachment to the college" (p. 523). In service to this argument, I draw upon data from recent studies and words or narratives from interview participants to illustrate the relationship between involvement and sense of belonging in college, to identify the ways in which involvement facilitates (or, conversely, undermines) sense of belonging in college, and to recommend strategies that college student educators can employ on their campus to promote conditions that engender students' sense of belonging in college. These are the primary purposes of the present chapter.

INVOLVEMENT AND ENGAGEMENT DEFINED

Before laying out the main premises of my argument for the relationship between students' involvement in college and their sense of belonging in that context, I think it's important to clarify a few terms, namely involvement and engagement (see Chapter 2 for a complete discussion). By "involvement," I refer to Astin's (1999) formulation of the concept that refers to the amount of physical and psychological energy that college students devote to the academic experience. His conception of involvement, as I mentioned earlier, is behavioral, referring to what students *do*, rather than what they merely *think* or *feel*. It follows, then, that synonyms of Astin's involvement include vigilance, effort, time on task, "cathexis" (a Freudian concept), and even to "engage in" (p. 519). Plainly, Astin clarified, "It is not so much what the individual thinks or feels, but what the individual does, how he or she behaves, that defines and identifies involvement" (p. 519). Generally speaking, the more involved the student is in the academic and social activities of college, the more successful he or she will be.

Student "engagement," on the other hand, is defined as "the time and energy that students devote to educationally purposeful activities and the extent to which the institution gets students to participate in activities that lead to student success" (Kezar & Kinzie, 2006, p. 150). Indeed, extensions of this definition abound (e.g., Kuh, Palmer, & Kish, 2003) and many scholars have studied the impact of engagement on college student learning and development, paying close attention to differences between the sexes, race/ethnicity variations, and the role of campus racial composition on outcomes (e.g., Bridges, Kinzie, Nelson Laird, & Kuh, 2008; Harper, 2003; Strayhorn, 2008b). Despite differences in operational definitions of engagement, the weight of empirical evidence supports the conclusion that engagement promotes college student learning (Carini, Kuh, & Klein, 2005).

So, what's the relationship between involvement and engagement? Some scholars argue that "these terms are in many ways distinct," while others use them interchangeably (Wolf-Wendel, Ward, & Kinzie, 2009). I tend to agree with others that there are important nuances to the definitions of these terms, although it's not my purpose to "split hairs" over each and every distinction between them. For instance, *involvement* typically connotes behaviors and actions—that is, what students do and how they behave in college. It's also important to note that *involvement* refers to both academic and social (e.g., extracurricular) activities; the investment of physical and psychological energy into different objects or activities, which occurs along a continuum; as well as the quantity (i.e., amount) and quality (i.e., nature) of students' investment in experiences designed to produce desired outcomes. Involvement theory, then, relates to the behavioral mechanisms or processes that facilitate students' development or satisfaction of a psychological state. Activities such as "working on campus, living on campus, *engaging with peers*, being a member of clubs, and socializing with faculty members are the types of involvement typically measured under this theory" (Wolf-Wendel, Ward, & Kinzie, 2009, p. 411).

Engagement is conceptually distinct in at least two ways. First, engagement refers to the amount of time and effort students devote to their academic responsibilities (i.e., studies) and other activities (e.g., sports, clubs) that "lead to the experiences and outcomes that constitute student success" (Wolf-Wendel, Ward, & Kinzie, 2009, p. 412). Sounds like *involvement*, doesn't it? Note, however, that engagement presupposes student success; it's completely feasible to be *involved in* an academic or social activity of college while failing to succeed in that endeavor. Second, engagement relates to how institutions invest resources and structure learning opportunities to "encourage students to participate in and benefit from such activities" (Wolf-Wendel, Ward, & Kinzie, 2009, p. 413). In consonance with the definition of engagement in the *Oxford English Dictionary* (i.e., "to bargain, make a contract, an agreement that parties enter into"), college students' engagement has two key elements: what institutions do and what students do. Interestingly, Astin (1999) made the exact opposite point when explaining involvement; involvement, he said, turns attention from what educators (or institutions) do to what the student does. A consistent stream of studies has shown that high levels of student engagement in a wide range of educationally purposeful activities (e.g., faculty–student collaborations, service-learning, study abroad) are positively associated with student learning and development across a variety of domains including appreciation of diversity, critical thinking, social responsibility, and character development, to name a few (Bridges, Kinzie, Nelson Laird, & Kuh , 2008; Kuh, 1993; Kuh, Kinzie, Schuh, Whitt, & Associates, 2005; Strayhorn, 2008b).

In light of these conceptual distinctions, I focus on *involvement* (i.e., what students do) in this chapter and the role that involvement plays in facilitating students' sense of belonging in college. Later, I turn my attention to identifying what college student educators and their employing institutions can do (i.e., engagement) to encourage students' involvement in programs and services designed to produce desired outcomes. I hope you found this discussion useful in clarifying the differences between these two terms. Now, let's talk about the studies that inform the present chapter.

THE STUDIES

Since I was interested in examining the relationship between involvement and students' sense of belonging in college, I drew upon several studies that provided information related to that topic. Specifically, I accessed data from four research studies in which I have been engaged over the past six years. The first of these was a national analysis of survey data from the College Students Experiences Questionnaire (CSEQ). The CSEQ consists of 191 items designed to measure the quality and quantity of students' involvement in college activities and their use of college facilities. For example, several items elicited information about students' involvement in a series of college activities (e.g., studying, working on research, discussing problems with faculty) that have been shown to contribute positively to college students' learning and development (Astin, 1993; Kuh, Vesper, Connolly, & Pace, 1997). In keeping with the theoretical assumptions discussed in the previous section (as well as Chapter 2 of this volume), the CSEQ instrument was developed based on the notion that "the more effort students expend in using the resources and opportunities an institution provides for their learning and development, the more they benefit" (Gonyea, Kish, Kuh, Muthiah, & Thomas, 2003, p. 14). The survey has consistent reliability and validity across various student samples and I have used it extensively in my prior research (Pascarella & Terenzini, 2005; Strayhorn, 2008b, 2008d).

Despite its widespread use and my familiarity with the CSEQ, I grew (and continue to grow) increasingly frustrated with the limits of using existing surveys in college impact research generally and in "sense of belonging research" specifically. To be sure, existing surveys can be mined in rigorous and meaningful ways to yield findings that advance our collective understanding of an important topic. In fact, I highly recommend the use of existing surveys and secondary databases in college student research elsewhere (Strayhorn, 2009b). But even then, I note that gains associated with using existing surveys or national databases (e.g., increased generalizability, time saved from piloting and testing new scales) "come at the expense of specificity to some degree" (Strayhorn, 2009b, p. 111). Researchers who use existing surveys and scales have limited options available from which to operationalize certain constructs; their choices are constrained by decisions made by the survey's designers. When using locally constructed surveys, however, "researchers have more control over the way in which variables are measured" (p. 111). So, in 2009, I set out to develop a *sense of belonging in college* scale that better fitted the needs of my research program and reflected more closely my conceptual, literal, and theoretical understanding of the concept. Much of this has been published elsewhere (e.g., Strayhorn, 2011a, 2011b), so suffice it to say that I developed a multi-item measure of college students' sense of belonging, each item typically placed on a seven-point scale ranging from "strongly disagree" to "strongly agree." Sample items included: *I feel a sense of belonging on campus*; *My friends would miss me if I left college*; and *I feel cared about by someone at* [said institution], to name a few. The second study discussed in the next section was designed to elicit information from over 700 colleges students using this newly created scale.

A third study consisted of extensive one-on-one or group interviews with college students on multiple campuses across the country, hoping to understand the nature of their academic and social experiences in higher education contexts. In short, I worked with members of my research teams to conduct in-depth interviews with willing participants over a 12-month period. Interviews were conducted in a way to elicit stories from each participant about his or her experiences since stories reflect human consciousness (Vygotsky, 1987). On average, interviews lasted 70 minutes, ranging from as few as 45 to as many as 200 minutes. Some interviews took longer because some participants needed more time to explain their collegiate experiences, clarify the meaning and significance of "critical" moments (e.g., "turning points" for them), and/or to work through strong emotions (e.g., deep sighs, crying) that were evoked by their recollections. Ambiguities and contradictions were resolved by follow-up correspondence with interviewees by phone, email, or in person where possible. As we wished our interviews to be candid, we promised all participants confidentiality. In the next section, I use pseudonyms selected by the student to share verbatim quotes that reflect their belonging experiences.

The fourth and final study referenced in this chapter was based on Astin's (1999) suggestion for researchers to use "time diaries" to determine "the relative importance of various objects and activities to the student" (p. 527). Specifically, I recruited a sample of 60 college students from two large, four-year, predominantly White institutions and 20 students from a four-year, private, historically Black college located in the southern region of the country. Participants were asked to keep a "time diary" (i.e., a log of their daily activities) for two weeks, using an electronic calendar provided to them by the researcher. Using an electronic calendar system made it easy for students to log their information wherever convenient for them; all participants logged information at some point during the two weeks. Follow-up interviews were conducted with participants to explore *why* they devoted time to the activities noted on their log. While everyone submitted "some" information during the online time diary phase, only 45 students reported complete information for both phases. In the next section, I use descriptive statistics to summarize how college students use their time and qualitative techniques to reveal *why* they devote time and energy to such activities, with a particular eye toward sense of belonging in college.

INVOLVEMENT AND SENSE OF BELONGING

Findings from the CSEQ analysis can be grouped into two major themes. First, I uncovered consistent evidence to support my initial hypothesis that there is a positive relationship between involvement in academic and social activities and students' belonging in college. Translated, this simply means that students who report being frequently involved in meaningful college activities also tended to report a greater sense of belonging in college, as measured by the CSEQ. Correlations between various involvement activities and students' sense of belonging in college ranged from –0.006 to 0.469. For instance, students who were involved in campus clubs, organizations, and committees tended to have a greater sense of belonging in college than their peers who were not involved in clubs or were involved less frequently. Figure 10.1 illustrates this positive relationship graphically, using data from 8000 students who responded to the CSEQ national administration.

Involvement in campus sport-related activities also was positively correlated with sense of belonging in college. Said differently, students who devoted time and energy to using "campus recreational facilities" or playing "team sport[s]" also tended to feel a stronger sense of belonging in college than their peers who reported less involvement in such activities. Figures 10.2 and 10.3 illustrate this relationship.

Not only do students benefit in terms of sense of belonging when they engage their peers in educationally purposeful ways (e.g., through clubs and sport-related activities), but students may also derive a sense of belonging from socializing with faculty members outside of class. Socializing with faculty encompasses a variety of activities and experiences, ranging from a mere conversation over coffee (one of my favorite pastimes!) to attending a social gathering at their home, just to name a few. Figure 10.4 summarizes this information in visual form.

Interestingly, I uncovered a convex relationship between the number of hours students devote to out-of-class academic work and their sense of belonging in college, as Figure 10.5 indicates. Results suggest that students benefit in terms of sense of belonging when they devote time and energy to out-of-class academic work up to the point of 20 hours per week, which

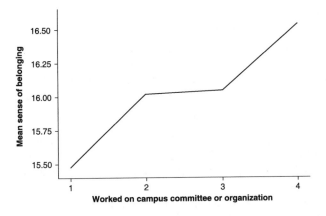

Figure 10.1 Graphic representation of the relationship between the frequency with which students worked on a campus committee or organization and their sense of belonging in college, as measured by the CSEQ.

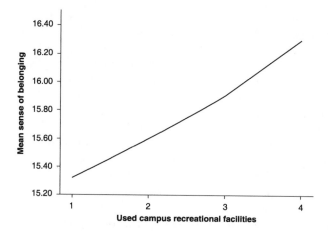

Figure 10.2   Graphic representation of the relationship between the frequency with which students used campus recreational facilities and their sense of belonging in college, as measured by the CSEQ.

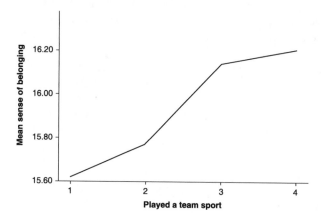

Figure 10.3   Graphic representation of the relationship between the frequency with which students played a team sport and their sense of belonging in college, as measured by the CSEQ.

represents a sort of "tipping point" beyond which the benefits of studying turn into "costs" or a loss of a sense of belonging in college. It is also interesting to muse about what happens at the 30 hours or more mark, where belonging scores rise again.

A second major theme of results from the CSEQ analysis is that involvement has a direct influence on students' sense of belonging in college. I have mentioned this a few times earlier in the book, but the weight of statistical evidence (e.g., correlations, regression, and structural equation modeling)

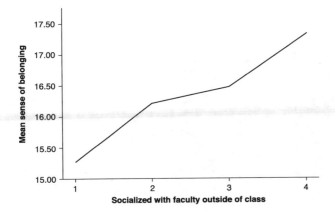

Figure 10.4 Graphic representation of the relationship between the frequency with which students socialized with faculty outside of class and their sense of belonging in college, as measured by the CSEQ.

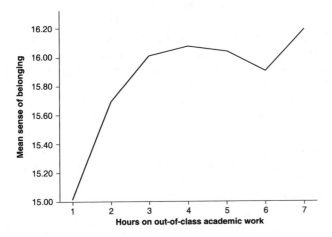

Figure 10.5 Graphic representation of the relationship between the number of hours students devote to out-of-class academic work and their sense of belonging in college, as measured by the CSEQ.

suggests that students who devote sufficient physical time and psychological energy to college activities subsequently feel a stronger sense of belonging in college. Path coefficients ranged from 0.14 to 0.33.

Other data were collected using the sense of belonging scale that I developed. Specifically, I designed a survey to elicit information about students' pre-collegiate personal histories, involvement experiences in college, and their subjective evaluations of college. Findings from this study lend further support to my initial hunch that there was a positive relationship between

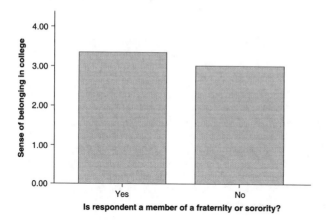

Figure 10.6   Sense of belonging in college by fraternity/sorority member status.

involvement and students' sense of belonging in college, even when using a newer multi-item scale. Correlations in this study ranged from –0.010 to 0.571. For instance, students who were involved in fraternities or sororities, as well as athletic teams, tended to have a greater sense of belonging in college than their peers who were not involved in such activities or were involved less frequently. Figure 10.6 summarizes this information in visual form.

To build upon the survey findings discussed to this point, I analyzed data from a set of semi-structured interviews that I conducted with college students a few years ago, paying particular attention to cues about their involvement experiences and sense of belonging in college. Three major findings are worth noting here. First, interview participants seemed to believe that involvement in campus activities facilitated their sense of belonging in college; in several instances participants referred to sense of belonging as their primary motivation for "becoming involved on campus." Second, stories from participants revealed four ways that involvement engenders students' sense of belonging in college: (1) connecting students with others who share their interests, values, and commitments; (2) familiarizing students with the campus environment and ecology; (3) affirming students' identity, interests, and values as "a part of campus" (in the words of a participant); and (4) generating feelings among students that they matter and others depend on them. Third, some participants spoke, at length, about the fact that "not all involvement is good" and some forms or levels of involvement can diminish, if not remove, one's sense of belonging in college. Several of these themes are discussed in more detail, along with verbatim quotes, in the next section.

Comments from participants lend additional support to my claim that involvement is positively related to students' sense of belonging in college. A majority of the participants shared that they did not begin to feel like "part of the campus" until they were involved in a few clubs, organizations, or campus activities such as student government, intramural sports, fraternities/sororities, or connected to others through class activities. Others referred to sense of belonging as their primary motivation for "joining clubs," "attending meetings," or "becoming involved on campus." For instance, Janice and Flip are both juniors (i.e., third-year students) at a medium-sized liberal arts college in the Midwest. When asked about their collegiate experiences, they shared the following:

> Well, I grew up in Pine Grove, Alabama [a pseudonym] ... it's a small town with only like a thousand residents. It's rural and a lot of the people in my neighborhood growing up worked at this cardboard manufacturing plant or one of the fast food joints in the town. Very few had gone to college and I'm definitely the first in my family to go to college. When I got here, I was really worried ... wondering if I would make friends with people, if they'd accept me although I don't have a lot of money like some of them, and if I would even want to stay around after my first year. I definitely wanted to fit in, so I got involved and joined a couple of organizations like the 4-H club, a reading club, and the pre-vet society.
>
> *(Janice)*

> A lot of the guys on my hall first year were upperclassmen, like juniors and seniors mostly. I would watch them come and go all day long and sometimes I'd stop one of them and ask, "What should I do to get adjusted around here?" A few of them would brush me off [laughing], but a couple of the guys plus my RA [resident assistant] encouraged me to get into a few clubs. I just remember going to the involvement fair thinking, "Here goes ... let's see if this will make me feel any better."
>
> *(Flip)*

By devoting physical time and psychological energy to becoming involved in college, students pursued and subsequently satisfied their goal or need to belong. In fact, some students are driven or motivated to become involved in college activities as a way of establishing a sense of belonging on campus. Mattering—"the feeling that others depend on us, are interested in us, are concerned with our fate, or experience us as an ego-extension" (Rosenberg & McCullough, 1981, p. 165)—can act as a motive in this way. Recall from Chapter 3 that mattering has several dimensions: attention, dependence, importance, and ego-extension.

Data from my interview participants revealed four ways that involvement engenders students' sense of belonging in college. Specifically, involvement was an important mechanism for (1) **community** or connecting students with others who share their interests, values, and commitments; (2) familiarizing students with the new campus environment and ecology; (3) **membership** or affirming students' identity, interests, and values as "a part of campus;" and (4) **mattering** or generating feelings among students that they matter and others depend on them. The following quotes illustrate these points in powerful ways:

> It really helped to meet other students through the organization. If I hadn't joined it, I don't think I would have ever met them because I wouldn't know how we would ever end up in the same place. Don't get me wrong, we share things in common but we really wouldn't have known that without the ensemble. It was definitely helpful for connecting me with them.
>
> *(Tiffanye, first-year undecided major)*

> Remember earlier when I was talking about being overwhelmed by the size of the place? [Interviewer mumbles yes] Well, that's what I mean. [Interviewer: Can you say more?] I mean that's just it ... I got involved so I could get to know the place, figure where stuff was located, and learn my way around and stuff.
>
> *(Henry, first-year pre-business major)*

> Black Voices is just what it says ... Black voices. With so many Black voices in a single place like [where the choir practices weekly] on any given Tuesday, singing songs like "Live Like It's Your Last Time" or "Look How Far We've Come," it's hard not to leave empowered with a sense of pride. All of the songs tell part of the story of Black people's struggle to make it. Man, I got chills at the spring concert ... so even though you're just singing a song or giving a concert, you feel connected to those around you ... in very real ways.
>
> *(Ty, fourth-year tourism and marketing major)*

> I don't think a lot of people know how it feels to be in [said organization], especially as a Black student here. It's easy to feel like you're alone when walking around campus because there are so few Black people here. As a music major, I don't even see Black students in most of my theory classes, and there's only one Black music professor and he's part-time. But [working with the club] helps me feel like I matter ... well, we [Black people] matter to [said university].
>
> *(Malika, second-year music and history double-major)*

Involvement in college enabled students to connect with other students, become familiar with the campus setting, and affirm their identities, interests, and values as a member of the campus community. All of this generated a feeling among students that they matter to others and others depend on them, which are main features of students' sense of belonging in college.

Before I turn attention to the time diary students, it's important to note an unanticipated finding from the interview study. Some participants spoke, at length, about the fact that "not all involvement is good" and some forms or levels of involvement can actually diminish, if not remove, one's sense of belonging in college. For instance, some women explained how devoting too much time to sororities, particularly during the "pledging" process, can divert attention from studying, reading for class, and socializing with peers

Table 10.1 Average time college students devote to various activities

Activity	Hours per week (mean)
Talking or texting on cellphone	13.0
Participating in sports or related activities	5.0
Working on campus/club committees	3.5
Using Facebook or MySpace	8.0
Studying for class	11.0
Sleeping	34.0

and faculty, all of which relate to college students' sense of belonging. As another example, some students of color talked about feeling like "one in the number," "strangers in an unknown land," or "the only [colored] face in a sea of Whiteness." For some, involvement provided a way to reduce, if not eliminate, such feelings. For others, involvement simply made them more aware of the differences between "us and them" (e.g., Black and White, rich and poor). Growing awareness of the differences seemed to heighten concerns about safety, support, and belonging.

Recall that the fourth study was based on Astin's (1999) suggestion for researchers to use "time diaries" to determine "the relative importance of various objects and activities to the student" (p. 527). Generally speaking, students devote considerable physical time and psychological energy to a vast array of activities in college. Table 10.1 presents a summary of this information.

As with the previous studies, there was an implied positive relationship between involvement in college and sense of belonging here. A number of participants explained that the impetus for their involvement in campus activities (e.g., sports, clubs) was forming a sense of belonging in college. Taken together, data from my four studies suggest that involvement in college engenders (or inhibits) sense of belonging for students.

DISCUSSION

Recall that the focus of this chapter was on involvement (i.e., what students do) and the role that involvement plays in facilitating students' sense of belonging in college. Using data from four studies, I examined the statistical association between students' involvement and their sense of belonging in college, as well as the reasons for their involvement in campus activities. Qualitative data were analyzed to unpack the meaning and significance of their involvement experiences. Key findings were identified and reported in the previous section. Here, I highlight a few of these findings and their implications for educational policy and practice. Specifically, I direct attention to identifying what college student educators and their employing institutions can do (i.e., engagement) to encourage students' involvement in programs and services designed to produce desired outcomes.

Involvement in college is positively associated with students' sense of belonging in college. Time and time again, I found statistically significant positive correlations between students' involvement in various campus activities (e.g., working on a committee/organization) and their perceived sense of support and belonging on campus. Like Astin (1999) and others after him (e.g., Kuh, Palmer, & Kish, 2003), I have found that the more involved students are in the academic and social activities of campus life, the more they gain from such involvement. Even more to the point, I have found that the more involved students are in college life (e.g., working with peers, socializing with faculty, using a campus recreational center), the greater their sense of support, acceptance, and—dare I say—*belonging* in college.

Not only have these studies provided substantial support to bolster my argument that involvement is positively correlated with sense of belonging in college, but they also produce persuasive evidence to suggest that involvement facilitates sense of belonging in college. In fact, for many college students, sense of belonging may serve as a motive or catalyst for their involvement in various campus activities. Echoing Baumeister and Leary (1995), I believe that sense of belonging characterizes an individual's need for frequent and consistent interactions with others to feel a part of something greater than themselves; sense of belonging is a motivation sufficient to drive human behavior. So, it's because students want to belong, to feel a part of, to feel valued, respected, and connected to others that they invest physical and psychological energy toward campus activities. It's because they want—no, *need*—to matter that some students take the initial step by attending involvement fairs, participate regularly on committees and task forces, or play on team sports. Generally speaking, involvement in campus activities engenders a sense of belonging in college.

It's important to point out two subtle, yet important, nuances in the story here. First, not all forms of involvement facilitate students' sense of belonging in college. And second, not all forms of involvement facilitate a stronger sense of belonging in college; some forms may actually exacerbate feelings of alienation. Recall that I uncovered a convex relationship between involvement in studying and sense of belonging, with optimal conditions being less than 20 hours per week. Devoting time beyond that threshold is not wise counsel. The same seems to be true for working off-campus, working more than 20 hours per week, and being rejected as a member of a fraternity or sorority. Of course, some of these are inevitable or beyond the control of students. So college student educators and academic spotters (see Chapter 8) are encouraged to be aware of how these experiences can diminish or disrupt students' sense of belonging and they may need additional triage or support.

These results have significant implications for policy and practice. First, education policymakers might consider this information when formulating new policies that encourage student involvement in campus life. For instance, policymakers could use information from this chapter to implement or justify policies that limit the number of hours that students can work (for pay) on- or off-campus. Of course, it would be unwise to enact such policies, which could disproportionately affect low-income and "no income" students, who enter college with a dire need to earn income. Institutions might offer need- and merit-based aid to make up for such restrictions.

Other policies might provide guidance to students about the important role that involvement plays in their academic success, as well as provide information to academic advisors, counselors, and faculty about the value that involvement adds to one's college experience. It has been my experience that some faculty, especially in science, technology, engineering, and math (STEM) fields, struggle to apprehend the value that involvement adds to students' experiences. The link and "secret sauce" may be our common desire for students to succeed.

Several implications for practice are worth noting. For instance, if involvement is positively correlated with students' sense of belonging in college, it might be important to identify students whose sense of belonging is low and to make special efforts early on to foster their inclusion through involvement and to help them develop academic and social skills. Consistent with the chapter's discussion of involvement and engagement, interventions aimed at increasing young adults' sense of belonging can be focused on the individual and organizational level. Individuals can be provided training in social skills, especially in cases where students' perceived low level of support is due to their inability to get along with others or to interact with others in constructive, purposeful ways. Armed with this information, I firmly believe that we can enact policies, enhance programs and services, as well as establish conditions on campus that matter for promoting students' sense of belonging.

By this point, you've likely realized that I have devoted a considerable amount of space to attempting to distinguish the differences between *involvement* and *engagement* in higher education. I did so to avoid conflating these terms as some previous authors have advised (Wolf-Wendel, Ward, & Kinzie, 2009) and to substantiate the claims that I made when describing the book's theoretical underpinnings (see Chapters 2 and 3). Although I would encourage readers to avoid losing sleep over these conceptual distinctions, I think they are instructive for our understanding of students' sense of belonging and should be preserved in future research on this phenomenon. Remember, even Astin (1999) admitted that "involvement ... should not be either mysterious or esoteric" (p. 518). He later shared with me, personally, that he's always thought the two terms were generally similar and shared a

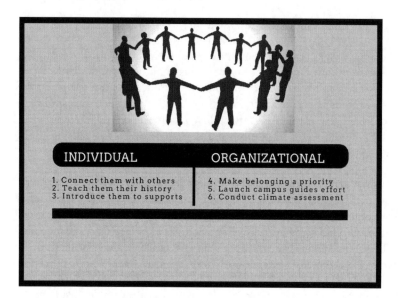

Figure 10.7   Belonging involvement strategies.

number of qualities in common (A. Astin, personal communication, March 13, 2011). Hopefully, one thing is fairly crystal-clear: that what students do (involvement) can engender or diminish students' sense of belonging in college, which may provide clues about what institutions can do (engagement) to encourage students' sense of belonging in college. Untangling that relationship is far more important to the purposes of this book than untangling the "tangled web of terms" (Wolf-Wendel, Ward, & Kinzie, 2009). Figure 10.7 offers a few more ideas for each plane of action.

Chapter 11

Epilogue

What better way to end the second edition of a book than to return to its beginning again. Recall that the book has several main purposes. First, the Introduction and leading chapters were designed to review the extant literature on sense of belonging and critique that literature in light of new and emerging theory. Second, the book's review of literature served as a foundation for synthesizing several theoretical threads and conceptual components that represent the book's overarching organizing framework or model in Chapter 3. Third, the book presents new and relatively recent research findings from quantitative, qualitative, and mixed-methods studies conducted by the author as a way of demonstrating empirical linkages between determinants of belonging, sense of belonging itself, and educational antecedents such as grades, self-efficacy, adjustment, retention, and satisfaction, to name a few. And, finally, *College Students' Sense of Belonging* offers college student educators what's really needed by translating research into better practice—practical recommendations for improving educational environments, practices, policies, and programs in ways that facilitate students' sense of belonging on campus.

Throughout this volume, I have argued the importance of college students' sense of belonging as a critical dimension of their success. Using findings from research as support, I framed sense of belonging as a basic human need that takes on heightened significance at times, posited a model for sense of belonging, and described the various ways in which sense of belonging relates to the collegiate experiences of various groups ranging from Latino students to gay men of color, from science, technology, engineering, and math (STEM) students to graduate students in higher education. To do this, a working definition of sense of belonging was needed and it is re-presented in the next section for review.

RECAP OF WORKING DEFINITION

Throughout this book, sense of belonging is framed as a basic human need and motivation, sufficient to influence behavior. Sense of belonging is part of a larger motivational framework and my approach to sense of belonging reflects a social cognitive perspective that is grounded in social psychology. Consequently, sense of belonging is believed to be created, constructed, experienced, imagined, and produced in reciprocal relationship with others. In terms of college, sense of belonging refers to students' perceived social support on campus, a feeling or sensation of connectedness, the experience of mattering or feeling cared about, accepted, respected, valued by, and important to the group (e.g., campus community) or others on campus (e.g., faculty, staff, peers). As discussed in the opening chapter, it is a cognitive evaluation that typically leads to an affective and/or behavioral response(s).

Sense of belonging is also relational and there's a reciprocal quality to relationships that provide a sense of belonging. Each member benefits from the group and the group benefits from the contributions of each member. It's the proverbial "I am we and we are each" phenomenon. Under optimal conditions, members feel that the group is important to them and that they are important to the group. The group satisfies the needs of the individual—in exchange for membership, they will be cared for and supported. For that, the individual offers the group time, energy, attention, and loyalty. Thus, in essence, sense of belonging is a "feeling that members matter to one another and to the group, and a **shared faith** that members' needs will be met through their commitment to be together" (McMillan & Chavis, 1986, p. 9). That's actually really powerful; think about it in terms of first-generation college students who enter college *trusting* that they will matter to the group (others on campus) and in exchange for becoming a "[fill in the name of any mascot/campus here]" they will be cared for and supported. Think back to the "Moving Email" episode in Chapter 2; if you've forgotten, look back now before moving on.

With this operational definition in plain view, it is clearly implied throughout the book that sense of belonging is not only a basic human need but a compelling motivation sufficient to drive behavior and beliefs or perceptions. Other core elements of sense of belonging were discussed earlier in the book and they are reviewed in the next section as a segue into the theoretical model.

CORE ELEMENTS OF BELONGING REVISITED

In Chapter 3, I identified seven core elements of sense of belonging and explained each in the context of existing literature and how they applied to the main thesis of this book. Here they are again for your reading pleasure. I've always thought that purposeful redundancy could be an effective teaching strategy; reviews of the first edition praised this aspect of the book so I preserved some of the redundancy *intentionally* in this edition.

1. *Sense of belonging is a basic human need.* The need for belongingness is universal and applies to all people. Satisfying the need for belonging is a necessary precondition for higher-order needs such as the desire for knowledge, understanding, and self-actualization (Maslow, 1962), all of which are related to the consummate goals of higher education. Everybody wants to belong. College students and K-12 students alike. Students who score high on the ACT exam and those who score single digits want to feel cared about and valuable. Student leaders, athletes, high-achievers, and even those who are frequently "in trouble" want to matter and be celebrated for good reasons. It's not a matter of race—all students, White, Black, Latino, Asian, Native American, mixed race, and more want to feel a sense of belonging in college. It is not always an *expressed need*, but it is a clear and present need of all people.

2. *Sense of belonging is a fundamental motive, sufficient to drive human behavior.* Sense of belonging is not only a basic human need, but it also is a motive that can affect human behavior(s). Needing to belong compels individuals to act in ways that can be appropriate, healthy, and productive as well as anti-social, unhealthy, and risky. All people want to feel cared about, needed, important, and valued; most are willing to do whatever it takes to satisfy this need. In pursuit of it, some people will scale a wall, jump from Mt. Everest, marry a partner (or divorce one), join a club or gang, pay dues for a fraternity or tuition for college, enter the military or enter university as a returning military veteran. Remember, even "Uncle Sam" uses the message of belonging to compel others to come (see Figure 11.1).

3. *Sense of belonging takes on heightened importance* (a) *in certain contexts*, such as being a newcomer to an otherwise established group, (b) *at certain times*, such as (late) adolescence when individuals begin to consider who they are (or wish to be), with whom they belong, and where they intend to invest their time and energies in the future (Chickering & Reisser, 1993; Sanford, 1962), and (c) *among certain populations*, especially those who are marginalized or inclined to feel excluded, invisible, irrelevant, or "left out" in said context (for more, see Goodenow, 1993a). The experience of belonging is context-dependent, such that sense of belonging in a particular context like a department or classroom has the greatest influence on outcomes such as adjustment, achievement, or learning in *that* area. Applied to

higher education, I have argued that some college students face serious difficulty in attending to tasks like studying, learning, or retaining information until they resolve one of their most fundamental needs—a need to belong. Part of this makes good sense in terms of classic psychological theory—when students do not feel like they belong some *cognitive resources* are taken up mulling over the absence of that basic need and even more energy is exhausted thinking through how to find it. All those resources are preoccupied with this process and, thus, cannot be used for other purposes like focusing on the lecture, completing

Figure 11.1 Sign displaying "You Belong Here" with Uncle Sam.

the lab, acing the test, running for student office, making new friends, interviewing well for a job, or simply staying in college.

4. *Sense of belonging is related to, and seemingly a consequence of, mattering.* The weight of empirical evidence, much of it cited in this volume, lends fairly persuasive evidence to support the idea that mattering matters. Interactions with others that are affectively positive or pleasant are necessary but not sufficient for experiencing belongingness. To satisfy the need for belongingness, the person must believe one cares selflessly about their welfare and success. Mattering has several major components: attention, dependence, ego-extension, importance, and sometimes, appreciation. Figure 11.2 presents key elements.

5. *Social identities intersect and affect college students' sense of belonging.* Although the need for belongingness is universal and applies to all people, it does not necessarily apply to all people equally. Quite often, social identities converge and intersect in ways that simultaneously influence sense of belonging. To understand students' belonging experiences, one must pay close attention to issues of identity, identity salience or "core self," ascendancy of certain motives, and even social contexts that exert influence on these considerations.

6. *Sense of belonging engenders other positive outcomes.* Satisfying the need to belong leads to a plethora of positive and/or prosocial outcomes such as engagement, achievement, wellbeing, happiness, and

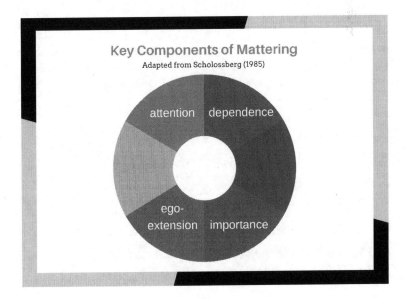

Figure 11.2   Mattering elements.

optimal functioning in a particular context or domain. Failure to satisfy this need often leads to depression, grief, unhappiness, loneliness, or suicidal ideation and attempts (Baumeister & Leary, 1995; Joiner, 2010). It's almost that simple.

7. *Sense of belonging must be satisfied on a continual basis and likely changes as circumstances, conditions, and contexts change.* The need to belong can be satisfied by a few meaningful attachments that engender feelings of appreciation, love, and respect that ultimately fuel belongingness. Over time and through various experiences, students' sense of belonging, of personal acceptance, or having a rightful, valued place in a particular social context tends to stabilize and consistently influence one's beliefs, commitments, feelings, and behaviors. Keep in mind that perceived belongingness may change as context, circumstances, settings, and people change. A college students' closest friend or faculty-advisor could change institutions overnight or students could transfer institutions between semesters and finding a sense of belonging starts all over again.

This is just a brief summary of the seven core elements of sense of belonging (see Figure 11.3). Consider these as you contemplate the proposed model of college students' sense of belonging, which is lightly covered in the next section.

Belonging Model Revisited

In an attempt to avoid redundancy, I'm not going to say much about the book's model, which was outlined in Chapter 3. If questions linger or you need to be reminded of a key component, I encourage you to flip back a

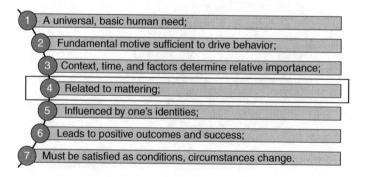

1. A universal, basic human need;
2. Fundamental motive sufficient to drive behavior;
3. Context, time, and factors determine relative importance;
4. Related to mattering;
5. Influenced by one's identities;
6. Leads to positive outcomes and success;
7. Must be satisfied as conditions, circumstances change.

Figure 11.3   Key elements of sense of belonging.

few pages and re-read that section. And, for ease, here's another graphical representation of the model (Figure 11.4).

Generally speaking, the model suggests the essence of college students' sense of belonging, using Maslow's (1954) hierarchy of needs as a foundation around which I wrapped additional theoretical insights about the consummate goal of higher education and the maximum potential of students. Students enter various social spaces associated with college life (e.g., classroom, department, club/organization, off-campus group) longing for these basic needs and that motivates or drives behavior(s) to satisfy those needs. Satisfaction of physiological and safety needs, for example, gives way to belongingness needs (in college) and, should these more fundamental needs be satisfied, individuals achieve esteem and self-actualization and even higher-order needs like creativity, spontaneity, self-authorship, and integrity. Deprivation of belongingness needs can lead to unhealthy or negative outcomes, prevent individuals from dealing with the academic tasks at hand (e.g., knowledge, writing), and thwart personal growth. Concerns about safety that arise can lead to regression from higher needs to more basic needs, as outlined in the model.

College students' needs emerge in various college contexts. Some attempt to whet their "belonging appetite" by becoming involved in campus clubs and organizations (see Chapter 10), establishing relationships with supportive others, learning the values of the profession to which they aspire (see Chapter 8), or engaging in any number of belonging experiences, as shared in short vignettes throughout the book. Altogether, sense of belonging serves as a determinant of students' behaviors, recruiting all capacities of the individual in service to achieving that feeling in college. Those who satisfy their need to belong in college are rewarded by positive outcomes such as achievement, growth, persistence, and happiness. Since publication of the first edition, I have met literally hundreds of alumni across the

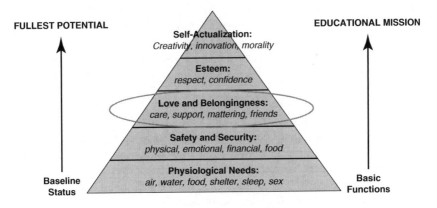

Figure 11.4 Revised model of college students' sense of belonging.

country whose reflections converge on a single point: students who feel a sense of belonging in college become happy, *generous* alumni; those who do not, don't.

With all of this back in your mind, let me make several recommendations for practice and move to future directions for this work.

RECOMMENDATIONS FOR POLICY, PRACTICE, AND RESEARCH

A careful review of each and every sentence in this book would reveal that applications to policy, practice, and research are countless. By this point in the book, I have recommended hundreds of ways in which policy decisions, educational practices, and research studies can facilitate college students' sense of belonging. Federal policymakers making tough decisions like expanding the size and amount of Pell Grants is not just a way of opening access for economically disadvantaged students, but also signaling to them that they matter *even on the minds of* politicians in Washington. Building accessible buildings on campus for students living with disabilities isn't just about compliance with ADA legislation but it satisfies students' safety, security needs, and core elements of sense of belonging theory like feeling cared about, thought of, and included. And since writing the first edition of this book, I have given hundreds of lectures on belonging in front of campus leaders and policymakers alike who have helped me think about multiple ways to "legislate belonging," as I like to say. For instance, policies that establish new or expand existing summer bridge, early outreach, TRIO, or peer mentoring programs respond to findings that show how important these interventions can be for fostering students' sense of belonging in college. Federal policies that aim to make college campuses more safe and secure, like Title IX or the Clery Act, help improve students' sense of belonging in the long run; remember, it's impossible to feel like you belong in a place that's unsafe and threatening. And while *all students have insecurities* of some sort, physical insecurity about the campus or classroom and their sense of belonging in college shouldn't be one of them. Figure 11.5 provides a starting point for more ideas.

Sense of belonging has implications for campus strategic planning. Most administrators have led, participated in, or been involved in strategic planning. If one hasn't yet, just keep living, as they say—it is almost inevitable because strategic planning in higher education almost always accompanies organizational changes like getting a new president, provost, dean, supervisor, or any new-wave effort to attempt climbing higher in the *U.S. News & World Report* rankings. Strategic planning, done well, can be highly effective. And I think strategic planning executed effectively becomes the

Ways to "Legislate Belonging" in Higher Education

Since the first edition of this book, there has been tremendous interest in college students' sense of belonging as a strategy for "moving the needle" on student success rates. College presidents, provosts, deans, and even university trustees have expressed strong support for the idea and crave recommendations for "doing something" about it. But, quite honestly, I have struggled to think of clear policy connections until now. Working to finish this edition opened my eyes to new and different ways to "legislate belonging," as I like to say. Here's a list of a few ideas to jump-start the thinking of others:

1. Food policies that promote equitable access to fresh foods and produce, even for homeless, hungry, or foster youth in college help to foster belonging by satisfying students most basic needs first;
2. Campus conduct policies that reduce bias, prohibit discrimination, and reduce social isolation of students, especially ethnic minorities, LGBTQ, undocumented, and immigrants can impact sense of belonging by ensuring safety and security: implicit bias training, safe zones, inclusive non-discrimination clauses are recommended;
3. Funding policies that ensure equitable distribution of resources to all student groups—regardless of popularity or power—help to "level the playing field" between majority groups and smaller clubs that provide a sense of belonging for minoritized groups;
4. HR policies for staff evaluation that acknowledge and reward time/energy devoted to helping students, connecting with families, or going "beyond the call of duty" can help encourage a focus on belonging;
5. Tenure and promotion policies that encourage intrusive advising, faculty mentoring, and time-intensive work with students help to foster sense of belonging.

Figure 11.5   Ideas about legislating belonging.

framework for day-to-day management of an academic unit, campus, or school. Over the last few years, I have consulted with nearly two dozen campuses where sense of belonging was the focus of their strategic plan. Campuses like Colgate University, Kent State University, Triton College, and the University of Missouri System, to name a few, all have taken strategic steps to make their campus more welcoming, supportive, and familiar to students as a way of creating sense of belonging. In most cases, the need for improving sense of belonging on campus came from institutional efforts to assess campus climate, the nature of relationships, or students' experiences. Figure 11.6 is a screenshot from a university's printed strategic plan that clearly shows how importantly it ranked.

EPISODE 11.1

Sense of Belonging in Action

"Campus Strategic Plans"

Strategic planning executed effectively becomes the framework for day-to-day management of the unit. With this information in mind, respond to each of the following:

1. Where does sense of belonging fit within the larger goals/objectives of the campus shown in Figure 11.6?
2. Strategic plans vary in the extent to which they reference the literature upon which most assertions stand; what's the literature that supports the primacy of sense of belonging in college?
3. How might the book's theoretical model serve as a logic model for developing steps to belonging for all students?

There are many implications for practice and countless examples have been shared to this point in the book. For instance, since so many students turn to campus clubs and organizations to meet their belonging needs, institutions would do well to offer a broad menu of clubs for students to join. Faculty members spend a lot of time with students and sometimes are in a position to make recommendations to students who might be struggling to find a sense of place on campus. Generally speaking, faculty don't have a good sense of all the support services and clubs available to students on campus—organizations for poets, parents, military veterans, dancers, LGBTQ, pre-law, formerly incarcerated, and students in recovery for instance. Institutions would do well to create a list of available support resources and clubs for faculty and staff members as a way of helping to build belonging.

One aspect of belonging or feeling a sense of membership on a college campus is merely *feeling part of* something and knowing something about the place. For instance, when studying the summer bridge program at the

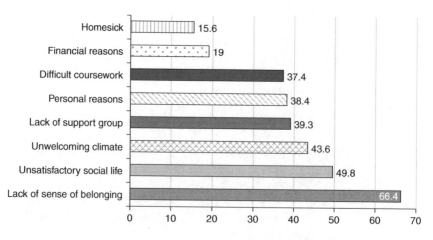

Top reasons why students seriously considered leaving

Reason	Value
Homesick	15.6
Financial reasons	19
Difficult coursework	37.4
Personal reasons	38.4
Lack of support group	39.3
Unwelcoming climate	43.6
Unsatisfactory social life	49.8
Lack of sense of belonging	66.4

Figure 11.6 Sense of belonging ranks at top for student departure causes.

University of Tennessee, Knoxville, I was impressed with the clear sense of confidence that exuded from participants in the semester immediately following the five-week program. Students shared how happy they were to help their fellow freshmen during "move-in weekend" or the first few weeks of school as so many of their peers did not know where the library was located, how to get their student ID, or even where to pick books; bridge participants learned all of this during the program and, thus, were in a position to help their peers navigate the campus. "Just that ... feeling like I already knew something about [the campus] and now could help my friends helped me feel like I really did belong there maybe," as one student explained.

There are other things that college educators can do to help students "know things" about campus or to answer their questions as a way to facilitate sense of belonging. For example, I have visited dozens of campuses and learned about online student support services. For instance, at Cornell University, there's an "Ask Ezra" website named after Ezra Cornell, the university's namesake. "Ask Ezra" uses a corpus of volunteer writers to pose and answer questions that come up for members of the campus community like: When is fall break? Where can I find tutoring? Where can I see my grades? How do I apply as an international student? For more, see Figure 11.7 and go to: www.askezra.cornell.edu. Similar websites exist or were in development (at the time of this writing) at Oregon State University, SUNY Binghamton, and Georgia State according to reliable sources.

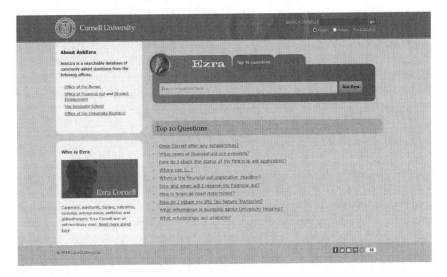

Figure 11.7   Screenshot of Ask Ezra website at Cornell University.

In keeping with this idea that sense of belonging is enhanced when students know about the institution's history, where support services are located, how to access them, and where to turn when they have questions, there is another recommended practice that I have witnessed in action: campus guides programs. Think about it. Many readers will be familiar with the experience of walking into the grocery store and someone greets you at the door asking: "May I help you?" In fact, at Walmart, the multi-national retail corporation founded by Sam Walton in the 1960s, staff greeters can be identified easily by their blue apron-like vest that reads: "How may I help you?" No matter what you're looking for or *who you are*—whether you're looking for smart TVs, doggy training pads, or K-cups by *Keurig* to stay up all night studying for physics—shoppers know they can find someone in the blue apron and ask for help. What would this look like if applied to higher education campuses? Well, one does not need to imagine this; there are examples across the country like the "Student Success Advocates" and "Outreach Ambassadors" at the University of Utah. Not only can students develop close ties with peer advocates or ask them questions, but advocates are available to "walk students to the building" or "introduce them to financial aid staff" when they're really lost or afraid. For more, visit the website: www.studentsuccess.utah.edu.

It may be less apparent but common reading programs also support sense of belonging for students. I have explained that belonging is closely connected with community—that is, a state, experience, or feeling of fellowship with others due to sharing common attitudes, beliefs, customs, interests, values, and goals. Educational communities, as Boyer (1990) explained, should be open, just, educationally purposeful and collaborative. By sharing a book in common (e.g., Ron Suskind's [1998] *Hope in the Unseen*), students have a shared experience, develop a common language about the text, can share different opinions and perspectives, and, quite frankly, have something other than "How's the weather" to jump-start casual conversation. The effects of common reading experiences are likely enhanced when organized as part of a larger, living-learning community.

Sense of belonging is correlated with college student success. Some students don't succeed because they never feel like they belong in college in the first place. It's hard to feel like you belong in a place where you don't know the rules, how things get done, and you're not even sure what is required. Several years ago, I was asked to deliver a keynote about belonging at a conference for the *deaf and hard of hearing* (DHH) community. It was my first time doing something with the DHH community and I was really anxious about it, especially since I did not know what to expect (or what was expected of me really). About a week passed after the invitation and the organization scheduled a "prep call" where we talked about various aspects of the conference: where I would stand, where the interpreter would stand, the pace at which I should speak, and where I could turn for help if I get lost. All of this reduced my anxieties, restored my confidence, and helped me feel like I mattered enough for them to coach me and set me up for success. The same is true in higher education; we help students find belonging and succeed when we're clear about our policies, expectations, what counts, and what's required for them to excel and graduate. Student orientation programs, curricular alignment efforts, transparency about campus rules (both hidden and obvious) all work to impact sense of belonging.

Creating high-touch environments where all students get at least one meaningful interaction with a faculty or staff member is another way to foster college students' sense of belonging. This need not be difficult. Knowing students' names and using them (correctly) helps build belonging. Like the old TV show *Cheers*, everybody wants to go where somebody knows their name; the same is true for college students. But there can be more. Consider the work of staff members at "Single Stop" at Monroe Community College who helped students like Tasha Gray overcome feelings of insecurity, self-doubt, and social isolation. How did they do this? Calling her by her name rather than "hey, student" or "miss" or imply that she was just another in the number. They also helped her belong by acknowledging her strengths, celebrating her successes, giving her hugs, and going out of their way to make her feel welcome. In fact, in an interview, Tasha shared that "Single Stop" staff often told her that they were "proud of [her]," which reflects *ego-extension*, a core element of mattering.

Recommendations for belonging practices also apply to the important work of academic advisors and counselors. For example, if you accept that one's mind is a major battlefield for belonging where many thoughts arise leading one to be uncertain about whether or not they belong, then one way to help facilitate belonging is to reduce such uncertainties, strengthen confidence, and affirm one's belief that they belong in college. Academic advisors and counselors can be highly effective here in helping students. Consider Dweck's (2007) notion of fixed and growth mindset. In her book, she tells the story of Loretta who migrated to the United States and tested into the non-elite kindergarten class. Later, after improved performance, Loretta was transferred to the *elite* class ("The Eagles") but never actually felt like she belonged despite achievement, awards, and high performance. Although she was physically *in* the elite class, she was *psychologically removed* (perhaps even barred) from the class, which impacted her feelings (affective) and actions (behavioral). Though in the same class, Loretta couldn't soar with the other "Eagles" (pun intended).

One thing is crystal clear: our words matter and can powerfully influence the ability of students to "see themselves" as capable, bona fide members of schooling communities. Advisors, counselors, and faculty alike would do well to avoid labeling students in ways that diminish their sense of efficacy and self: at-risk, endangered, high-risk, troubled, borderline, illegal, alien, and more. Of course, we all know that placement exams and tests scores are commonly used to make decisions about when and where students enter postsecondary education. Educators would do well to help students remember that placement doesn't predict promise or potential. That is, "where you start doesn't dictate where you'll end up," as I often say in public lectures. Students have a hard time with this—in fact, lots of people do. Left to their own devices, people often confuse the incident with intelligence—that is, if you "fail" the test then you must *be a failure*. They have a hard time distinguishing the unit from the universe. If I "lose" points on the quiz, then it follows that I must *be a loser*. The can't separate the moment from the monumental. The action (or experience) from the actor (or identity). This is where academic advisors, counselors, mentors, parents/guardians, and student personnel administrators (e.g., club advisors) can be very helpful by talking candidly with students about the difference between performance on a single assessment and potential for their ability in life. Encouraging growth mindedness over a fixed mindset may be effective in opening college students' up to the possibility of finding belonging on campus. Helping them see setbacks as motivations, effort as fuel for achievement, failure as part of the apparatus of success, and themselves as works in progress are all empirically supported strategies for nurturing growth mindedness.

There is also fairly consistent evidence suggesting proven ways for increasing students' self-efficacy or building confidence, which is correlated positively with sense of belonging. Confidence building strategies include verbal persuasion; vicarious experiences; and mastery experiences. To help college students feel like they belong, educators can persuade them verbally—just tell them that they belong. "You belong here." Or, "if I haven't told you this semester, I want you to know that you matter and belong here." In fact, I heard from a community college professor via email who heard me lecture about belonging; she shared the steps she took to communicate belonging to her students (see Figure 11.8).

FUTURE DIRECTIONS

Having written so much about college students' sense of belonging in previous journal articles and this book specifically, you might wonder what more can be said. Each chapter ends with a discussion of broader implications for the work on educational policy, practice, and, at times, research. I think it goes without saying that some strategies mentioned in this book can be difficult to mount or far too expensive to implement overnight, especially in times of financial exigency. For example, designing and implementing new summer bridge programs or STEM support centers requires money to pay instructors, meet overhead or administrative costs,

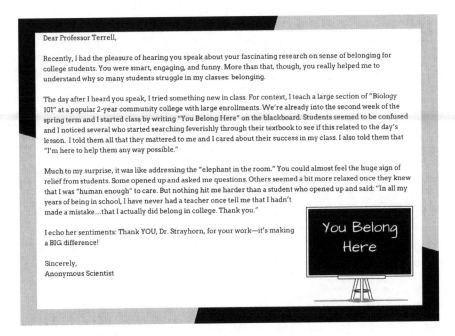

Dear Professor Terrell,

Recently, I had the pleasure of hearing you speak about your fascinating research on sense of belonging for college students. You were smart, engaging, and funny. More than that, though, you really helped me to understand why so many students struggle in my classes: belonging.

The day after I heard you speak, I tried something new in class. For context, I teach a large section of "Biology 101" at a popular 2-year community college with large enrollments. We're already into the second week of the spring term and I started class by writing "You Belong Here" on the blackboard. Students seemed to be confused and I noticed several who started searching feverishly through their textbook to see if this related to the day's lesson. I told them all that they mattered to me and I cared about their success in my class. I also told them that "I'm here to help them any way possible."

Much to my surprise, it was like addressing the "elephant in the room." You could almost feel the huge sign of relief from students. Some opened up and asked me questions. Others seemed a bit more relaxed once they knew that I was "human enough" to care. But nothing hit me harder than a student who opened up and said: "In all my years of being in school, I have never had a teacher once tell me that I hadn't made a mistake...that I actually did belong in college. Thank you."

I echo her sentiments: Thank YOU, Dr. Strayhorn, for your work—it's making a BIG difference!

Sincerely,
Anonymous Scientist

Figure 11.8 Email from community college professor.

and offer stipends to encourage student participation, as well as to alleviate their financial burden to work. Training all faculty to use culturally relevant teaching strategies or bias-free examples in their classrooms can be costly, requiring money for training curricula, materials, supplies, and consultants to facilitate that growth. Even building new cultural centers or centralizing connected support services so that students have a "wrap-around service" or "one-shop stop" experience can cost millions in renovations. Still, educators are urged to consider the recommendations shared throughout the volume, thinking of new ways to fund or support such effective interventions. Promoting college students' sense of belonging, however, need not be cost-prohibitive or resource-draining. In fact, I've said to my students and while lecturing across the country that what we lack most in such instances is not human or financial resources, it's not legal backing to pursue a compelling interest, and it's not creativity to design conditions that promote college students' sense of belonging on campus. Rather, what we tend to lack most is a collective will to do what's needed to help all students, especially those most in need. Goodwill is hard to find and even harder to manufacture; but, where there's a will, there's a way to sense of belonging.

It is my hope that this new volume has given research, policy, and practice in this area a new impetus, a sort of "shot in the arm." I urge current and future researchers, practitioners, and policymakers to sustain and build upon this momentum by extending work in this area in directions that hold promise for advancing our understanding of *College Student's Sense of Belonging: A Key to Educational Success for All Students*. If you remember nothing, remember this: every student wants to belong; with our help, they will.

Appendix A—Chapter 6

GUIDING QUESTIONS FOR SUMMER BRIDGE PROGRAM DEVELOPMENT

PHILOSOPHY

- What overarching purpose or goal does the program aim to support?
- Who is it for? (And who is it not for?)
- What would success look like, in terms of the program?
- The program is a bridge to where—summer term, academic year, undergraduate study, or the major?
- In the program in competition or collaboration with other programs and efforts on- or off-campus? List all competitors and collaborators; discuss the role they play in connection with the program under development.

PROGRAM

- What's the program's name?
- How long will it last in terms of duration—a day, a week, three weeks, five weeks, year-round?
- When will it start and when will the program end?
- Will it be residential, commuter, or some other arrangement?
- What will be the size of the program's cohort—in other words, how many students will be served?

- What will you need to successfully launch the program; think in terms of:
  - Space and residence halls
  - Course instructors
  - Courses (i.e., credit or non-credit)
  - Marketing, publicity
  - Social activities

PERSONNEL

- Who will staff the program?
- Are they paid, volunteer, or combination of both?
- Who will serve as the management team?
- Who will serve as the implementation team?
- And, who will serve as the communications/outreach team?
- Do you have someone (or a group) identified to serve as the assessment/evaluation team?

Appendix B—Chapter 6

SAMPLE SCRIPT FOR MANAGING HOME TIES

EVALUATION OF TIES

1. List relationships that are most important to you overall.
2. List relationships that are most important to you (from #1 above) in order of *significance*.
3. List relationships that are most important to you (from #1 above) in order of *proximal distance* (i.e., how close you are to them).
4. List relationships that are most important to you (from #1 above) in order of *security*—that is, the extent to which you feel secure in that relationship and its ability to persist despite distance and time.
5. Identify any relationships that are HIGH on your list in terms of *significance* but LOW on your list in terms of *security*. What does this reveal to you?
6. What else does this evaluation of relationships reveal to you?

SCRIPT FOR MANAGING TIES

1. **Identify a relationship that is significant to you, but also far away (*proximal distance*).** Usually any stress felt in this situation can be reduced by *affirming* the significance of the relationship and *acknowledging* the impact of distance on *how* that significance gets communicated. For instance, two best friends who attended the same high school might hang out after class, walk to school together, and

even share lunch when they are nearby; this becomes difficult, if not impossible, with distance. Here are a few prompts that might be helpful to students: "I want you to know that I value our friendship and, though we're apart, I still want to hear about all your fun ventures." "Now that I'm away in college, you might think it's 'out of sight, out of mind.' Well, it's not. I value our friendship and can't wait to see you when I come home for Fall Break. Until then, let's also FaceTime when you're not busy and I'm not studying."

2. Identify a relationship that is significant to you, but also LOW on your list in terms of *security*. Usually any stress felt in this situation can be reduced by *affirming* the significance of the relationship and *acknowledging* feelings of insecurity. Fill in the blank: "Hey, [put name here], I value our friendship but I'm worried that [e.g., *you'll forget about me*] while I'm in college. I don't want to let that happen and I'm willing to do what's necessary to prevent it."

References

Adelman, C. (1999). *Answers in the toolbox: Academic intensity, attendance patterns, and bachelor's degree attainment.* Washington, DC: US Department of Education, Office of Educational Research and Improvement.

Agronick, G., O'Donnell, L., Stueve, A., Doval, A. S., Duran, R., & Vargo, S. (2004). Sexual behaviors and risks among bisexually- and gay-identified young Latino men. *AIDS and Behavior, 8*(2), 185–197.

Anant, S. S. (1966). The need to belong. *Canada's Mental Health, 14,* 21–27.

Anderman, L. H. (2003). Academic and social perceptions as predictors of change in middle school students' sense of belonging. *Journal of Experimental Education, 72,* 5–23.

Anderman, L. H., & Freeman, T. M. (2004). Students' sense of belonging in school. In M. L. Maehr & P. R. Pintrich (Eds.), *Advances in motivation and achievement: Vol. 13. Motivating students, improving schools: The legacy of Carol Midgley* (pp. 27–63). Greenwich, CT: Elsevier.

Anfara, V. A., & Mertz, N. T. (2006). *Theoretical frameworks in qualitative research.* Thousand Oaks, CA: Sage.

Arbona, C., & Nora, A. (2007). The influence of academic and environmental factors on Hispanic college degree attainment. *Review of Higher Education, 30*(3), 247–269.

Astin, A. W. (1984). Student involvement: A developmental theory for higher education. *Journal of College Student Personnel, 25,* 297–308.

Astin, A. W. (1993). *What matters in college: Four critical years revisited.* San Francisco, CA: Jossey-Bass.

Astin, A. W. (1999). Student involvement: A developmental theory for higher education. *Journal of College Student Development, 40*(5), 518–529.

Astin, A. W., & Sax, L. J. (1998). How undergraduates are affected by service participation. *Journal of College Student Development, 39*(3), 251–263.

Battle, J., & Bennett, M. (2000). Research on lesbian and gay populations within the African American community: What have we learned? *African American Research Perspectives, 6*(2), 35–47.

Baumeister, R. F., & Leary, M. R. (1995). The need to belong: Desire for interpersonal attachment as a fundamental human motivation. *Psychological Bulletin, 117,* 497–529.

Bean, J. (1982). Student attrition, intentions, and confidence: Interaction effects in a path model. *Research in Higher Education, 17*(4), 291–320.

Berelson, B. (1960). *Graduate education in the United States.* New York, NY: McGraw-Hill.

Berger, J. B. (1997). Students' sense of community in residence halls, social integration, and first-year persistence. *Journal of College Student Development, 38,* 441–452.

Berger, J. B., & Milem, J. F. (2002). The impact of community service involvement on three measures of undergraduate self-concept. *NASPA Journal, 40*(1), 85–103.

Besnier, N. (1995). The appeal and pitfalls of cross-disciplinary dialogues. In J. A. Russell, J. M. Fernandez-Dols, A. S. R. Manstead, & J. C. Wellenkamp (Eds.), *Everyday conceptions of emotion: An introduction to the psychology, anthropology, and linguistics of emotion* (pp. 559–570). Dordrecht, The Netherlands: Kluwer Academic Publishers.

Bettinger, E. P., & Long, B. T. (2005). *Addressing the needs of underprepared students in higher education: Does college remediation work?* NBER Working Paper No. 11325. Cambridge, MA: National Bureau of Economic Research.

Bettinger, E. P., & Long, B. T. (2009). Addressing the needs of underprepared students in higher education: Does college remediation work? *Journal of Human Resources, 44*(3), 736–771.

Bollen, K. A., & Hoyle, R. H. (1990). Perceived cohesion: A conceptual and empirical examination. *Social Forces, 69,* 479–504.

Boyer, E. L. (1990). *Campus life: In search of community.* Princeton, NJ: Carnegie Foundation for the Advancement of Teaching.

Boyle, P., & Boice, B. (1998). Best practices for enculturation: Collegiality, mentoring, and structure. In M. S. Anderson (Ed.), *The experience of being in graduate school* (pp. 87–94). San Francisco, CA: Jossey-Bass.

Bragg, A. K. (1976). *The socialization process in higher education.* Washington, DC: American Association of Higher Education.

Braxton, J. M. (2000). Reinvigorating theory and research on the departure puzzle. In J. M. Braxton (Ed.), *Reworking the student departure puzzle* (pp. 257–274). Nashville, TN: Vanderbilt University Press.

Brazzell, J. C. (2001). A sense of belonging. *About Campus,* January/February, 31–32.

Breneman, D. W. (1998). Remediation in higher education: Its extent and cost. In D. Ravitch (Ed.), *Brookings papers on education policy* (pp. 359–382). Washington, DC: The Brookings Institute.

Bridges, B. K., Kinzie, J., Nelson Laird, T. F., & Kuh, G. D. (2008). Student engagement and student success at historically Black and Hispanic serving institutions. In M. Gasman, B. Baez, & C. S. V. Turner (Eds.), *Understanding minority-serving institutions* (pp. 217–236). Albany, NY: State University of New York Press.

Brim, O. G. (1966). Socialization through the life cycle. In O. G. Brim & S. Wheeler (Eds.), *Socialization after childhood* (pp. 3–49). New York, NY: Wiley.

Brown, E., II (2005). We wear the mask: African American contemporary gay male identities. *Journal of African American Studies, 9*(2), 29–38.

Burgess, R. G. (1997). The changing context of postgraduate education in the United Kingdom. In R. G. Burgess (Ed.), *Beyond the first degree: Graduate education, lifelong learning, and careers* (pp. 3–17). Buckingham, UK: Open University Press.

Carini, R. M., Kuh, G. D., & Klein, S. P. (2005). Student engagement and student learning: Testing the linkages. *Research in Higher Education*, 47(1), 1–32.

Carter, D. F., & Hurtado, S. (2007). Bridging key research dilemmas: Quantitative research using a critical eye. In F. K. Stage (Ed.), *Using quantitative data to answer critical questions* (pp. 25–35). San Francisco, CA: Jossey-Bass.

Carter, P. L. (2005). *Keepin' it real: School success beyond Black and White*. New York, NY: Oxford University Press.

Cass, V. C. (1984). Homosexuality identity formation: Testing a theoretical model. *Journal of Sex Research*, 9(1/2), 105–126.

Castellanos, J., & Jones, L. (2003). Latina/o undergraduate experiences in American higher education. In J. Castellanos & L. Jones (Eds.), *The majority in the minority: Expanding the representation of Latina/o faculty, administrators, and students in higher education* (pp. 1–14). Sterling, VA: Stylus Publishing.

Chickering, A. W., & Reisser, L. (1993). *Education and identity* (2nd edn.). San Francisco, CA: Jossey-Bass.

Choenarom, C., Williams, R. A., & Hagerty, B. M. K. (2005). The role of sense of belonging and social support on stress and depression in individuals with depression. *Archives of Psychiatric Nursing*, 19, 18–29.

Clark, B. R. (Ed.) (1993). *The research foundations of graduate education*. Berkeley, CA: University of California Press.

Clark, C. M. (1992). Deviant adolescent subcultures: Assessment strategies and clinical interventions. *Adolescence*, 27, 283–293.

Crenshaw, K. (1991). Mapping the margins: Intersectionality, identity politics, and violence against women of color. *Stanford Law Review*, 43(6), 1241–1299.

Cuyjet, M. J. (Ed.) (1997). *Helping African American men succeed in college*. San Francisco, CA: Jossey-Bass.

Cuyjet, M. J. (2006). African American college men: Twenty-first-century issues and concerns. In M. J. Cuyjet & Associates (Eds.), *African American men in college* (pp. 3–23). San Francisco, CA: Jossey-Bass.

D'Augelli, A. R. (1991). Gay men in college: Identity processes and adaptations. *Journal of College Student Development*, 32, 140–146.

Deci, E. L., & Ryan, R. M. (2000). The "what" and "why" of goal pursuits: Human needs and the self-determination of behavior. *Psychological Inquiry*, 11, 227–268.

Deci, E. L., Vallerand, R. J., Pelletier, L. G., & Ryan, R. M. (1991). Motivation and education: The self-determination perspective. *Educational Psychologist*, 26(3/4), 325–346.

Díaz, R. M., Ayala, G., Bein, E., Henne, J., & Marin, B. V. (2001). The impact of homophobia, poverty, and racism on the mental health of gay and bisexual Latino men: Findings from three US cities. *American Journal of Public Health*, 91(6), 927–932.

Dill, B. T., & Zambrana, R. E. (2009). Critical thinking about inequality: An emerging lens. In B. T. Dill & R. E. Zambrana (Eds.), *Emerging intersections: Race, class, and gender in theory, policy, and practice* (pp. 1–21). New Brunswick, NJ: Rutgers University Press.

Dweck, C. (2007). *Mindset: The new psychology of success*. New York, NY: Ballatine Books.

Einfeld, A., & Collins, D. (2008). The relationships between service-learning, social justice, multicultural competence, and civic engagement. *Journal of College Student Development*, 49(2), 95–109.

Elliott, K. M., & Shin, D. (2002). Student satisfaction: An alternative approach to assessing this important concept. *Journal of Higher Education Policy and Management, 24,* 197–209.

Ellis, E. M. (2001). The impact of race and gender on graduate school socialization, satisfaction with doctoral study, and commitment to degree completion. *Western Journal of Black Studies, 25*(1), 30–45.

Fassinger, R. E. (1991). The hidden minority: Issues and challenges in working with lesbian women and gay men. *Counseling Psychologist, 19,* 157–176.

Ferguson, A. A. (2000). *Bad boys: Public schools in the making of Black male masculinity.* Ann Arbor, MI: University of Michigan Press.

Fleming, J. (1981). Special needs of Blacks and other minorities. In A. W. Chickering & Associates (Eds.), *The modern American college: Responding to the new realities of diverse students and a changing society* (pp. 279–295). San Francisco, CA: Jossey-Bass.

Fleming, J. (1984). *Blacks in college: A comparative study of students' success in Black and White institutions.* San Francisco, CA: Jossey-Bass.

Flowers, L. A. (2004). Examining the effects of student involvement on African American college student development. *Journal of College Student Development, 45,* 633–654.

Furman, G. C. (1998). Postmodernism and community in schools: Unraveling the paradox. *Educational Administration Quarterly, 34*(3), 298–328.

Gardner, S. K. (2010). Contrasting the socialization experiences of doctoral students in high- and low-completing departments: A qualitative analysis of disciplinary contexts at one institution. *Journal of Higher Education, 81*(1), 61–81.

Gasman, M. (2008). Minority-serving institutions: A historical backdrop. In M. Gasman, B. Baez, & C. S. V. Turner (Eds.), *Understanding minority-serving institutions* (pp. 18–27). Albany, NY: State University of New York Press.

Gilmore, P. (1985). "Gimme room": School resistance, attitude, and access to literacy. *Journal of Education, 167*(1), 111–128.

Glenn, D. (2005). Remedial courses help college students complete degrees, study finds. *Chronicle of Higher Education, 51*(43), A31.

Gloria, A. M., & Robinson Kurpius, S. E. (1996). The validation of the cultural congruity scale and the university environment scale with Chicano/a students. *Hispanic Journal of Behavioral Sciences, 18,* 533–554.

Gonyea, R. M., Kish, K. A., Kuh, G. D., Muthiah, R. N., & Thomas, A. D. (2003). *College Student Experiences Questionnaire: Norms for the fourth edition.* Bloomington, IN: Indiana University Center for Postsecondary Research, Policy, and Planning.

Goodenow, C. (1993a). Classroom belonging among early adolescent students: Relationships to motivation and achievement. *Journal of Early Adolescence, 13,* 21–43.

Goodenow, C. (1993b). The psychological sense of school membership among adolescents: Scale development and educational correlates. *Psychology in the Schools, 30,* 79–90.

Gregory, J. F. (1997). Three strikes and they're out: African American boys and American schools' responses to misbehavior. *International Journal of Adolescence and Youth, 7*(1), 25–34.

Guiffrida, D. A. (2003). African American student organizations as agents of social integration. *Journal of College Student Development, 44,* 304–319.

Guiffrida, D. A. (2004). Friends from home: Asset and liability to African American students attending a predominantly White institution. *The NASPA Journal, 24*(3), 693–708.

Guiffrida, D. A. (2005). To break away or strengthen ties to home: A complex question for African American students attending a predominantly White institution. *Equity and Excellence in Education, 38*(1), 49–60.

Hagerty, B. M. K., Lynch-Bauer, J., Patusky, K., Bouwsema, M., & Collier, P. J. (1992). Sense of belonging: A vital mental health concept. *Archives of Psychiatric Nursing, 6*, 172–177.

Hagerty, B. M. K., Williams, R. A., & Oe, H. (2002). Childhood antecedents of adult sense of belonging. *Journal of Clinical Psychology, 58*, 793–801.

Harper, S. R. (2003). Most likely to succeed: The self-perceived impact of involvement on the experiences of high-achieving African American undergraduate men at predominantly White universities. *Dissertation Abstracts International, A64*(6), 1995.

Harper, S. R. (2006). Enhancing African American male student outcomes through leadership and active involvement. In M. J. Cuyjet & Associates (Eds.), *African American men in college* (pp. 68–94). San Francisco, CA: Jossey-Bass.

Harper, S. R., & Quaye, S. J. (2007). Student organizations as venues for Black identity expression and development among African American male student leaders. *Journal of College Student Development, 48*(2), 127–144.

Hausmann, L. R. M., Schofield, J. W., & Woods, R. L. (2007). Sense of belonging as a predictor of intentions to persist among African American and White first-year college students. *Research in Higher Education, 48*(7), 803–839.

Hazan, C., & Shaver, P. R. (1994a). Attachment as an organizational framework for research on close relationships. *Psychological Inquiry, 5*, 1–22.

Hazan, C., & Shaver, P. R. (1994b). Deeper into attachment theory. *Psychological Inquiry, 5*, 68–79.

Herek, G. M. (1993). Documenting prejudice against lesbians and gay men: The Yale sexual orientation study. *Journal of Homosexuality, 25*(4), 15–30.

Hirt, J. B. (2006). *Where you work matters: Student affairs administration at different types of institutions.* Lanham, MD: University Press of America.

Hirt, J. B., Amelink, C. T., Bennett, B. R., & Strayhorn, T. L. (2008). A system of othermothering: Relationships between student affairs administrators and students at historically Black colleges and universities. *The NASPA Journal, 45*(2), 210–236.

Hoffman, M., Richmond, J., Morrow, J., & Salomone, K. (2002–2003). Investigating sense of belonging in first-year college students. *Journal of College Student Retention: Research, Theory, and Practice, 4*(3), 227–256.

Holloman, D. B., & Strayhorn, T. L. (2010). College bound sons: Exploring parental influences on the pre-entry attributes of African American males. In T. L. Strayhorn & M. C. Terrell (Eds.), *The evolving challenges of Black college students: New insights for policy, practice and research* (pp. 161–178). Sterling, VA: Stylus Publishing LLC.

Huebner, D. M., Rebchook, G. M., & Kegeles, S. M. (2004). Experiences of harassment, discrimination, and physical violence among young gay and bisexual men. *American Journal of Public Health, 94*(7), 1200–1203.

Hurtado, S., & Carter, D. F. (1997). Effects of college transition and perceptions of campus racial climate on Latino college students' sense of belonging. *Sociology of Education, 70*(4), 324–345.

Icard, L. D. (1996). Assessing the psychosocial well-being of African American gays. *Journal of Gay and Lesbian Social Services, 5*(2), 25–50.

Icard, L. D. (2008). Reaching African American men on the "Down Low": Sampling hidden populations: Implications for HIV prevention. *Journal of Homosexuality, 55*(3), 437–449.

Icard, L. D., & Nurius, P. S. (1996). Loss of self in coming out: Special risks for African American gays and lesbians. *Journal of Loss and Trauma, 1*(1), 29–47.

Jacoby, B., & Garland, J. (2004–2005). Strategies for enhancing commuter student success. *Journal of College Student Retention: Research, Theory, and Practice, 6*(1), 61–79.

Jakobson, R. (1987). On realism in art. In K. Pomorska & S. Rudy (Eds.), *Language in literature* (pp. 25–26). Cambridge, MA: Harvard University Press.

Johnson, D. R., Soldner, M., Leonard, J. B., Alvarez, P., Inkelas, K. K., Rowan-Kenyon, H., & Longerbeam, S. D. (2007). Examining sense of belonging among first-year undergraduates from different racial/ethnic groups. *Journal of College Student Development, 48*(5), 525–542.

Joiner, T E. (2005). *Why people die by suicide.* Cambridge, MA: Harvard University Press.

Joiner, T. E. (2010). *Myths about suicide.* Cambridge, MA: Harvard University Press.

Jones, S. R., & McEwen, M. K. (2000). A conceptual model of multiple dimensions of identity. *Journal of College Student Development, 41*(4), 405–414.

Justiz, M. J., & Rendón, L. I. (1989). Hispanic students. In M. L. Upcraft, J. N. Gardner, & Associates (Eds.), *The freshman year experience: Helping students survive and succeed in college* (pp. 261–276). San Francisco, CA: Jossey-Bass.

Karner, T. X. (1998). Professional caring: Homecare workers as fictive kin. *Journal of Aging Studies, 12*(1), 69–82.

Kezar, A. J., & Kinzie, J. L. (2006). Examining the ways institutions create student engagement: The role of mission. *Journal of College Student Development, 47*(2), 149–172.

Kimbrough, W. M., & Hutcheson, P. A. (1998). The impact of membership in Black Greek-letter organizations on Black students' involvement in collegiate activities and their development of leadership skills. *Journal of Negro Education, 67*(2), 96–105.

King, J. L. (2004). *On the down low: A journey into the lives of "straight" Black men who sleep with men.* New York, NY: Harlem Moon.

Kissane, M., & McLaren, S. (2006). Sense of belonging as a predictor of reasons for living among older adults. *Death Studies, 30*, 243–258.

Kuh, G. D. (1993). In their own words: What students learn outside the classroom. *American Educational Research Journal, 30*, 277–304.

Kuh, G. D., Kinzie, J., Schuh, J. H., Whitt, E. J., & Associates (2005). *Student success in college: Creating conditions that matter.* San Francisco, CA: Jossey-Bass.

Kuh, G. D., Palmer, M., & Kish, K. (2003). The value of educationally purposeful out-of-class experiences. In T. L. Skipper & R. Argo (Eds.), *Involvement in campus activities and retention of first-year college students* (pp. 19–34). Columbia, SC: University of South Carolina, National Resource Center for the First-Year Experience and Students in Transition.

Kuh, G. D., Vesper, N., Connolly, M. R., & Pace, C. R. (1997). *College Student Experiences Questionnaire: Revised norms for the third edition.* Bloomington, IN: Indiana University Center for Postsecondary Research and Planning.

LaPidus, J. B. (1997). Issues and themes in postgraduate education in the United States. In R. G. Burgess (Ed.), *Beyond the first degree: Graduate education, lifelong learning, and careers* (pp. 21–39). Buckingham, UK: Open University Press.

Lee, C. C. (1994). Adolescent development. In R. B. Mincy (Ed.), *Nurturing young Black males: Challenges to agencies, programs, and social policy* (pp. 33–44). Washington, DC: Urban Institute Press.

Locks, A. M., Hurtado, S., Bowman, N. A., & Oseguera, L. (2008). Extending notions of campus climate and diversity to students' transition to college. *Review of Higher Education, 31*(3), 257–285.

Maestas, R., Vaquera, G. S., & Zehr, L. M. (2007). Factors impacting sense of belonging at a Hispanic-serving institution. *Journal of Hispanic Higher Education, 6*(3), 237–256.

Majors, R., & Billson, J. (1992). *Cool pose: The dilemmas of Black manhood in America.* New York, NY: Touchstone.

Maslow, A. H. (1954). *Motivation and personality.* New York, NY: Harper & Row.

Maslow, A. H. (1962). *Toward a psychology of being.* New York, NY: von Nostrand Reinhold.

Massey, D. S., Charles, C. Z., Lundy, G. F., & Fischer, M. J. (2003). *The source of the river: The social origins of freshmen at America's selective colleges and universities.* Princeton, NJ: Princeton University Press.

McLaren, S. (2009). Sense of belonging to the general and lesbian communities as predictors of depression among lesbians. *Journal of Homosexuality, 56,* 1–13.

McMillan, D. W., & Chavis, D. M. (1986). Sense of community: A definition and theory. *Journal of Community Psychology, 14,* 6–23.

Merriam, S. B. (1998). *Qualitative research and case study applications in education.* San Francisco, CA: Jossey-Bass.

Mincy, R. B. (Ed.) (1994). *Nurturing young Black males: Challenges to agencies, programs, and social policy.* Washington, DC: Urban Institute Press.

Museus, S. D., & Maramba, D. C. (2011). The impact of culture on Filipino American students' sense of belonging. *Review of Higher Education, 34*(2), 231–258.

National Research Council (2006). *Rising above the gathering storm: Energizing and employing America for a brighter economic future.* Washington, DC: National Academies Press.

Nerad, M., & Cerny, J. (1993). From facts to action: Expanding the graduate division's educational role. In L. L. Baird (Ed.), *Increasing graduate student retention and degree attainment* (pp. 27–39). San Francisco, CA: Jossey-Bass.

Nerad, M., & Miller, D. (1996). Increasing student retention in graduate and professional programs. In J. Haworth (Ed.), *Assessing graduate and professional education: Current realities, future prospects* (pp. 61–76). San Francisco, CA: Jossey-Bass.

Nettles, M. T., & Millett, C. M. (2006). *Three magic letters: Getting to Ph.D.* Baltimore. MD: Johns Hopkins University Press.

Nora, A., Rendón, L. I., & Cuadraz, G. (1999). Access, choice, and outcomes: A profile of Hispanic students in higher education. In A. Tashakkori, S. H. Ochoa, & A. E. Kemper (Eds.), *Education of Hispanics in the United States: Politics, policies, and outcomes* (pp. 175–199). Readings on Equal Education Vol. 16. New York, NY: AMS Press.

Oliver, M. L., Rodriguez, C. J., & Mickelson, R. A. (1985). Brown and black in white: The social adjustment and academic performance of Chicano and Black students in a predominantly White university. *The Urban Review, 17*(1), 3–23.

Ortiz, A. M. (2004). Promoting the success of Latino students: A call to action. *New Directions for Student Services, 105,* 89–97.

Osterman, K. F. (2000). Students' need for belonging in the school community. *Review of Educational Research, 70*(3), 323–367.

Ostrove, J. M. (2003). Belonging and wanting: Meanings of social class background for women's constructions of their college experience. *Journal of Social Issues, 59,* 771–784.

Ostrove, J. M., & Long, S. M. (2007). Social class and belonging: Implications for college adjustment. *Review of Higher Education, 30*(4), 363–389.

Palmer, R. T., & Gasman, M. B. (2008). "It takes a village to raise a child": The role of social capital in promoting academic success of African American men at a Black college. *Journal of College Student Development, 49*(1), 52–70.

Parker, C. A. (1977). On modeling reality. *Journal of College Student Personnel, 18*(5), 419–425.

Pascarella, E. T., & Terenzini, P. T. (1991). *How college affects students.* San Francisco, CA: Jossey-Bass.

Pascarella, E. T., & Terenzini, P. T. (2005). *How college affects students: A third decade of research* (Vol. 2). San Francisco, CA: Jossey-Bass.

Perna, L. W., & Titus, M. A. (2005). The relationship between parental involvement as social capital and college enrollment: An examination of racial/group differences. *Journal of Higher Education, 76*, 486–518.

Pettigrew, T. F. (1998). Intergroup contact theory. *Annual Review of Psychology, 49*, 65–85.

Pierce, C. (1995). Stress analogs of racism and sexism: Terrorism, torture, and disaster. In C. V. Willie, P. Rieker, B. Kramer, & B. Brown (Eds.), *Mental health, racism, and sexism* (pp. 277–293). Pittsburgh, PA: University of Pittsburgh Press.

Poock, M. C. (1999). Students of color and doctoral programs: Factors influencing the application decision in higher education administration. *College and University, 74*(3), 2–7.

Rendón, L. I., Jalomo, R. E., & Nora, A. (2000). Theoretical consideration in the study of minority student retention in higher education. In J. M. Braxton (Ed.), *Reworking the student departure puzzle* (pp. 127–156). Nashville, TN: Vanderbilt University Press.

Rhee, B. (2008). Institutional climate and student departure: A multinomial multilevel modeling approach. *Review of Higher Education, 31*(2), 161–183.

Roach, R. (2001). Where are the Black men on campus? *Black Issues in Higher Education, 18*(6), 18–24.

Rosenberg, M., & McCullough, B. C. (1981). Mattering: Inferred significance and mental health among adolescents. *Research in Community Mental Health, 2*, 163–182.

Ryan, R. M., & Stiller, J. (1991). The social contexts of internalization: Parent and teacher influences on autonomy, motivation, and learning. In P. R. Pintrich & M. L. Maehr (Eds.), *Advanced in motivation and achievement: Goals and self-regulatory processes* (Vol. 7, pp. 115–149). Greenwich, CT: JAI Press.

Sanford, N. (1962). Developmental status of the entering freshman. In N. Sanford (Ed.), *The American college* (pp. 253–282). New York, NY: Wiley.

Schlossberg, N. K. (1985). *Marginality and mattering: A life span approach.* Paper presented at the Annual Meeting of the American Psychological Association, Los Angeles, CA.

Seymour, E. (1992). "The Problem Iceberg" in science, mathematics, and engineering education: Student explanations for high attrition rates. *Journal of College Science Teaching, 21*(4), 230–238.

Seymour, E., & Hewitt, N. M. (1997). *Talking about leaving: Why undergraduates leave the sciences.* Boulder, CO: Westview Press.

Sigelman, L., & Tuch, S. A. (1997). Metastereotypes: Blacks' perceptions of Whites' stereotypes of Blacks. *Public Opinion Quarterly, 61*(1), 87–101.

Solórzano, D. G., Ceja, M., & Yosso, T. (2000). Critical race theory, racial microaggressions, and campus racial climate: The experiences of African American college students. *Journal of Negro Education, 69*, 60–73.

Stage, F. K. (Ed.) (2007). *Using quantitative data to answer critical questions.* San Francisco, CA: Jossey-Bass.

Steele, C. M. (1997). A threat in the air: How stereotypes shape intellectual identity and performance. *American Psychologist, 52*, 613–629.

Strauss, A. (1995). *Qualitative analysis for social scientists.* Cambridge, UK: Cambridge University Press.

Strauss, A., & Corbin, J. (1998). *Basics of qualitative research: Techniques and procedures for developing grounded theory* (2nd edn.). Thousand Oaks, CA: Sage.

Strayhorn, T. L. (2005). Democratic education and public universities in America: A literature review. *Journal of College and Character, 6*(3). Retrieved from: www. collegevalues.org/articles.cfm?id=1366&a=1.

Strayhorn, T. L. (2006). Factors influencing the academic achievement of first-generation college students. *NASPA Journal, 43*(4), 82–111.

Strayhorn, T. L. (2008a). Fittin' in: Do diverse interactions with peers affect sense of belonging for Black men at predominantly White institutions? *Journal of Student Affairs Research and Practice, 45*(4), 501–527.

Strayhorn, T. L. (2008b). How college students' engagement affects personal and social learning outcomes. *Journal of College and Character, X*(2), 1–16. Retrieved from: http://collegevalues.org/pdfs/Strayhorn.pdf.

Strayhorn, T. L. (2008c). The role of supportive relationships in facilitating African American males' success in college. *NASPA Journal, 45*(1), 26–48.

Strayhorn, T. L. (2008d). Sentido de pertenencia: A hierarchical analysis predicting sense of belonging among Latino college students. *Journal of Hispanic Higher Education, 7*(4), 301–320.

Strayhorn, T. L. (2008e). The invisible man: Factors affecting the retention of low-income African American males. *National Association of Student Affairs Professionals Journal, 11*(1), 66–87.

Strayhorn, T. L. (2008f). Teachers' expectations and urban Black males' success in school: Implications for academic leaders. *Academic Leadership Journal, 6*(2). Retrieved from: www.academicleadership.org/emprical_research/Teacher_Expectations_and_Urban_Black_Males_Success_in_School_Implications_for_Academic_Leaders.shtml.

Strayhorn, T. L. (2009a, October). *Academic and social barriers to Black and Latino male collegians in engineering.* Paper presented at the 39th Annual Frontiers in Education (FIE) Conference, San Antonio, TX.

Strayhorn, T. L. (2009b). Accessing and analyzing national databases. In T. J. Kowalski & T. J. Lasley, II (Eds.), *Handbook of data-based decision-making in education* (pp. 105–122). New York, NY: Routledge.

Strayhorn, T. L. (2009c). The burden of proof: A quantitative study of high-achieving Black collegians. *Journal of African American Studies, 13*(4), 375–387.

Strayhorn, T. L. (2009d). Different folks, different hopes: The educational aspirations of Black males in urban, suburban, and rural high schools. *Urban Education, 44*(6), 710–731.

Strayhorn, T. L. (2010). When race and gender collide: The impact of social and cultural capital on the academic achievement of African American and Latino males. *Review of Higher Education, 33*(3), 307–332.

Strayhorn, T. L. (2011a). Bridging the pipeline: Increasing underrepresented students' preparation for college through a summer bridge program. *American Behavioral Scientist, 55*(2), 142–159.

Strayhorn, T. L. (2011b). Sense of belonging and African American student success in STEM: Comparative insights between men and women. In H. T. Frierson,

Jr. & W. F. Tate (Eds.), *Beyond stock stories and folktales: African Americans' paths to STEM fields* (pp. 213–226). Diversity in Higher Education Vol. 11. New Milford, CT: Emerald Books.

Strayhorn, T. L. (2011c). Singing in a foreign land: An exploratory study of gospel choir participation among African American undergraduates at a predominantly White institution. *Journal of College Student Development, 52*(5), 137–153.

Strayhorn, T. L. (in press a). "And their own received them not": Black gay male undergraduates' experiences with White racism, Black homophobia. In T. E. Dancy, M. C. Brown, II, & J. E. Davis (Eds.), *Educating African American males: Contexts for consideration, possibilities for practice.* Washington, DC: Peter Lang.

Strayhorn, T. L. (in press b). Quantifying the socialization process for Black male doctoral students and its influence on sense of belonging. *Journal of Higher Education.*

Strayhorn, T. L. (Ed.) (2013). *Living at the intersections: Social identities and Black collegians.* Charlotte, NC: Information Age Publishers.

Strayhorn, T. L. (2015). Reframing academic advising for student success: From advisor to cultural navigator. *NACADA Journal, 35*(1), 56–63.

Strayhorn, T. L., Blakewood, A. M., & DeVita, J. M. (2008). Factors affecting the college choice of African American gay male undergraduates: Implications for retention. *National Association of Student Affairs Professionals Journal, 11*(1), 88–108.

Strayhorn, T. L., Blakewood, A. M., & DeVita, J. M. (2010). Triple threat: Challenges and supports of Black gay men at predominantly White campuses. In T. L. Strayhorn & M. C. Terrell (Eds.), *The evolving challenges of Black college students: New insights for policy, practice and research* (pp. 85–104). Sterling, VA: Stylus.

Strayhorn, T. L., & Mullins, T. G. (2012). Investigating Black gay male undergraduates' experiences in campus residence halls. *The Journal of College and University Student Housing, 39*(1), 140–161.

Strayhorn, T. L., & Saddler, T. N. (2009). Gender differences in the influence of faculty–student mentoring relationships on satisfaction with college among African Americans. *Journal of African American Studies, 13*(4), 476–493.

Strayhorn, T. L., & Terrell, M. C. (2007). Mentoring and satisfaction with college for Black students. *The Negro Educational Review, 58*(1/2), 69–83.

Suskind, R. (1998). *Hope in the unseen: An American odyssey from the inner-city to the ivy league.* New York, NY: Broadway Books.

Swail, W. S., Cabrera, A. F., & Lee, C. (2004). *Latino youth and the pathway to college.* Washington, DC: Educational Policy Institute.

Swail, W. S., & Perna, L. W. (2002). Pre-college outreach programs: A national perspective. In W. G. Tierney & L. S. Hagedorn (Eds.), *Increasing access to college: Extending possibilities for all students* (pp. 15–34). Albany, NY: State University of New York Press.

Taylor, C. M., & Howard-Hamilton, M. F. (1995). Student involvement and racial identity attitudes among African American males. *Journal of College Student Development, 36*, 330–335.

Taylor, J. R., Turner, R. J., Noymer, A., Beckett, M. K., & Elliott, M. N. (2001). A longitudinal study of the role and significance of mattering to others for depressive symptoms. *Journal of Health and Social Behavior, 42*, 310–325.

Thomas, S. L. (2000). Ties that bind: A social network approach to understanding student integration and persistence. *Journal of Higher Education, 71*, 591–615.

Thomas, S. L., & Perna, L. W. (2004). The opportunity agenda: A reexamination of postsecondary reward and opportunity. In J. C. Smart (Ed.), *Higher education: Handbook of theory and research* (Vol. 19, pp. 43–84). Dordrecht, The Netherlands: Kluwer Academic Publishers.

Thoreau, H. D. (1971). *Walden*. Princeton, NJ: Princeton University Press.

Tinto, V. (1993). *Leaving college: Rethinking the causes and cures of student attrition* (2nd edn.). Chicago, IL: University of Chicago Press.

Tovar, E., & Simon, M. A. (2010). Factorial structure and invariance analysis of the sense of belonging scales. *Measurement and Evaluation in Counseling and Development, 43*, 199–217.

Turner, C. S. (1994). Guest in someone else's house: Students of color. *Review of Higher Education, 17*, 355–370.

US Bureau of Census (2000). *Census 2000 demographic profile highlights* (Vol. 2006). Washington, DC: US Bureau of Census.

US Department of Education, National Center for Education Statistics (2000). *The condition of education 2000* (NCES 2000-062). Washington, DC: US Government Printing Office.

US Department of Education (2006). *A test of leadership, charting the future of US higher education: A report of the commission appointed by Secretary of Education Margaret Spellings*. Washington, DC: US Department of Education.

US Department of Education, National Center for Education Statistics (2010). *The condition of education 2010*. NCES Report No. 2010-081. Washington, DC: US Government Printing Office.

US Department of Education, National Center for Education Statistics (2011). *The condition of education 2011*. NCES Report No. 2011-033. Washington, DC: US Government Printing Office.

US Department of Education, National Center for Education Statistics (2016). *The condition of education 2016*. NCES Report No. 2016-042. Washington, DC: US Government Printing Office.

Villalpando, O., & Solórzano, D. G. (2005). The role of culture in college preparation programs: A review of the research literature. In W. G. Tierney, Z. B. Corwin, & J. E. Colyar (Eds.), *Preparing for college: Nine elements of effective outreach* (pp. 13–28). Albany, NY: State University of New York Press.

Vygotsky, L. (1987). *Thought and language* (A. Kozulin, trans.). Cambridge, MA: MIT Press.

Walton, G. M., & Cohen, G. L. (2007). A question of belonging: Race, social fit, and achievement. *Journal of Personality and Social Psychology, 92*(1), 82–96.

Warburton, E. C., Bugarin, R., & Nunez, A. M. (2001). *Bridging the gap: Academic preparation and postsecondary success of first-generation students*. NCES Report No. 2001-153. Washington, DC: US Department of Education, National Center for Education Statistics.

Weidman, J. C., & Stein, E. L. (2003). Socialization of doctoral students to academic norms. *Research in Higher Education, 44*(6), 641–656.

Weidman, J. C., Twale, D. J., & Stein, E. L. (2001). Socialization of graduate and professional students in higher education: A perilous passage? *ASHE-ERIC Higher Education Report* (Vol. 28, pp. 25–54). San Francisco, CA: Jossey-Bass.

Weiss, R. (1973). *Loneliness: The experience of emotional and social isolation*. Cambridge, MA: MIT Press.

White, J. L., & Cones, J. H. (1999). *Black man emerging: Facing the past and seizing a future in America*. New York, NY: Freeman.

Winkle-Wagner, R. (2010). College as life or death: The college choice and transition process of African American women. In T. L. Strayhorn & M. C. Terrell (Eds.), *The evolving challenges of Black college students: New insights for policy, practice and research* (pp. 26–48). Sterling, VA: Stylus Publishing.

Wolf-Wendel, L., Ward, K., & Kinzie, J. L. (2009). A tangled web of terms: The overlap and unique contribution of involvement, engagement, and integration to understanding college student success. *Journal of College Student Development, 50*(4), 407–428.

Zea, M. C., Reisen, C. A., & Poppen, P. J. (1999). Psychological well-being among Latino lesbians and gay men. *Cultural Diversity and Ethnic Minority Psychology, 5*(4), 371–379.

Index

Page numbers in **bold** denote tables, in *italic* denote figures